Brown on Brown

Brown on Brown

Chicano/a Representations of Gender, Sexuality, and Ethnicity

FREDERICK LUIS ALDAMA

University of Texas Press ◆ Austin

First edition, 2005

Requests for permission to reproduce material from this work should be sent to Permissions, University of Texas Press, P.O. Box 7819, Austin, TX 78713-7819.

⊗ The paper used in this book meets the minimum requirements
of ANSI/NISO Z39.48-1992 (R1997) (Permanence of Paper).

Library of Congress Cataloging-in-Publication Data

Aldama, Frederick Luis, 1969–
  Brown on brown : Chicano/a representations of gender, sexuality, and ethnicity / Frederick Luis Aldama.— 1st ed.
    p.   cm.
  Includes bibliographical references.
  Contents: Introduction : narrative, sexuality, race, and the self — Querying postcolonial and borderland queer theory — John Rechy's bending of brown and white canons — Arturo Islas's and Richard Rodriguez's ethnosexual re-architexturing of metropolitan space — Ana Castillo's and Sheila Ortiz Taylor's bent Chicana textualities — Edward J. Olmos's postcolonial penalizings of the film-image repertoire — Conclusion : re-visioning Chicano/a bodies and texts.
        ISBN 0-292-70940-4 (pbk. : alk. paper)
    1. American literature—Mexican American authors—History and criticism.   2. Gays' writings, American—History and criticism.   3. Homosexuality and literature—United States.   4. Mexican American gays—Intellectual life.   5. Mexican Americans—Intellectual life.   6. Mexican Americans in literature.   7. Gender identity in literature.   8. Ethnicity in literature.   9. Sex role in literature.   10. Gays in literature.   I. Title.
  PS153.M4A435 2005
  810.9'353—dc22
                                                                              2005003912

Contents

Acknowledgments

I wish to acknowledge the many conversations with queer Chicano/a writers such as Luis Alfaro, Francisco X. Alarcón, Michael Nava, Ricardo Bracho, and Cherríe Moraga; they have shed much light on how their creative acts reframe reality in ways that engage their various audiences anew. I am grateful to my friends and colleagues who have provided extremely insightful readings of drafts of specific chapters: Herbie Lindenberger, Susann Cokal, David William Foster, Viet Nyguyen, and Donald Morton. I would like to thank those who've had a great influence on my work that encouraged my intellectual explorations generally: Henry Abelove, Porter Abbott, Robert Alter, José Aranda, Alfred Arteaga, Emilio Bejel, Nancy Easterlin, Barbara Foley, Zulfikar Ghose, Marcial González, Carl Gutiérrez-Jones, Patrick Colm Hogan, Ben Sifuentes-Jáuregui, Seth Lehrer, Theresa Meléndez, Jim Phelan, Ralph Rodriguez, Rafael E. Saumell, María Herrera-Sobek, José and Ramón Saldívar, Werner Sollors, Alan Williams, and Lisa Zunhsine, among others. For their indefatigable moral support, many thanks go to my colleagues at the University of Colorado, Boulder, Leke Adeeko, John-Michael Rivera, Cheryl Higashida, Daniel Kim, Ruben Donato, Vince Woodard, and Arturo Aldama (also my big brother). I look forward to the next phase of my journey, as a scholar at Ohio State University. Finally, Theresa May and Allison Faust of the University of Texas Press deserve special recognition for their generous support and patience with this project.

Brown on Brown

Narrative, Sexuality, Race, and the Self

I write: In the beginning was the Act.

—JOHANN WOLFGANG VON GOETHE, *FAUST*

Do not read any more—look!
Do not look any more—go!

—PAUL CELAN, *ENGFÜHRUNG*

My subject here is sex, sexuality, gender, ethnicity, and the self. Notwithstanding its multifaceted difficulties and complexities, I see it as a joyous, lively, complex, frequently surprising, and altogether gratifyingly controversial topic. One that has been treated in literature, cinema, and the arts from every angle of vision and from all ideological perspectives and yet remains as fresh and as inexhaustible as ever. One that bears a very close and concrete relationship with every aspect of our social existence, activity, and status and that is nonetheless often concealed or shut away in the private sphere or approached in mainly "universal," "impersonal," and more or less "deterministic" terms that variously characterize it as either a biological feature (male and female genitals, hormones, genes), an instinct (sexual energy, drive, libido, a certain entity situated between the somatic and the mental), or a fundamentally unintentional/unconscious component of life.[1] One that plays an essential defining role for every human being as a "self," as a unique and independent agent/subject to which criteria such as those of freedom of will, responsibility, and accountability apply. And yet it continues to be largely terra incognita in the empirical and testable research fields of the social sciences and even psychology. Lastly, the topic has been the object of much speculative theorizing in poststructuralist cultural and literary studies on the basis of certain untested, untestable, and speculative ideas taken from philosophy, psychoanalysis, and sociolinguistics.

This topic of the self that oft appears as a labyrinthine collection of enigmas and contradictions I approach from a particular standpoint to explore closely the work of several *queer* (in its expansive connotation) Chicano/a authors and one film director. I chose the work of Ana Castillo, Sheila Ortiz Taylor, John Rechy, Richard Rodriguez, Arturo Islas, and Edward James Olmos not only out of admiration for and enjoyment of their significant contribution to literature and cinema, but also because their work creatively represents and complexly reflects the multiform struggle against homophobic, heterosexist, and xenophobic practices today.

Re-presenting Sexuality

I want to begin this book by mapping briefly the representational contours of the ethnosexualized self and then moving more extensively into a biological-and social-based discussion of ontology. I do so at the outset to provide a refined understanding of the ethnosexual self which will inform the literary and filmic interpretation that follows and that makes up the main body of *Brown on Brown: Chicano/a Representations of Sexuality, Gender, and Ethnicity*.

It is obvious that we are still benefiting from the large degree of freedom of expression gained in the 20th century. Many of yesteryear's taboo sexual expressions and experiences have moved from representational margins to mainstream centers in just a few decades. The Marquis de Sade's 18th-century orgiastic extravaganzas, James Joyce's Bloom masturbating to images of Gerty McDowell, Thomas Mann's Aschenbach spiraling into dizzying spells of desire for the still-pubescent Tadzio, Vladimir Nabokov's Humbert Humbert lusting for the archetypal ingénue Lolita—to recall a few examples taken from literature—are now evoked nonchalantly in everyday conversations. Madonna's gyrating with whip and studded collar has become commonplace in music videos; S&M leather-clad, body-pierced bad guys make a nonchalant appearance in the Wachowski brothers' *Matrix Revolutions;* many an "independent" film now makes commonplace the cybernetic voyeuristic delights seen in earlier films such as David Cronenberg's *Crash*. In photography, Mapplethorpe's post-AIDS shock queer iconography, which had generated heated controversy and was even censored in the 1980s, appeared not only in many a contemporary art museum but later, in book form, on many a coffee table. Following the lead of several European cities, Manhattan has opened a museum of sex. Novels, music videos, films, photographs, and museums are unceasingly opening hitherto closed doors; acts formerly characterized as supremely transgressive are more and more mainstreamed (and internationally exhibited) as ordinary, everyday manifestations of the American sociocultural framework.

The same is also true to a large extent for representations of bisexual and gay/lesbian self and experience. Queer sexuality has played a central role in popular American film and TV series and in some of the most innovative English-penned fictions of the 20th century. Certain ever-popular cable television melodramas such as *Queer as Folk* can now be rented in video and DVD formats at nationwide chains like Blockbuster, along with Jim Fall's queer-exalting film *Trick* and Richard Glatzer and Wash West's gay porn-industry tale *The Fluffer*. The lipstick-lesbian Showtime melodrama "The L Word" is now also widely available at video rental stores. Concerning the canonizing of erstwhile taboo novels, I think readily of Djuna Barnes's same-sex desiring characters in *Nightwood*, William Burroughs's polysexual, racially hybrid denizens of his "interzone" in *Naked Lunch* and Jeanette Winterson's bi/queer narrator/protagonist in *Written on the Body*.

Unfortunately, quite often the most widely publicized representations are also the ones that do the least to engage the public in a serious reflection and understanding of gay/lesbian and bisexual experiences and identity. Wittingly or not, most devolve into clichés that continue to reproduce age-old stereotypes of gender and ethnosexual identity. For example, in *The Fluffer* the physical love denouement between bisexual Sean (played by Michael Cunio) and straight, gay-for-pay Johnny Rebel (played by Scott Gurney) takes place only after they have crossed the U.S. border into Mexico, a country that the audience is expected to identify as a "natural" locus for the occurrence of transgressive sexual acts; it has been stereotyped as just such a transgressive, "primitive" space in many a film and in many a well-known novel by such authors as D. H. Lawrence, Malcolm Lowry, and Jack Kerouac, to name a few. Generally, audiences and readers are expected to recognize and easily accept such a myth because, very often, queer feelings, queer self-concepts, queer social identities, and queer behaviors have been and continue to be inscribed within a binary that ultimately Otherizes certain (dark-skinned) subjects and certain spaces (the economically and politically subordinate countries). In this binary, the so-identified Third World figures implicitly as dark and primitive, a site where "instinctual gratification" is more "natural and commonly accepted," and the "First World" figures implicitly as enlightened and civilized, a site of "sexual repression."

At the opposite pole of this racist and homophobic stand are the bisexual, gay/lesbian literary and filmic depictions that have been created in the last thirty-plus years by gay/lesbian Chicano/a novelists, poets, playwrights, and directors. I think readily of *Ya vas, Carnal* and *Tattoo*, the first collections of poems that queer Chicano poet Francisco X. Alarcón published in 1985, and *The Little Death*, the first mystery novel focused on a gay Chicano, published by Michael Nava in 1986. By that time, of course, lesbian Chicana poets, fiction writers, and playwrights Gloria Anzaldúa, Cherríe Moraga, and Alicia Gaspar de Alba had come into their own as shapers of a so-identified Xicana queer sensibility. And much more recently, representing and complicating bi/queer Chicano sexuality in the movies, there is film director Miguel Arteta. I think here also of the queer representations that have entered the Latino cinematic mainstream: Hector Babenco's critically acclaimed film adaptation *Kiss of the Spider Woman* (1985), director Alfonso Cuarón's crossover success *Y Tu Mamá También* (2001), and Marcel Piñeyro's award-winning *Plata Quemada* (2001) that brought to life the true story of the romantic love affair between bank robbers Angel and El Nene.

At the same time that such writers and directors have been representing a complex gay/lesbian Chicano/a identity and experience, interested scholars have begun to reframe their scholarship with a more broadly inclusive critical outlook. In the mid-1980s, Juan Bruce-Novoa made a call to be inclusive rather than exclusive of gay, lesbian, and bisexual themes and characters when theorizing a Chicano/a canon, as this would allow Chicano/a scholars to forge a more "humane Chicano identity" ("Homosexuality and the Chicano Novel," 105). His essay aimed to provide a schematic overlay that would help create a "progressive space of dialogue" between early Chicano writers like José Antonio Villarreal and the newer, gay and/or lesbian identifying authors such as John Rechy, Arturo Islas, and Sheila Ortiz Taylor.

The approach recommended by Bruce-Novoa has been heeded and can be seen at work in a number of theoretical incursions: the essays included in a special issue of *The Bilingual Review* (1996) that employed a queer analytic rubric for readings of Chicano/a literature; the volume of essays titled *Chicano/Latino Homoerotic Identities* (1999), edited by David William Foster, which included groundbreaking analyses of writers such as Francisco X. Alarcón, Alma Luz Villanueva, Gloria Anzaldúa, and Alicia Gaspar de Alba; the more recent volume edited by Arturo J. Aldama, *De-colonial Voices* (2002), which includes very valuable queer postcolonial theorizations; and Mary Pat Brady's *Extinct Lands, Temporal Geographies*, which explores powerfully the work of Chicana lesbian authors such as Terri de la Peña. Other important explorations and evaluations include Yvonne Yarbaro-Bejarano's seminal book-length study of Cherríe Moraga titled *The Wounded Heart* (2001) and the research by Chicana scholars such as Luz Calvo, María Herrera-Sobek, Chela Sandoval, Deena González, Emma Pérez, Susana Chávez-Silverman, Cecilia Rosales, Catrióna Rueda Esquibel, and Alicia Gaspar de Alba, which has made visible a complex array of Chicana/ Latina lesbian representations in literature, film, and cultural iconography. (For a more comprehensive bibliography of Chicano/a lesbian, gay, and bisexual criticism, see Manuel de Jesús Hernández-Gutiérrez's "Building a Research

Agenda on U.S. Latino Lesbigay Literature and Cultural Production: Texts, Writers, Performance, and Critics" and the appendix to David William Foster's edited *Chicano/Latino Homoerotic Identities*.) Of course, these and other scholars have begun to transform the Chicano/a cultural studies map. However, the necessary critical work is far from finished. Much new remapping remains to be done.

Brown on Brown aims to contribute to this immense and indispensable project of excavating, analyzing, and tracing a new cartography for queer (by and about) Chicano/a literature and film.

Back to the Future

In an effort to refine our understanding of ethnosexuality as textualized in the realm of queer Chicano/a literature and film, I want to reassess at length some assumptions about the basic property of our existence: the constitution of self. Here, I do not aim to have the last word on defining the self and its constitutive ethnic, sexual, and gendered elements, nor do I seek to replay those vacuously abstract and obscurantist formulations in vogue for quite a while now. Instead, I aim to formulate an emerging understanding of the self based on the way it is both biologically and sociohistorically constituted. I propose that verifiable information and scientific hypotheses can provide the raw material needed for us to pour a solid foundation for the building of a theory of what constitutes the self (ethnosexual or otherwise). Science (mostly pseudo) has certainly been used by oppressive elites to justify racism and bigotry, but this does not belie the fact that truth and scientific knowledge are essential for subaltern subjects worldwide to fight successfully against exploitation and oppression. It is in the spirit of this latter position that I wish to work.

Now, an important caveat. To base an understanding of the self in the empirically verifiable and material conditions that make up our past and present reality[2] doesn't mean that I seek to elevate to the level of science my central interest: the analysis of queer Chicano/a literature and film. Nor does it suggest that my analysis of queer Chicano/a literature and film will help advance those scholarly fields I draw from, such as neuroscience and cognitive science, history, linguistics, and psychology. Nor is it meant to level the playing field between science and, say, history or literary analysis in the manner of a social constructivism that proposes all aspects of our reality to be equal. I intend such scholarly research outside of my primary field to serve as ancillary tools (a few among many others available) that clarify and make sense of how power, knowledge, and subjectivity really work in the real world. I turn to such tools as a way to lift a foreboding silence that has blanketed straightforward discussion of the subject of the self (subject/identity) as a result of in-vogue contentless formulations.

While this first section of the book deals primarily with questions of ontology, the overall thrust is to know better how Chicano/a authors and film directors organize aesthetically (via discourse or diegesis, theme, and characterization, for example) their representations of sexuality and its many expressions (especially gay/lesbian and bisexual). However, even to analyze the representation of ethnoqueer Chicano/a selves, we first have to determine what identity is. After all, how can we even identify "Chicano/a" and "queer" (as either characters or real authors) if we do not first determine what differences make them different from everyone else?

Here we must hold two ideas in our minds. These are that narrative fiction is always in the final instance a representation of reality, even when (as in science fiction and other fantastic genres) the components in the diegesis differ from those biological and socially instituted facts that make up the real world; and that, though fiction ultimately refers to the real *hors texte*, it follows its own rules of organization.

Subject of the Self

Prima facie, the notion of the self implies the notion of a living human organism. At the most basic level, this means that the self is a bounded, living being formed by billions of organized cells. At this biological level, the self is a metabolizing entity which functions by distinguishing between what is *in* and what is *out*. This separate and bounded body is a natural kind (it belongs to the human species—and shares its biological blueprint or genome) while at the same time being unique (different from all other bodies and entities).

Though the brain's complex biochemical, neuronal, and affective processes have yet to be mapped completely, scientific research on the brain can help us refine this initially crude formulation of the self. Its advances *poco a poco* have provided a solid, material basis for understanding the self's constitution and function.[3] I think here of the scientifically grounded and testable hypotheses formulated by those scholars included in *The Self from Soul to Brain* (LeDoux, Debiec, and Moss, eds., 2003). Such pathbreaking scholars and scientists as Antonio Damasio, Erik Kandel, Naomi Quinn, Henry Moss, Jacek Debiec, and Joseph E. LeDoux further establish how the brain's total cognitive and affective processes (the neuronal, synaptic, and biochemical activity that allows for the selection, storing, and retrieval of memory and emotion) constitute the self. This and other such scholarship identifies the importance of the brain/body's necessary engagement with objects and organisms other than itself both at the cellular level (metabolic regulation and basic learned response mechanisms) and at the more-general social level; the self is the result of the complete workings of hardwired activity in the brain and simultaneously the result of engagement with that outside of itself. Our individual mind/body's engagement with the world leads to different behaviors and habits unique to each one of us; this is what we commonly call personality. Morphological and phenotypical variation aside, this is why every person we encounter is different to an infinite degree as each of us can behave and subscribe to ideas in an infinite number of ways. I don't mean to posit that personality (individual behavior, opinion, and so on) is a phenomenological manifestation of the self, but rather that it results from that cluster of traits (good or bad, and so on) that constitute the self of the person.

Although there are many differences (personality traits) from person to person, there is much that remains stable and the same in the organic blueprint of the self. We are individual, unique, and changing (even at the cellular level), but we are also biologically and socially constant. That we are predictable provides practical everyday advantages. If we were to behave in unpredictable and inconsistent ways, we would face some serious survival problems. Would we risk driving a car if we couldn't predict the behavior of others? So, while we might experience personal epiphanies and transformations of opinion or might change chameleon-like within different social spheres (the way I act at work is not the same as at home), such transformations don't alter fundamentally the blueprint of our biogenetic (cognitive and neural) self. Stability at the social and biochemical level supersedes individually willed self-transformations.

The sociobiological self experiences a constancy in change. In *The Feeling of What Happens* (1999), Antonio Damasio further elaborates, identifying the interaction between a "core self" that is a "transient entity [that is ceaselessly] re-created for each and every object with which the brain interacts" (17) and the "autobiographical self" that is "a nontransient collection of unique facts and ways of being which characterize a person" (17). In *Homo sapiens sapiens,* both core and autobiographical selves work seamlessly as one self as a result of our higher-order consciousness, which is in turn formed by our engagement with the social; that is, our sense of a coherent narrative unit as both ceaselessly regenerative and bounded as a self-reflexive (acting) agent in a past, present, future world.

For our discussion of the human self (core, autobiographical, and higher consciousness) to mean anything, it must be distinguishable from everything else. Simply identifying it as different doesn't make the self a self, so what we must do is make a distinction between the self and that which is not the self. For example, we can distinguish the chemical property of oxygen from that of, say, hydrogen, but we don't refer to oxygen or hydrogen as having a self.

That is, in understanding what constitutes the self we must focus on how its difference makes a difference (see Leibniz's principle of identity).[4] That is, we must take into account not just distinctiveness and separation (isolation), but in the case of the human self, the notion of agency and responsibility. The action of, say, bacteria that causes another organism like ours to have a digestive problem is not an action with agency; hence, we never refer to the "self of a bacteria" because while it acts, its actions lack the component of agency and responsibility central to the constitution of the human self. When we do identify an amoeba as a pathological "agent" for dysentery we use the word in a technical sense that excludes any attribution of moral responsibility: no amoeba will be condemned in a court of law for causing dysentery.

Agency and responsibility are the difference that make a difference in determining the constitution of the human self. In the concluding essay of *The Self from Soul to Brain*, Joseph E. LeDoux and Jacek Debiec have identified this central property not only as an adaptive function that arises out of our being social animals, but one that gives rise to higher-order consciousness that becomes our guide to "authorship of action"—and "authorship of emotion" (309). They elaborate, "The person who feels will for action typically then feels responsibility for that action, and so will also be susceptible to moral emotions such as pride or guilt depending on the action's effects" (309). Our self is biologically constituted, and it has agency (responsibility) and the capacity for knowledge of self. So while our organic biochemical makeup differs from other "minded organisms" that regulate life functions in response to the outside world, what makes a difference is how our biological organism develops necessarily within the social. Yes, our self is grounded in our organism's specific biological, physical, and chemical components. However, the way these elements work together determines the engagement (and sense of belonging) with the material (physical, chemical, biological) and social world. Without appropriate and adequate neural stimulation, gene expression doesn't occur and so those elements that constitute extended or higher-order conscious selves don't develop. This is why child-rearing practices share much in common cross-culturally: all seek to create social environments that will most effectively trigger cognitive and emotive responses to allow for the healthy development of a sense of higher-functioning self (self-reflexive, responsible, and so on). Without stimulus reinforcement and other conditioning responses (at the neuronal level), necessary gene expression would not occur; the growth of synaptic connections necessary for learning, for example, might not develop. And, likewise, the self of the person who suffers from chronic depression might experience a diminished will to live; the biochemical and the social interact in such a way as to create a less-than-vital experience of the world and engagement with it.

Do people such as schizophrenics whose biological functions do not allow for a sense of agency and responsibility lack a self? This is not so much an ethical or ontological question as it is a question of the presence or not of a higher-consciousness self. Organisms that have a basic "mental *concern* over the organism's own life" (Damasio 25, emphasis his) in their regulation of metabolism and conditioned learning exhibit what Damasio identifies as "core consciousness"; we might identify this as a protean self where the organism is aware of the absolute "now" of itself only in the absolute now of time and space. While this might be the case in schizophrenics (and other non-normal functioning people), this is not the normal functioning, evolutionarily speaking, of *Homo sapiens sapiens*. Our organism's normal functioning is not that of a "minded organism" (cf. Damasio), but rather that which includes the full development of cognitive modules such as language, memory, and reason that make up our higher-consciousness self—a self aware of itself in a present, past, and future as well as with an awareness of self-agency within a world beyond its boundaries (our imaginative capacity). It is a self that has developed a capacity for imagining (worldmaking), grammar, memory, and empathy (that amplification of feeling for those separate from us), and for creating maps of its own maps (as delineated in these pages, even).[5] Our organism's normal functioning self is of a higher order. This does not mean that those organisms whose biological hardwiring or social development has precluded this possibility have any lack of self; they simply lack this higher-order self. It is this difference that makes a difference between us and other organisms as well as between those selves functioning as per a healthy evolutionary trajectory and those selves that have been left behind in the adaptive order of things.

Natural/Social Self

As discussed, as organisms we are both "basic-minded" (in terms of our habitual and "unconscious" biological functions like homeostatic regulation, metabolism, breathing, and so on) and "higher-minded" (self-reflexive, imaginative, responsible, and so on). We have evolved a protean-minded self that regulates and monitors everyday biological functions and that is an emanation of the body much like urine and mucus, as well as a higher-minded self that is the product of our engagement with the material and social world. I will turn to a discussion of those differences that make a difference in terms of this latter, higher-minded self as developed in the social.

One way or another, many fashionable formulations of the self (subject/identity) theorize it as boundary-less (disembodied) and/or self-written/

written-upon; one way or another, they formulate the self as either willed or written into existence and/or as occupying all that exists in the universe. According to the basic principle of discernibility, this leads us nowhere in further refining our understanding of the self. Rather, as I've begun to formulate, the human minded self is distinguishable from other organic and nonorganic entities, and it is so not just biologically (as discussed above), but because of this important and necessary element of the social. The human self that is one way or another unable to have a healthy engagement with the social never develops what we've identified as a higher-minded self. We don't need to look to the example of schizophrenics to see this. We know from Piaget's work with children that those who are precluded from healthy social patterning (parenting, reward/punishment systems of learning) fail to develop healthy neurochemical brain functions (memory and language) that in turn allow for the development of a higher-minded self. The age-old case in point, Caspar Hauser, who was raised completely in isolation from the social world, never developed some of those necessary elements (symbolic representation) that would allow him to develop a higher-minded self. Of course, the mind/body's development of a higher-minded self begins much earlier in our development. We know from children conceived in countries where there is a shortage of food and basic health care, that even before the child is born it has been deprived of the basic nutrients necessary for its healthy biological development. It is our species' blueprint that determines that we can only exist, develop, and evolve as organisms intimately tied to other members of our species. Hence, in the case of the fetus developing in social conditions of insufficient nourishment, the social has already influenced the biological architecture to such a degree that once the child is born, its development of self has been already marked by such social conditions. So, while it is our organism's evolutionary strategy to develop a higher-minded self, the social conditions do not necessarily guarantee its formation.

Our higher-minded self is the healthy development and interplay between our biological makeup and our social engagement. The social is all that is man-made and all of nature that we transform according to our given needs and concepts of our time. Hence, the configurations of the social change not just from place to place (the poor of Zimbabwe versus the rich of the United States), but also historically. The self is formed in history, beginning with our ancestors' first organization into social units. There is a difference between the self conceived, born, and developed in the 21st century and the pre-agricultural self formed ten centuries ago.[6] The self is not the same when free as it is when enslaved or when it exists in a feudal society. The self that developed after the French Revolution swept away all remains of feudalism and the bourgeoisie rose to power is not the same self as that before the revolution. More generally, the self is not the same when living in a capitalist society where economics of private property determine everyday movement or restrictions of movement. The conception of self shifts along with the shifts of social transformation that make history and that result from the massive movements of people. So, in discussing the self, we must also keep an eye directed to its formation within the class struggle (to protect both one's individual and collective rights as worker and as owner of means of production). For example, today in the United States, where only 10 percent or less of the working class are unionized, the self is not the same as it was in the late-19th century. And, because the modern self formed within the framework of the modern nation-state, which, as a result of the working-class struggle, has had to guarantee rights and protections, to destroy this nation-state would be to destroy this self.[7] The self under the tyrannical dictatorship of a Hitler, a Franco, or a Pinochet is one that, like the defenseless child of abusive parents, exists in a state of total subordination. Finally, the self is not the same if one is a person first bound to Mexico nationally, then second bound to the United States; nor is it the same for the Mexican who today crosses borders for gainful employment as it was for the homebound Mexican of yesteryear.

The understanding of the self (ethnosexual or otherwise) requires an understanding of the different ways that society has been organized in time and space. And each of these historical moments is shaped differently because of the different relations established between us in order to survive and develop as we metabolize nature for our survival; since the human being is part of nature, by transforming nature it transforms itself as nature. Moreover, we are unique in that our metabolizing of all of nature takes place necessarily in association with other members of the species: society. It is this metabolizing of nature within the time and place of the social that allows us to establish that the self is constituted both biologically and socio-materially.

In understanding the self as formed in the social, we must further distinguish between society/culture and the nonhuman world. As a part of nature, *Homo sapiens sapiens* is capable of reflecting on all aspects of nature as well as of modifying all of nature that surrounds him/her. This transformation, achieved through labor/work/practical activity that seeks to sustain itself and to perpetuate itself, has to transform all the nature exterior to it. Then you have a valid distinction between society and man, culture and nature, and so forth. Culture is the whole product of man's activities: language, cars, art, and bombs. The distinction between nature and culture is based on what is man-made and not man-made.

However, all that is man-made is based on nature because man is a biological organism. This self-generating of man—that is, one part of nature—through his/her work produces what we call society and culture, society being the specific form in which this part of nature can self-generate itself by association with other members of the same self-generating part of nature. In sum: society is simply the collective formed by individuals—humans—in order to be able to self-generate and self-reproduce. If man were not by necessity, and therefore biologically, hardwired to be gregarious, if man were an animal that had been hardwired to be isolated from the other animals, there would be no culture, no society, no man. *Homo sapiens sapiens* can only accomplish self-generation and reproduction as a species by forming collectives. What separates man from other animals in the animal kingdom is man's specific mode of existence, the specific mode of self-generation and reproduction that leads to the production of what we call culture and society. Just as the spider is inseparable from its web (the mode of existence that allows it to reproduce and eat and continue living) so, too, does man have to spin out culture and society to live. When talking about the self of humankind, then, we are also talking about nature.

That the self is a socially and biologically constituted entity means that the very conception of humankind (and maybe even our immediately pre–*Homo sapiens sapiens* ancestors) is that it is one fragment of nature. In order to subsist and to maintain our existence evolutionarily speaking, we self-generate and self-reproduce ourselves by producing society and culture. Just as spiders continue existing and reproducing themselves for hundreds of thousands of years by secreting, so, too, do humans secrete society and culture to survive.

We have nature and only nature. Within this nature we have differentiation in the way that living organisms perpetuate themselves: the spider secretes its web and humans secrete culture and society to survive evolutionarily. If we diagrammed this as a series of sets, nature would be the largest circle, and within this circle we would have the circle of animal kingdom (all living life from microbes to *Homo sapiens sapiens*), and within this smaller circle we would have mammals, and within the circle of mammals we would have mankind. All of these circles are included within the larger set: nature. Within this large set of living nature all living organisms manifest different ways of maintaining their existence (reproducing themselves) over time both individually and as a species. This is to say that the sociobiological self is formed within the social, which is a part of this larger set we identify as nature. This is what makes us unique and individual (social beings) as well as what makes us a complete set as individual members that form the same species.

Why talk about all of this? Much of the theoretical formulation of the self circulating in the humanities today is completely devoid of a social materialist (historical) purview; many believe that the motor for historical shift is an abstracted movement from one idea to the next; others believe that an atomized performative self can resist oppressive hegemonic master narratives. The human (higher-minded) self is a self as formed in a society that is itself formed in history, which in recent times has been formed by the class struggle. So even before the self is ethnic or gendered, it is formed in relation to the class struggle (in which guaranteed rights and laws are opposite to the interests of a ruling class) within the framework of the modern nation-state. To understand today's self is to subordinate gender and ethnicity to an understanding of it as formed and developed within a capitalist society. It is also to see that capitalism is not a determined element of a natural (biologically determined) human self. It is to see the human self historically and as arising within these social conditions.

Does Identity Matter?

The question of the self and its identities is complex and yet very simple. When we speak of queer Chicano/a selves, we identify aspects that make up an individually and socially constituted self. Here, however, when talking of the self and its identities, I want to sidestep formulations of the self as performative and in flux because to get to this point one must necessarily believe that everything that exists in the world is indeterminate. That is, there would be no difference that makes a difference in this infinitely regressive formulation: "borderland," "hybrid," and so on can be infinitely mixed and matched when talking about gay Chicano identity. Instead, I want continue to follow the basic principle of discernability to refine our understanding of queer Chicano/a identity.

Of course, as I've already discussed regarding our cellular and atomic constitution, nothing remains fixed and identical in the universe. However, this doesn't mean there isn't coherence and a sense of permanence. Not one single atom that made up my bounded self at the moment of writing this book will exist when it is finally in print, yet we can still identity me as Frederick Luis Aldama constantly. If there weren't a sense of coherence, we wouldn't be able to refer to me as Frederick Luis Aldama, nor drive a car, nor study matter (the distinguishing between A and B in biology, physics, chemistry), nor use language and writing to make a study of queer Chicano/a literature and film. At this most basic level, then, we must be able to identify the difference between A and B not subjectively, as a notion that is invented and that depends on my existence, but objectively.

Let me clarify further. For the human being to survive and to exchange information with the world (its vital function as a biological organism), it has to develop a sense of self. This development includes the forming of an awareness of the difference between its self and the rest of world; as this sense of difference develops we also develop a purposeful and intentional sense of acquiring and giving back information directly to the world. This world is constituted by all that exists outside of the human self; that is, if we were to disappear altogether as a species, rocks would still be rocks and they would still be different from water, which would still be different from fire, and so on. The existence or disappearance of that outside the self doesn't depend on my existence nor on my higher-minded self making distinctions. Even at this most basic level of understanding, we know then that there is a material and objective basis to establishing differences and therefore to identity.

Following this principle, then, we can't assert that, for example, it is biology that determines a queer Chicano/a identity. In the mapping of the human genome, we have determined genes for blood group, skin and eye color, and the like, and we have even been able to use such genetic information to follow ancestry: the genetic composition of a Native blood type in North America corresponds to that of a group in Asia, and thus we trace a line of descent for Native North Americans back to Asia. However, such a study doesn't alter the way the human race is characterized by a single genome that singularly characterizes our species and that first came out of Africa thousands of years ago. Namely, subordinate to my identification as queer and Chicano (or right-handed with dark hair and a medium build) is my sociobiological self as determined by genetic composition as a member of the human race.

Identities matter, of course. How they matter, however, varies greatly depending on whether we are talking about identities that have become socially instituted, like ethnicity and gender, or are talking about the biological. From a nuts-and-bolts bio-evolutionary perspective, the identity that makes a difference is sexual. Here I mean sexual in the sense of sexual reproduction, and not sexual preference. My sexual preference might be for those of the same sex, but if I choose to reproduce biologically, then I will necessarily have to involve (via in vitro fertilization, say) a member of the opposite sex. So, sexual identity—that which identifies a man as different from a woman in terms of differently evolved and functioning sexual organs—is an identity that makes a difference in the evolutionary scheme. To reproduce the species, we must have the exchange of XX and XY chromosomal information and subsequent mitosis, whether in sexual copulation or by other means. There is no way around this as biological fact; this is how evolution has taken place. It is a material reality that preexists human beings; it preexists society. In this sense, then, the sexual—overtly identified by physical differences that mark every individual member of *Homo sapiens sapiens*—is an elemental identification that, in the case of evolution, matters.

What does sexual (biological) identity mean on an everyday level? As already mentioned, it means that if one desires to be with those of the same sex as well as to reproduce biologically, one must contend with biological fact. It means that to declare sexuality a performative construct neglects the biological material facts. It means that to replace "gender" for "sexuality" in an effort to emancipate women, or to "trouble gender" by performing constructs of the feminine, changes little for ordinary people like a farmer in Mexico or a factory worker in the United States. Evolutionarily speaking, my identification as Chicano doesn't matter; what matters is whether or not I function to reproduce the species. From an evolutionary perspective, sexual reproduction is the biological sine qua non to continued survival and development of the *Homo sapiens sapiens* self.

What of identification of the self based on what sex we desire? Again, from an evolutionary point of view, we must strip down desire—the sexual drive—and understand its biological function. Human beings have in-built sexual instincts (sexual drive) like other animals (although ours are perennial and theirs seasonal) that include a corresponding excitation of sexual organs. Evolutionarily speaking, this excitation happens for the purpose of reproduction and so a sexual drive has evolved that directs an attraction toward those of the opposite sex. Sexual drive, arousal, and this feeling of desire are parts of a very primitive biological mechanism that has evolved since our distant ancestors transcended the uni-cellular stage of cell reproduction. This doesn't mean that there is anything morally wrong when one desires someone of the same sex. It means simply that desire is not a difference that makes a difference in evolution and therefore in terms of the biologically constituted self.[8]

For human beings everywhere, to exist is to reproduce existence not just biologically but socially. As already discussed, we exist and in our existence we transform nature, which process in turn transforms us. So, while biological reproduction is the minimum condition for survival of the human species, this does not mean that how we have sex or who we desire, for example, is evolutionarily predetermined. What is predetermined is the machinery that we need in order to biologically reproduce.

As I've begun to establish, the social and biological are intimately intertwined in the development of the human self. Today we have arrived at a stage in our evolution where we have created social institutions (the census, for example) that identify us as Chicano, Caucasian, African American, Filipino, Native American, and so on. Ethnic identity is the product of our transformation of the social. We see this with the official census forms that determine demographics that in turn determine public and social policy. Within this context, we have established many ways of identifying social differences. Some have led to the instituting of racist and homophobic exclusionary practices (one can say that those born in Mexico and their descendants will not have the right to sell their capacity to work, for example). Others aim to reform such practices; within a capitalist system where exploitation and oppression are the rule, much political organizing and action have helped advance otherwise exploited groups of people. Take, for example, the effects of the working-class–based civil rights movement, which has led to affirmative action programs and the creation of scholarships by institutions like the Ford Foundation that award them to those who historically suffered as a result of institutional discrimination: for example, Alaska Natives, Blacks/African Americans, Mexican Americans (Chicanos/as), Puerto Ricans, Native American Indians, and Native Pacific Islanders. The civil rights movement also opened doors for erstwhile socially discriminated against groups to finally have equal access to education. In this positive sense, it's because of social identification that I can write a book that focuses on queer Chicano/a literature and film.

Identity Matters ... by Degree

Many literary and cultural critics (Chicano/a or otherwise) have explored the race/class/gender nexus. And many do base their understanding in material fact. For example, as Chicana lesbian scholar Alicia Gaspar de Alba sums up, "Sex and race are biologically determined, the genitalia and racial DNA with which we were born" (*Velvet Barrios,* ix). For Gaspar de Alba, gender and ethnicity are socially constituted and only inflect the biological facts of our differently sexed bodies. As she suggests, we must identify ethnic and sexual preference categories precisely because they have become institutionalized; that is, to fight oppression and exploitation based on these socially instituted categories, we must necessarily make visible such categories. At an even more basic and necessary level of self-identification, however, we must identify the self as it exists within today's society characterized by an economic system of capitalism: the making of all peoples and all relations dependent on the market for the most basic needs, which requires the bourgeoisie to maintain social order and conditions favorable for the accumulation of profit by means of exploitation. Class is thus a fundamental identification of self and an identification that makes a difference. Namely, without identification of class, we can't identify the huge portion of society made dependent on this economic structure that includes all exploited minorities—the working class, women, gays, lesbians, Mexicans, and so forth. Historically, it is what allowed women and gays, lesbians, and Chicanos to struggle effectively against institutionalized exploitation of women in their demands for rights such as equal pay and access to health care. A brief look at the women's struggle for equal rights—the right to vote, to work, to hold property, to divorce, for example—demonstrates its concrete link to the general workers' movement. In the United States we had the anarchist Emma Goldman, and in Germany the suffragette Clara Zetkin. Women have had to organize themselves within the labor movement to demand not just job security, social security, equal pay, and health benefits, but also basics like day-care centers.

Identity politics has become a projection of an expression of a very obscurantist, retrograde, reactionary way of thinking. Instead of isolating myself as a Chicano, I would do better to acknowledge that I am one among many who make up a collective experience of institutional discrimination, and therefore need to organize to form their own political parties to struggle alongside all the other people who have a vested interest in overthrowing capitalism. While identity politics makes visible those who have become targets of institutionalized homophobic and racist policies, for social transformation to take place, we must reach beyond our particular experiences to form solidarity with others who experience exploitation and oppression. For real transformation to take place, the struggle needs to be against capitalism. If we isolate our causes from one another, we simply supply capitalists with the weapons for our own destruction. Cesar Chávez knew this when he helped form trade unions in the fight to institutionalize equal pay for all members of the working class.

Just as social identification matters because we all are social animals, so too do ideas matter. For example, as Henry Abelove discusses, "to say what they wanted to say politically about same-sex eroticism and the global history of their times" (*Deep Gossip*, xviii), writers like Elizabeth Bishop, Paul Bowles, William S. Burroughs, and Allen Ginsberg circulated same-sex eroticism and ideas that fed into gay/lesbian struggles of the 1960s and 1970s. And, Abelove writes, those of the Gay Lesbian Front (GLFers) saw in Baldwin's *Giovanni's Room* "their own reflections, searched for the means to comprehend the ties imagined at the start of the book between colonialist conquest and the denial and betrayal of love, and searched too for the imitation of what they might yet need to learn to 'redeem sex' and, as they often put it, to decolonize America" (81). Abelove identifies how these writers and their ideas allowed the GLFers to see beyond their unique cause and to create bonds with larger communities of oppressed and exploited working-class groups.

Speaking more basically, whether or not one's boss thinks a person is lazy or stupid because he or she is Chicano and/or queer will not change if one decides to wear a Che Guevara and/or Gay Pride T-shirt to work. The worker will continue to be exploited until the individual organizes along with other individuals to create the massive material force necessary to transform the capitalist economic system that exploits the working class worldwide. Ideas only really matter when ideas materialize in the massive unification of millions of people that creates the material force necessary for transformation of the policies of the dominant class. So, while queer Chicano/a literature and films may encourage people in their struggles, they cannot be said to cause the struggles or determine their outcome. We must keep this in mind when analyzing queer Chicano/a literature and films as well as when determining a real politics of social transformation.

Initial Conclusions

According to the original caveat, concepts are objective and true when they correspond to reality, in the same way that a map's adequacy is determined by its correspondence to a given territory, even when the features it picks out are selected according to particular purposes or interests. But in its postmodern (relativistic and constructivist) new guise, the "territory" has lost all objective existence and the "map" is but an illusion; the world is no longer that which is out there, whether I or the whole human race exist or not, it is what I and the society I live in "make" of it and say it is. It is "that" which is "constructed" by society or "conceived" by language, through language, within the limits of language at a certain time and place. Accordingly, ideas are arbitrary in the sense that their contents are determined not by an independently existing reality but by the kinds of expressions authorized by language and society, which ultimately means that there is no escape from totalitarianism. For constructivism there is no objective truth, no objective reality, thus no universality of science: ideas are condemned to be perpetually held in a viselike grip by social, historical, and linguistic constraints, and only those ideas can be formulated that society, tradition, language, and the unconscious allow to be formed. Thus both Nietzsche's perspectival stand and postmodern relativism and constructivism are "deterministic," despite their claims to the contrary, and inadvertently side with the political status quo. Everything we do is realized within society—therefore within certain social conditions.

It was against this constructivist backdrop that I sought to establish a materialist basis for understanding the ethnosexual self. Hence, this introduction's turn to an understanding of the self as socially and biologically constituted. However, such knowledge gleaned from scientific and nonscientific domains is intended only to provide a materialist background for what is the focus of this book: the aesthetic construction (storytelling technique, mood, and genre) of fictional (imaginary) objects and selves that include perspectives and themes that speak to the real-world issues of politics, history, and culture of gay/lesbian and bisexual Chicano/a experiences in a contemporary United States. This isn't to say that ethnoqueer novels and films do not have a determinate ontological status; after all, as cultural objects, they are part of the "stuff" that makes up reality and necessarily "point" to it. Yet, it is important to keep in mind that they are at the same time truth-independent.

Such a difference is the basis upon which I build the central concern of *Brown on Brown:* to explore how each of the authors and directors concerned invents a fictional world that engages its audience through a variety of storytelling genres and styles and that also disengages by expanding radically the Chicano/a and American literary and filmic narrative landscape and image repertoire.

In Chapter 1, "Querying Postcolonial and Borderland Queer Theory," I take stock of a number of queer theories (Chicano/a or otherwise) that bring us to a crossroads in the mapping of queer subaltern literary and filmic theory. I examine several main threads in queer theory (formulated via the work of Jacques Lacan, Jacques Derrida, and Michel Foucault) that seem to lead us down blind alleys.

In Chapter 2, "John Rechy's Bending of Brown and White Canons," I ask, What are the necessary ingredients for one to identify a writer like John Rechy as a Chicano and gay writer? To answer this, I trace the genealogy of ethnic criticism that has deliberated his inclusion. I then explore Rechy's use of narrative technique and characterization in such novels as *Numbers, This Day's Death, Sexual Outlaw,* and *The Miraculous Day of Amalia Gómez.* As I show, not only does Rechy engage with established authors (John Dos Passos, Julio Cortázar, and James Joyce, among others) to provide narrative means and generic containers, but he also disengages from the canon in his texturing of bisexual and gay Chicano/a figures such as Jim Girard, Johnny Rio, and Amalia Gómez. As such, Rechy gives his reader much more than the representation of a Chicano (variously queered and gendered) experience and identity as he engages then redeploys world literary themes and narrative techniques.

In Chapter 3, "Arturo Islas's and Richard Rodriguez's Ethnosexual Re-architexturing of Metropolitan Space," I explore how their respective protagonists emplace and re-spatialize new ways of existing within a number of different metropolitan centers: Los Angeles, Mexico, Tijuana, and San Francisco. I analyze *La Mollie and the King of Tears* and Islas's use of the fast-paced tempo associated with the technique used in noir detective stories and Rodriguez's employment of an investigative journalist voice in *Days of Obligation.* I show how these gay Chicano authors engage and disengage their respective genres: Islas's noir is revised as the storytelling frame shifts from the white, hetero-masculine protagonist à la Chandler to the pachuco, caló-speaking protagonist Louie Mendoza; Rodriguez's journalistic-styled narration fictionalizes fact to richly texture a series of contradictory narrating voices.

In Chapter 4, "Ana Castillo's and Sheila Ortiz Taylor's Bent Chicana Textualities," I look into the way Castillo in her novels *So Far from God* and *Peel*

My Love Like an Onion and her short stories in *Loverboys,* as well as Ortiz Taylor in her novel *Coachella,* variously employ genre and narrative technique to strategically engage, seduce, then disengage a reading public that might otherwise resist entering into their queer/lesbian border-erotic worlds.

In Chapter 5, "Edward J. Olmos's Postcolonial *Penalizings* of the Film-Image Repertoire," I analyze how Olmos invents a filmscape that engages with and critically disengages from Chicano and mainstream film reels that have historically relegated brown women and same-sex-desiring brown men to silent margins. I read *American Me* as a self-reflexive critique of the process by which certain Euro-Spanish colonial models of subjugation are internalized. When the protagonist, Santana, shows signs of "weakness," the film's connotative schema provides a map for us to decode this as his moving into a more ambiguous top/bottom, *activo/pasivo,* strong/weak identification that threatens the male-male (unquestionably macho) scripts of Chicano prison/gang *vida.*

In the concluding chapter, "Re-visioning Chicano/a Bodies and Texts," I close the book with a discussion of the problems of confusing language with cultural phenomena, as well as narrative fiction with ontological fact. I then assert the importance of distinguishing between aesthetic organization, history, language, and the sociopolitical material facts that make up our reality. I end this chapter by suggesting that for us to move forward in a productive manner in the study of queer (and straight) Chicano/a literature and film, we must sidestep the mystical formulations whereby *verba* (word) magically transforms *res* (thing); we must identify those differences that make a difference. This will allow us to avoid missteps that undermine the "real" social and political programs based on empirical fact that lead to the making of a "real" democratic polity. It will also allow us to enrich and further advance our understanding of one of our many activities: the making of and engagement with queer (and straight) Chicano/a literary and film narratives.

CHAPTER 1

Querying Postcolonial and Borderland Queer Theory

Chicano/a Queer Mappings

In *Brown: The Last Discovery of America,* literary agent provocateur Richard Rodriguez renders visible his experiences as queer and Chicano in a so-identified post-Protestant/Catholic postcolonial Americas. In his trademark fast-paced and highly stylized journalese mode, Rodriguez textures an identity he variously dubs as *brown* and "third man" (125) that occupies "the passing lane in American demographics" (125). In his creative autobiographical reinvention, he appears as a shape-shifter of sorts who inhabits the slipstreams of a third space that is neither black nor white but queer "Catholic Indian Spaniard" (35). The Rodriguez of *Brown* is a Chicano queer subject who is both of the past (pre-Columbian/colonial) and of a future (postcolonial) that points to new ways of seeing ethnic and sexual relationalities.

Rodriguez's creative texturing of a "bifocal" (his term) precolonial/post-colonial–visioning, Chicano, queer subjectivity mirrors much of the theoretical work being done in Chicano/a, Latino/a, and postcolonial queer theory today, which results from the hard-won battles of yesteryear's postcolonial gay/lesbian and feminist Chicano/a, Latino/a scholars and creative artists.

In the 1980s a critical mass of queer Chicano/a artists and intellectuals such as Gloria Anzaldúa, Luis Alfaro, Francisco X. Alarcón, Alicia Gaspar de Alba, Angie Chabram, Cherríe Moraga, Michael Nava, John Rechy, and Sheila Ortiz Taylor, to name a few, forced open the gates to an otherwise generally homophobic *raza*-nationalist (late-1960s and 1970s) political movement. In their creative and intellectual work such figures complicated representations of the Chicano/a experience and exploded an erstwhile Us/Them binary opposition: Anglo vs. brown, male vs. female, queer vs. straight. This shift is best exemplified by the publication of Moraga and Anzaldúa's edited *This Bridge Called My Back* in 1981, the production of Moraga's first play ("Giving

Up the Ghost") in 1984, and the Chicano/a studies near-immediate canonizing of Anzaldúa's *Borderlands/La Frontera* after its appearance in 1987.[1] As testament to their importance in redirecting the flow of Chicano/a studies, all three texts remain in print today. This new wave of Chicana feminist and queer poetry, fiction, and creative nonfiction sought to destabilize binary paradigms such as white vs. brown, straight vs. queer, and the United States vs. Mexico. In their imaginatively recontoured Aztlán, women were no longer imprisoned within patriarchally inscribed cultural spaces (brown and white), nor were queer individuals cast from the Chicano/a fold. Aztlán was reconfigured as a borderland space inclusive of *atravesados* (see Anzaldúa) where the wounds inflicted by patriarchal oppression could heal, then reopen to embrace all subjects. It was a space where the memory of colonial violence and racialized inequality and domination would not be forgotten in the postcolonial moment.

The creative queering of Aztlán identified a hybrid and queer inclusive space and, arguably, acted as the springboard for the 1990s remapping of a Chicano/a critical terrain. That decade witnessed more formal recognition of this space as "Borderland" Chicano/a studies inclusive of queer and feminist subjectivities. Indicative of this are Norma Alarcón's essay "Conjugating Subjects: The Heteroglossia of Essence & Resistance" in Alfred Arteaga's *An Other Tongue* (1994) and later the "mestiza consciousness" formulations of Sonia Saldívar-Hull in *Feminism on the Border* (2000). Borderland studies radically exploded the Chicano/a critical purview. In *Border Matters* (1997), José Saldívar explores a host of Chicano/a cultural phenomena—from Arturo Islas's novels to the parodic performances of El Vez to *rock en español*—as sites of borderland reinhabitation and expressive of hybrid subjectivities.

This is also the time when we begin to see the solidification of the critical interface of Chicano/a studies with British postcolonial cultural studies. In José Saldívar's introduction to *Border Matters*, many such critics, Paul Gilroy and Stuart Hall among them, are referred to as influences. Since then, a great number of important self-identified postcolonial borderland scholarly works have appeared on the critical horizon. I think here, for instance, of Raúl Villa's *Barrio-Logos*, Arturo J. Aldama's *Disrupting Savagism* (along with *De-Colonial Voices*, edited with Naomi Quiñonez, and his edited volume *Violence and the Body*), Catrióna Rueda Esquibel's *With a Machete in Her Hand*, Carl Gutiérrez-Jones's *Race Narratives*, Monica Brown's *Gang Nation*, Paula Moya's *Learning from Experience* (and her coedited *Reclaiming Identity*), Curtis Marez's *Drug Wars*, Ralph Rodriguez's *Brown Gumshoes*, and Michael Hames-García's *Fugitive Thought*. Such borderland scholarship continues to complicate and foreground the multiform expressions of exile and dislocation for Chicano/as living within the United States. Each writer articulates a borderland space (with varying degrees of explicitness) that resonates loudly with a postcolonial interstitial "third space" of inhabitation and resistance within otherwise exclusionary spaces. (See Homi Bhabha, "The Third Space," and Amritjit Singh and Peter Schmidt's essay "On the Borders Between U.S. Studies and Postcolonial Theory" in *Postcolonial Theory and the United States*, which they coedited.)

Concerns with globalization and its impact on Chicano/a and subaltern peoples configurate the comparative "transethnic" scholarship that characterizes queer borderland studies today.[2] The collection of essays *Chicano/Latino Homoerotic Identities* (1999), edited by David William Foster, stretches wide and further deepens our understanding of gay Chicano poets such as Francisco Alarcón and performance artists like Luis Alfaro; here also the term *chueco* (Spanish for "crook/crooked" and Mexican slang for "transvestite") is used to identify a racial- and gender-resistant performativity (see Cecilia Rosales, "Chueco Sexualities"). In *Velvet Barrios* (2003) Alicia Gaspar de Alba brings together a series of scholarly essays that expand the domain of Chicano/a borderland studies by inquiring into the various explorations of an *"alter-Native"* (xxi) "erotic *travesías*" (xxv) in previously unexplored (and underexplored) Chicana/o gay and lesbian textual re-visions. The publication of *Chicana Feminisms* (Gabriela F. Arredondo et al, eds., 2003) further solidified the central presence of a queer (feminist) critical slant in borderland studies; here, Chicana lesbian scholar Ellie Hernández, for example, shows how Emma Pérez's *Gulf Dreams* embodies a "different historical preaccount of the cultural representation of Chicana lesbian sexuality by making visible the traumatic psychological ruptures of colonial memory in Chicana/o discourse" (155). Finally, to these significant collections of essays (the list is by no means exhaustive), we must add Rosa Linda Fregoso's book *meXicana encounters* (2003), which reconstructs alternative Latina filmspaces to identify traces of queer performance in Mexican mainstream and Chicano/a avant-garde films. We must also keep centrally in mind the vitalizing presence of Mary Pat Brady's *Extinct Lands, Temporal Geographies* and of Yvonne Yarbro-Bejarano's *The Wounded Heart*, which both explore issues of space, desire, and bodies as they crisscross a variety of lesbian mestiza textual practices.

Queer Recoveries

I have glossed the queer borderland re-visioning of Chicano/a studies to sketch some of the central scholarly and creative work that has emplaced the presence of gay, lesbian, and bisexual representations in the cultural domain. Such work puts to pasture erstwhile nonrepresentations of queer Chicano/a artistic expressions and cultural production and both engages and disengages with Euro-Anglo–identified queer theory. It provides us with a critical framework to question and critique contemporary queer theorists such as Leo Bersani, as well as gay European authors such as André Gide, who uncritically reproduce a Western-gazing subjectivity that turns Third World subjects into objects.[3] Also, the queer borderland transethnic critical purview allows us to see the differences between diversely informed (historical and cultural) expressions of postcolonial queer subjectivities. The scenario of gay Mexican novelist Luis Zapata that represents "straight" machos having sex with men (*passivos*/bottoms) and yet identifying as "straight" and macho within the community most likely would not appear in a queer Euro-Anglo textual configuration. And such building of queer transethnic bridgings allows us to explore a sameness and difference with other postcolonial queer relationalities. For example, the identification of a common history of dislocation within an oppressive globalizing capitalism has led several queer postcolonial scholars to identify politically and culturally based queer alliances among gays and lesbians in Bangkok, Manila, Seoul, Budapest, Mexico City, and San Francisco. In this case, such theorists ultimately identify a queer agency that wrests control from global capitalism by using media/internet technologies to gather and share information and to build transnational political coalitions. In their introduction to *Queer Globalizations*, Arnaldo Cruz-Malavé and Martin F. Manalansan IV, for example, detect a space of resistance and collectivity within the global manufacture and consumption of the Carlos and Billy dolls as well as in the production of films such as *The Crying Game, Strawberry and Chocolate, Fire,* and *To Wong Foo.* For Cruz-Malavé and Manalansan, while global capitalism develops conspicuous consumption of all cultural artifacts to generate profits, it can simultaneously create "multiple opportunities for queer political intervention through an equally globalized coalition politics" (1).

To summarize thus far: Much queer borderland and postcolonial theory today seeks to recuperate and/or identify otherwise outlawed epistemologies and ontologies. It begins to create transnational models of comparative analysis to make visible differences and affinities between those subjects traditionally marked as perverse and/or outlawed. Importantly, it seeks to engage and disengage same-sex–desiring representations within marginal and mainstream culture.

Here, I would like to take pause and question several assumptions that inform (to varying degrees) an often (sub)textual theoretical thread of thinking regarding how power, knowledge, and resistance are formulated in queer theory (borderland, postcolonial, and/or otherwise). To tease out and make explicit several underlying assumptions regarding what queer borderland and postcolonial cultural formulations can do and not do as forms of political and symbolic resistance in the actual transformation of our everyday, I now turn to a discussion of how the subject, power, and knowledge are theorized by Jacques Derrida, Jacques Lacan via Sigmund Freud, and, more fashionably perhaps, by Michel Foucault. As each has published a large number of theoretical works (Derrida more than seventy books), I've unthreaded only those strands that rub frictively against issues of central importance to queer borderland and postcolonial theory. Rather uncharacteristically, I often quote at length here to show—my filtering as diminished as possible—the oft-tautological and mercurial foundation their arguments sit upon.

Derrida's (Anti)Foundationalism

After a period of studying what I consider to be Jacques Derrida's most influential books on Western thought and literature—those commenting on G. W. F. Hegel, Edmund Husserl, Martin Heidegger, Ferdinand de Saussure, Sigmund Freud, Jean-Jacques Rousseau, Etienne Bonnot de Condillac, Karl Marx, Emmanuel Levinas, Claude Lévi-Strauss, Charles Baudelaire, Stéphane Mallarmé, Antonin Artaud, Georges Bataille, and Maurice Blanchot—I've narrowed my discussion to but a handful that propose several of the key theories that directly and indirectly inform the many ideas that we take for granted in queer ethnic (borderland and postcolonial) theory.

Much of Derrida's work shares the common formulation that meaning is always endlessly deferred. For example, in his deliberations on how the dictionary works he identifies how any signified is also in the position of a signifier, thus looking up one word always and necessarily implies the previous understanding of another word or words and so each consultation of an entry implies a previous knowledge of a lexicon ad infinitum. For Derrida, this lexical indexing directs us to the infinite semiosis of language as a system built on an infinitely regressive series of differences. It follows for Derrida that if there is no meaning in language, then there is no meaning—no Self, no Truth, no Reason, no Science, no Word of God—anywhere.[4] Hence his criticism of "logocentrism" and his mocking of the transcendental signifier—the ultimate grounds for meaning. And so, if "meaning" has no foundation then its construction can be infinitely deconstructed.

Such an anti-foundationalist stance is attractive, especially for those of us working in queer ethnic/postcolonial theory. It suggests that by deconstructing a constructed heterosexist Logos we can formulate an ethnoqueer subjectivity intra-dicta, or between those fissured cracks of discourses that naturalize difference. It is a position attractive generally to many academics that willy-nilly redeploy to articulate an "anti" stance: anti-capitalism, anti-patriarchy, anti-theology, and so on. A second, third, or fourth read, however, reveals this understanding of language and meaning not only to be untestable and to lack common sense, but also to show a foundationalist basis to Derrida's anti-foundationalist theories. Moreover, in a third or fourth reading, we see how Derrida's formulation reveals not only a tautology, but also a fundamental faith in the miraculous in his theorizing of an onto-theology.

On many occasions, Derrida has firmly rejected descriptions of his thinking as a form of laicized negative theology. Rather than take a side in this rather pointless debate, at least in my mind, we see rather plainly from the syntax and vocabulary Derrida employs that he uses forms of expression commonly seen in the writings of well-known exponents of the apophatic (or negative) theology, as he himself acknowledges. "Apophatic" or "negative" theology proceeds by descriptions of what God is not, rather than by what God is. God is described only by the absence of attributes: uncreated, infinite (not determined by space), eternal (not determined by time), invisible, incomprehensible, ineffable, incomparable, and so on; we see this also in the so-called cataphatic or "positive" theology. In a like spirit, Derrida's neologisms appear always as meaning both one thing and its opposite, as well as *neither* one thing *nor* its opposite.

To effect this doubling and/or infinitely regressive meaning-making maneuvering, he refuses to identify his neologisms as "concepts" but rather refers to them variously as "marks," "motifs," and "operators of generality." For Derrida, then, a key term like "dissemination" can "mean nothing, and cannot be reassembled into a definition" (*Positions*, 44). The same applies to arguably one of his most fundamental notions—"the motif of *différance*"—that he characterizes as being "neither a *word* nor a *concept*" (*Speech and Phenomena*, 130).[5] And, on another occasion, he characterizes *différance* as being that which "makes the opposition of presence and absence possible [and thus] produces what it forbids, makes possible the very thing that it makes impossible" (*Of Grammatology*, 143). Like the apophatic theological description of God as that which is not (rather than by what God is), so too is *différance* described as that which it is not.

The similarities between Derrida's thought and apophatic theology become particularly pointed if we continue to follow his characterization of the motif of *différance*. In *Speech and Phenomena* Derrida begins by stating that the motif of *différance* "cannot be *exposed*" since, as he continues to explain, "we can expose only . . . what can be shown, presented as a present, a being-present in its truth, the truth of a present or the presence of a present" (134). He continues (and I necessarily need to quote him at length here):

> However, if difference /is/ (I also cross out the 'is') what makes the presentation of being-present possible, it never presents itself as such. It is never

given in the present or to anyone. Holding back and not exposing itself, it goes beyond the order of truth on this specific point and in this determined way, yet is not itself concealed, as if it were something, a mysterious being, in the occult zone of a nonknowing. Any exposition would expose it to disappearing as a disappearance. It would risk appearing, thus disappearing.

Thus, the detours, phrases, and syntax that I shall often have to resort to will resemble—will sometimes be practically indiscernible from—those of negative theology. Already we had to note *that* différance *is not,* does not exist, and is not any sort of being-present (*on*). And we will have to point out everything *that* it *is not,* and, consequently, that it has neither existence nor essence. It belongs to no category of being, present or absent. And yet what is thus denoted as difference is not theological, not even in the most negative order of negative theology. The latter, as we know, is always occupied with letting a supraessential reality go beyond the finite categories of essence and existence, that is, of presence, and always hastens to remind us that, if we deny the predicate of existence to God, it is in order to recognize him as a superior, inconceivable, and ineffable mode of being. Here there is no question of such a move.

(*SPEECH AND PHENOMENA*, 134–135)

Indeed, both *dissemination* and *différance,* as well as other "operators of generality," such as the series of quasi-synonymous terms Derrida has used from 1967 on (the meaning he assigns to Plato's *pharmakon,* or his idiosyncratic use of terms such as "trace,"[6] "supplement," "hymen," "gram," "incision," "interval," etc.) appear functioning in ways that resemble uncannily the classical modus operandi of apophatic or negative theology (*Of Grammatology,* 47). It is not so surprising, then, that he should conclude the above discussion of difference as not only "irreducible to every ontological or theological—ontotheological—reappropriation, but it opens up the very space in which ontotheology—philosophy—produces its system and its history. It thus encompasses and irrevocably surpasses onto-theology or philosophy" (135).

As I've begun to show, Derrida articulates a procedure not based on concepts but on what he identifies in *Positions* as "undecidables," "unities of simulacrum," and "'false' verbal properties (nominal or semantic) that can no longer be included within philosophical (binary) opposition" (43). However, such "undecidables," et cetera, he continues,

> inhabit philosophical opposition, resisting and disorganizing it, *without ever* constituting a third term, without ever leaving room for a solution in the form of speculative dialectics (the *pharmakon* is neither remedy nor poison, neither good nor evil, neither the inside nor the outside, neither speech nor

writing; the *supplement* is neither a plus nor a minus, neither an outside nor the complement of an inside, neither accident nor essence, etc.; the *hymen* is neither confusion nor distinction, neither identity nor difference, neither consummation nor virginity, neither the veil nor unveiling, neither the inside nor the outside, etc.; the *gram* is neither a signifier nor a signified, neither a sign nor a thing, neither a presence nor an absence, neither a position nor a negation, etc.; *spacing* is neither space nor time; the *incision* is neither the incised integrity of a beginning, or of a simple cutting into, nor simple secondarity. Neither/nor, that is, *simultaneously* either *or*; the mark is also the *marginal* limit, the *march*, etc.).

(POSITIONS, 43)

As evinced here, Derrida's "undecidables" (and/or "marks," "motifs," and "operators of generality") share a common ground: all possess the quality of being "empowering," "creative," and/or "demiurgic."

Following from this, I ask, what do we make of the vexed question of Derrida's non-concept of the *hors-texte*? When discussing his "principles of reading," Derrida emphasizes the need to use "all the instruments of traditional criticism," for otherwise a critical reading would "risk developing in any direction at all and authorize itself to say almost anything" (*Of Grammatology*, 158). He also asserts the opposite—that a text cannot reflect or refer to a preexisting world. For example, he writes, "if reading must not be content with doubling the text, it cannot legitimately transgress the text toward something other than it, toward a referent (a reality that is metaphysical, historical, psychobiographical, etc.) or toward a signified outside the text whose content could take place, could have taken place outside of language. . . . *There is nothing outside of the text* [there is no outside-text; *il n'y a pas de hors-texte*]" (*Of Grammatology*, 158). And, Derrida reaffirmed this position five or so years later when he published *Dissemination,* wherein he declares, "There is nothing before the text; there is no pre-text that is not already a text" (328). And here again he explains, "If there is no extra-text, it is because the graphic—graphicity in general—has always already begun, is always implanted in 'prior' writing" (328).

In sum, for Derrida there is no referent, as he states, "at least if conceived as a real thing or cause, anterior and exterior to the system of general textuality" (*Dissemination*, 4). There is no presence, as he states, "in any of its modes (meaning, essence, existence—whether objective or subjective; form, i.e. appearance, content, substance, etc.; sensible presence or intelligible presence)" (5). And, finally, there is no "fundamental or totalizing principle," [no] "transcendental signified," [no] "extra-text which would arrest the concatenation of writing (i.e., that movement which situates every signified as a differential trace)" (5). As variously articulated in *Speech and Phenomena, Positions, Dissemination,* and *Of Grammatology, "il n'y a pas de hors-texte"*—there is nothing outside the text. Yet, in *Dissemination* Derrida warns against the temptation to claim that the traditional concept of the referent ("the classical system's 'outside'") has been done away with "by decree," for such a gesture would pose, he informs, "the risk of engaging in an interminable 'negative theology'" (5).

In disentangling certain of Derrida's key positions we see the following practical consequences. First, in positing that no text is supported by anything else but a text would mean, if taken seriously, an infinite regress from text to text. Second, in identifying "motifs," "marks," "operators of generality," and/or "undecidables" that "ground" the text but do not actually furnish it with a "foundation" that would stop the regress ad infinitum, he is proposing something both nonsensical and even counterproductive for those of us invested in the study and communication of ethnoqueer studies. If meaning of a text is always a context that has no beginning and no end (infinite in time and in its multiplicity), then in actual fact no communication could ever take place: every act of communication in all forms would always necessarily be deferred; every act of communication would always necessarily move back and forward in time and in space within the infinitude of its contexts. This position not only doesn't hold up against even our most basic everyday activities, but it puts forward a theory of language and meaning that one might expect more of fantastical storytelling—as with a boggled Alice after her run-in with Humpty Dumpty, who, within the fictional confines of Wonderland, declares himself the source of a meaningless and arbitrary lexicon.

On a practical level, Derrida's theory of infinite regress would render pointless the articulation of "Chicano/a" and "gay," for example. If meaning is this eternal deferral—*différance*—then there is no final meaning and thus one would have to exhaust the infinite amount of words present in the dictionary before being able to understand and communicate the word "Chicano" and/or "gay." Moreover, the sequence "gay," "rights," and "activism" would mean absolutely nothing.

Derrida's Onto-theological Turn

In Derrida's more recent work, we see a more explicit turn to the onto-theological as a way to ground such tautological formulations. In 1994, Derrida presented a long essay at a seminar he organized with Gianni Vattimo on the isle of Capri, Italy. (The essay was later published in translation as "Faith and Knowledge: The Two Sources of 'Religion' at the Limits of Reason Alone.") In his characteristically labyrinthine way, Derrida argues that faith (the appeal to the faith of the other and the pledge of faith) is the foundation of everything: language, culture, society, even republican democracy. For Derrida, this faith is performative—a "faith without dogma" that, he states, "cannot be contained in any traditional opposition, for example that between reason and mysticism" (18). It is a faith that is, as he writes, not "identifiable with religion, nor, another point, with theology. All sacredness and all holiness are not necessarily, in the strict sense of the term, if there is one, religious" (8–9). It is a secular faith.

This performative and secular identified faith is foundational—like a "desert" (16)—for Derrida. It is what "makes possible, opens, hollows or infinitizes the other" (16), providing that foundational grounding that precedes, he writes, "all determinate community, all positive religion, every onto-anthropo-theological horizon" (16). It is the glue that holds together, as he states, "pure singularities prior to any social or political determination, prior to all intersubjectivity, prior even to the opposition between the sacred (or the holy) and the profane" (17). It is the grounding of all originary human activities, habilities, and convenants. It is the container that holds together all of our activities. As he declares, "No discourse or address of the other without the possibility of an elementary promise. Perjury and broken promises require the *same* possibility. No promise, therefore, without the promise of a confirmation of the *yes*. This *yes* will have implied and will always imply the trustworthiness and fidelity of a faith" (47). In sum, Derrida's faith is belief, credit, the fiduciary or the trustworthiness, trust or confidence in general, fidelity, the promise, the sworn faith, the given word, the testimony (or the testimonial pledge), the experience of witnessing, the expectancy, and the opening towards the future and towards the Other. It is "the desert in the desert [that] liberates a universal rationality and the political democracy that cannot be dissociated from it" (19).

From the communication and universal rationality needed to form democracies to what he identifies as "the critical and tele-technoscientific reason" (*Religion*, 30) all such human activities are founded on faith that Derrida identifies as a "fiduciary experience presupposed by all production of shared knowledge, the testimonial performativity engaged in all technoscientific performance as in the entire capitalistic economy indissociable from it" (44). So, if all our activities, habilities, and convenants are founded on "the promise of keeping one's promise to tell the truth—and to have already told it!—in the very act of promising" (30), then faith is also the great ontological and epistemological democratizer. Religion and reason, then, are seen to develop "in tandem" because they draw from, as he elaborates, "this common resource: the testimonial pledge of every performative, committing it to respond as much *before* the other as *for* the high-performance performativity of technoscience" (28).

Derrida's discussion of the performative act of faith and/or trust—a Rousseau-like social contract—leads him to identify today's "phenomena of ignorance, of irrationality or of 'obscurantism' [as] residues, surface effects, the reactive slag of immunitary, indemnificatory or auto-immunitary reactivity [that] mask a deep structure or rather (but also at the same time) a fear of self, a reaction against that with which it is partially linked: the dislocation, expropriation, delocalization, deracination, disidiomatization and dispossession (in all their dimensions, particularly sexual—*phallic*) that the tele-technoscientific machine does not fail to produce" (45). Likewise, according to Derrida, critiques of the "tele-technoscientific machine" suppose "trustworthiness" (44) based variously on "an irreducible 'faith,' that of a 'social bond' or of a 'sworn faith' of a testimony ('I promise to tell you the truth beyond all proof and all theoretical demonstration, believe me, etc.')" (44). Such a critique based on reason (and that Derrida associates with the Enlightenment) is identified as a "performative of promising at work" (44) that also takes place when lying and committing perjury "without which no address to the other would be possible" (44). He sums up his faith-based formulation of the social contract as follows: "Without the performative experience of this elementary act of faith, there would neither be 'social bond' nor address of the other, nor any performativity in general: neither convention, nor institution, nor constitution, nor sovereign state, nor law, nor above all, here, that structural performativity of the productive performance that binds from its very inception the knowledge of the scientific community to doing, and science to technics" (44).

I end this discussion of Derrida and what amounts to a faith-based social contractualism with a rather lengthy quote wherein he describes the performative experience of witnessing and testimony. He writes:

> In testimony, truth is promised beyond all proof, all perception, all intuitive demonstration. Even if I lie or perjure myself (and always and especially when I do), I promise truth and ask the other to believe the other that I am, there where I am the only one able to bear witness and where the order of proof or of intuition will never be reducible to or homogeneous with the elementary trust, the "good faith" that is promised or demanded. The latter, to be sure, is never pure of all iterability nor of all technics, and hence of all calculability. For it also promises its repetition from the very first instant. It is involved in every address of the other. From the first instant it is co-extensive with this other and thus conditions every "social bond," every questioning, all knowledge, performativity and every tele-technoscientific performance, including those of its forms that are the most synthetic, artificial, prosthetic, calculable. The act of faith demanded in bearing witness exceeds, through its structure, all intuition and all proof, all

knowledge ("I swear that I am telling the truth, not necessarily the 'objective truth,' but the truth of what I believe to be the truth, I am telling you this truth, believe me, believe what I believe, there, where you will never be able to see nor know the irreplaceable yet universal-izable, exemplary place from which I speak to you; perhaps as my testimony is false, but I am sincere and in good faith, it is not false as testimony"). What therefore does the promise of this axiomatic (quasi-transcendental) performative do that conditions and foreshadows "sincere" declarations no less than lies and perjuries, and thus all address of the other? It amounts to saying: "Believe what I say as one believes in a miracle." Even the slightest testimony concerning the most plausible, ordinary or everyday thing cannot do otherwise: it must still appeal to faith as would a miracle.

(*RELIGION*, 63–64)

In his characteristic style that moves forward and backward through paradoxical and tautological twists and turns, Derrida is actually presenting a rather simplistic formulation: all modes of inquiry, social interaction—all our activities—are grounded in "faith," a belief in "miracle." As he states, "pure testimony, if there is such a thing, pertains to the experience of faith and of the miracle. Implied in every 'social bond,' however ordinary, it also renders itself indispensable to Science no less than to Philosophy and to Religion" (*Religion*, 64). Separating kernel from chaff, we see here Derrida's simple formulation that to be a human being is to be a social being and thus requires a belief in that which is foundational to everything: "miracles."

Of course, one need not look far nor reflect too deeply to realize that not all our activities are "miracle-based." According to the confirmable or infirmable accounts offered by different sciences (many of which I touch on in the book's introduction), *Homo sapiens sapiens* is simultaneously a natural and a social being—a being that transforms all of nature, including its own nature, through social life and thus through work accomplished socially in conditions that it changes (knowingly or unknowingly) in time and space (that is, historically).

At this point, I suggest that we would do well to reconsider basing our understanding of queer ethnosexuality on that which amounts to, at the end of the day, a faith-based foundationalism that dons the cloak of radical antifoundationalism. We might do well to be mindful of the onto-theological underpinnings—that our existence and all that exists in the world is based on "a belief in 'miracle'"—of a quick-silvery poststructuralism floating atop a pit of quicksand. Before we do so, however, let me unthread yet another frayed end from our contemporary theoretical (poststructuralist) tapestry.

The Other ... Jacques

As Jacques Lacan's poststructuralist psychoanalytic formulations are based on the already highly speculative metapyschological work of Sigmund Freud, let me turn first to the latter. In 1895 Freud wrote a manuscript (unfinished) titled, "Project for a scientific psychology." It is here that Freud began to formulate ideas regarding the foundations for a future neuroscience capable of explaining all major human conscious and unconscious processes by establishing correlates between brain and mind. On one occasion he writes, "The intention is to furnish a psychology that shall be a natural science: that is, to represent psychical processes as quantitatively determinate states of specifiable material particles, thus rendering those processes perspicuous and free from contradiction" ("Project for a Scientific Psychology," 87). Although Freud was never able to move in this direction, the (neuro)scientific impulse hummed constantly in the background to his ulterior theorizing. According to Karl H. Pribram, Freud's "Project for a scientific psychology" not only anticipated later developments in psychology as a scientific enterprise, but provided "the Rosetta stone for psychoanalytic theory and for psychoanalysis as a language-based practice" ("A Century of Progress?" 12).

This is only part of the story, for it overlooks the fact that the "Project for a Scientific Psychology" also contains *in nuce* Freud's "metapsychology"—a set of highly speculative theories fully realized in his post-WWI theoretical works. It also overlooks the fact that the "Project for a Scientific Psychology" presents a hydraulic descriptive vocabulary (energy flows; discharges that can be channeled, diverted, and/or blocked) and methodological framework (spinning out of Descartes's earlier mind/body formulations) that informed much of his post-WWI metapyschological formulations: the energies of the id, the ego, and the superego (the entity that determines the application of drives and that is the basis of a wide series of cultural, historical, sociological, and anthropological phenomena).

In most if not all of Freud's work, he describes the mind, its products, and its functioning, mainly (though not exclusively) in terms of a mechanistic "hydraulic" model: the mind as a reservoir containing a psychic energy that can flow, be blocked and/or channeled, and that might assume various shapes and experience various transformations. (For more on this, see Ernest Gellner's *The Psychoanalytic Movement: The Cunning of Unreason*[7].) For Freud, all mental phenomena have their origin in the circulation and distribution of the psychic energy obtained from the instincts that generate it in order to satisfy bodily needs or impulses. These bodily needs/impulses activate the instincts by releasing a quantum of energy stored in the body and are experienced by the individual as tensions (pain or discomfort) that he/she seeks to remove. Since the whole available psychic energy has an instinctual source, Freud concludes that the action of the instincts builds a sort of mental storage tank or original reservoir (the "id") from which psychic energy is withdrawn in order to form the two additional basic components ("agencies"): the "ego" and the "super-ego." Each of the "agencies" effect one another in a variety of ways and all possess mechanisms that operate automatically. Together they constitute the energy distributing "psychical apparatus."[8] And, since the accumulation of psychic energy causes pain or discomfort (conversely, its discharge produces pleasure), the sole function of the id is to divest itself of stimulation or energy and to seek pleasure. The id has no direct contact with the environment, does not recognize anything external to it, is innate and expands through the mechanism of repression (operated by the ego). The id does not follow laws of reason, logic, or causality, knows no order and succession in time and space, and ignores all values and morality. The id obeys only what Freud calls the "pleasure principle," wants immediate gratification, fulfills its wishes by imagination, fantasy, hallucinations, and dreams, and would tend to deplete its store of energy if there were no mechanisms to restrain it from immediate discharge in the face of any and all internal or external tensions, excitations, disturbances, or stimulations. Finally, for Freud the most important restraining mechanism in this respect is the ego, a portion of the id that becomes a separate agency without severing all contact with the id and is in charge of ensuring the survival of the individual and therefore of the species. In Freud's words, "The ego seeks to bring the influence of the external world to bear upon the id and its tendencies, and endeavors to substitute the reality principle for the pleasure principle which reigns unrestrictedly in the id. For the ego, perception plays the part which in the id falls to instinct. The ego represents what may be called reason and common sense, in contrast to the id, which contains the passions" (*The Ego and the Id*, 19).[9] Finally, the third agency composing the psychic apparatus—the superego—is the last to appear. As Freud explains, it "is in fact the heir to the Oedipus complex and only arises after that complex has been disposed of" (*An Outline of Psycho-Analysis*, 95).[10]

An understanding of the mind based on a "hydro-hermeneutic" (cf. Gellner) model is certainly creative—also highly speculative. Given that Freud expressed a deep interest in neuroscience-based research in 1895, why would he turn to such a speculative formulation of the mind? After all, neuroscience research was already well under way, so it wasn't for lack of a scientific community.[11] Yet, he decided not to follow a scientific method in his research. This is something that he reflects on retrospectively in his "Autobiographical Study," asking why he gave "free rein to the inclination . . . to speculation" (36). He even lists here what he considers to be his most speculative works: *Beyond the Pleasure Principle* (1920), *Group Psychology and the Analysis of the Ego* (1921), and *The Ego and the Id* (1923); and in his "Autobiographical Study" he candidly identifies what he considers to be his most speculative concepts, including the sexual and the death instincts as well as his division of the "mental apparatus" into "an *ego*, an *id*, and a *super-ego*" (31). Karl H. Pribram conjectures that Freud, who didn't publish his "Project for a Scientific Psychology" manuscript and who lost his place at the University of Vienna to Sigmund Exner, "was thrown back on his clinical practice and had to limit his research to his patients' verbal reports of introspection [because he] had no laboratory" ("A Century of Progress?" 12). And Lesley Chamberlain argues that while Freud had scientific ambitions and claimed a scientific status to his work, he was fundamentally an artist. That is, perhaps his considerable achievement should not have been judged as scientific, but rather as a creative expansion of durable myths and an artistic exploration of the imagination.

Whether we view Freud as "scientist" sans laboratory or as a creative artist, the fact remains that the founder of psychoanalysis had to limit his research to his "patients' verbal reports of introspection," which proved in and of itself to be a statistically insignificant sample that never led to the production of a body of work that could be submitted to controlled observations by other clinicians. Since he lacked a laboratory where he could do research and apply, profit from, and contribute to neuroscientific research, "neurology" was excised from what is considered to be his most influential work. The result for Freud: the slip from scientific research method to an ambitious and speculative philosophy. Moreover, it is upon this foundation that 20th-century Western psychoanalysis grew and became increasingly detached from real-world concerns: the ways in which human beings forge and transform their environment, their self, and their self-understanding.

Essentially the product of one man's mind, Freud's theories have made little or no scientific progress throughout century-old clinical practice. Contrary to usual practice in other fields, psychoanalysis has never been a therapeutic activity accompanied by a systematic investigation into the properties and functions of mental phenomena (pathological or not) accomplished by scientists submitting their clinical knowledge, experience, and skills to the test by peers in laboratory-like conditions. And, the fact that psychoanalysis became a "movement" almost a hundred years ago created the conditions for the birth of as many psychoanalytic "theories" as there were inventive and rhetorically skilled "psychoanalysts." These and certainly other factors confined psychoanalysis to a speculative status and rendered it more and more ad hoc and/or otherwise empirically unverifiable.

Seen from the point of view of the evolution of the psychoanalytic movement, Jacques Lacan's work, based on his proclaimed "return to Freud," exacerbates (bordering on caricature) Freud's most questionable speculations. The lack of empirical and logical constraints in Freud's metapsychology had already opened the way for claims as extravagant as those made by influential disciples such as Carl Gustav Jung and Alfred Adler who later created their own psychoanalytic splinter groups and the self-professed Freudian-Marxists Wilhelm Reich and Erich Fromm. While such psychoanalytic practitioners as Jung and Reich sought to give clear expression to their thoughts (even if speculative and mystical) and carried an intellectually healthy attitude toward critical dialogue, in the phase that followed—and with Lacan at the helm— this attitude toward clarity and self-critique changed radically. A quick glance at Freud or Jung reveals their use of an unpretentious and eminently accessible language—a sharp contrast to Lacan's willful obscurity, obsessive punning, dandyish mimicking of the Dadaists and Surrealists, incessant coining of new words with little or no factual content, and continuous abuse of mathematics. (See Alan Sokal and Jean Bricmont's *Fashionable Nonsense: Postmodern Intellectuals' Abuse of Science* for more on Lacan's confusion of mathematics; see also Thierry Simonelli, "La magie de Lacan: Une récréation mathématique.") This alone, in my opinion, is a very significant development; it shows a correlation between the extent of the intellectual decline in the theory and practice of psychoanalysis and the amount of attention given to Lacan's work in academic circles (mainly French and American) and to the psychoanalytic movement as a whole.

The work of Lacan is a complete revision of the basic framework in which Freud inserted all his other hypotheses, concepts, and speculations. So much so, that it is safe to say that Lacan's proclaimed "return to Freud" is simply a repackaging of certain terms used and made popular by Freud's work. In this repackaging, Lacan uses several key concepts from the work of Sartre, Heidegger, and Hegel, as well as Alexandre Kojève, Marcel Mauss, Claude Lévi-Strauss, Henri Wallon, Ferdinand de Saussure, and Roman Jakobson. It is well known, for example, that Lacan rejected the three-pronged psychical apparatus described by Freud and put in its place another ternary structure, formed by three fields that he named "the Real," "the Imaginary," and "the Symbolic." He adopted the terms used by Saussure in his theory of the sign as an inseparable unit of a signifier and a signified, and made nonsense of it by declaring that each component was separated by a gap and by stating that the signifier had priority in psychic life.[12] He borrowed from Jakobson the notion that pronouns are "shifters," since their referents change according to who is speaking, and turned this elementary fact into a wild speculation about the subject. And the "mirror stage" theory for which Lacan became known in the early part of his career comes from Henri Wallon. To quote Mikkel Borch-Jacobsen's perceptive study on Lacan, "as always with Lacan, [the mirror stage theory's] originality is in the nature of a generalizing combination. In short, Lacan mixed Wallon's examination of the mirror with Freud's narcissism and Hegel's dialectic, at the same time raising the psychologist Wallon's modest proposals to the level of a grandiose 'ontological structure of the human world'" (47).

Regardless of the fact that Lacan's notions are a repackaged melange of the concepts of other thinkers and built on the highly speculative workings of Freud, they have acquired massive currency and an academic cache. Such theories (as blended with Derrida's *différance* and Foucault's notion of power) have given way to formulations of sexuality as discursively produced within a discursively produced nation-state so that rather than search for a "truth" of subjectivity that repression may have kept from view, one must seek to identify a fragmented, nonautonomous (ethnosexual) subject. Of course, this (ethnosexual) subject must be a discursively (linguistically/socially) constructed, fragmented fiction, one that is acted upon but is not entirely assimilable by hegemonic power structures. In this schema, moreover, the formulation of the *queer*-desiring ethnosexual subject is likewise fragmented textually but is not predicated on lack—the lack of, say, a straight-identified Freudian Oedipal complex or Lacanian (linguistic) Phallus. The ethnosexual queer subject is a multiply desiring, fragmented fiction that exists for itself. Thus, the subject is both unfixed and fragmented and, because it doesn't lack (sidestepping fixity within a repressive law of the Freudian Oedipus complex and later superego and Lacan's Phallus as the linguistic sign that links signifier and signified to stabilize chains of ever-shifting meanings in society, for example), its desire is *full* and productive. (It being understood that, in order to make the subject and the world seem coherent and whole, those with power construct signifying systems that pretend wholeness all while naturalizing sexual difference.) As such, multiply desiring, discursively constructed ethnoqueer subjects are both produced by and have the power to unfix heteronormative, colonial/capitalist Euro-Anglo fields of signification.

The move into the realm of the Lacanian unconscious (mostly) to understand subjectivity superimposes the Saussurean signifier (acoustic image/phoneme) on the unconscious and the signifier (concept) on the conscious. And, within this conscious/unconscious or signifier/signified schema of formulating an ethnoqueer subjectivity, there is the recapitulation of a Derridean signifier/signified gap, slippage, or aporia. Namely, to come into consciousness is to come into the realm of the signifier. Once in the realm of chains of signifiers that infinitely reproduce and never reach true meaning, the subject is itself incoherent. In consciousness is fragmentation, but this is disavowed (Lacan's "misrecognition") by the subject in his/her fantasies of coherence. The queer subaltern subject inhabits the gaps between signifier and signified, or consciousness and unconsciousness, and so can destabilize the Imaginary where the ego/self is seemingly made to appear unified within dominant signifying systems. Because the Phallus is never attainable, and the ethnoqueer subject makes this visible, it also exposes how the Subject (straight/queer, Anglo/Other) is always in process of deferred becoming.

In sum: For postcolonial and borderland queer theorists, the ethnoqueer subject is not informed by material impulses and biological instincts—repressed and liberated—but by signs and meanings. Therefore, this subject is a discursively fragmented construct and it exists within chains of signifiers that promise consciousness but forever hold at bay the ultimate realizing of consciousness, or the primary signifier, the Phallus; precisely because it is a fragmented construct, such an ethnoqueer-desiring subject can detach itself, then reinhabit the gap between signifier/signified, or conscious/unconscious, and then refigure hetero-normalized discursively inscribed sites of desire.

Queer Performances

As already suggested, perhaps such speculative theories of the subject and onto-theological formulations might not be the best foundation for shedding light on what constitutes ethnic, racial, and sexual identification; they might not be the most solid foundation for identifying the real consequences of racism and homophobia and also our resistance to real oppression. I question, therefore, José Esteban Muñoz's notion of the discursively constructed queer Latino/a subject whose parodic (*"chusmaría"*) performance of race, sexuality, and/or gender radically transforms an otherwise oppressive (highly regulated discursively) world. Can the "willful mismatching of striped and floral print genre, and a loud defiance of a rather fixed order" (*Disidentifications*, 191) really enact "the actual making of worlds" (200), as Muñoz asserts? I ask the same of Silviano Santiago's affirmation of the "wily homosexual" and/or "homosexual rogue" whose "subjectivities in play" (18) expose and subvert signifying systems that naturalize heteronormativity in Brazilian society.

Derrida and Lacan's formulations prove speculative at best and thus we have to question whether or not we are indeed discursively constructed and whether or not we can indeed destabilize regulative fictions that control desire in ways that are socially and politically transformative. We must here look to yet another articulation of the performative to understand where Muñoz et al might be going astray. The "performative" is often (directly and indirectly) identified with Judith Butler, especially as articulated in her *Gender Trouble*, and that identifies its spinning anew of J. L. Austin's formulation of a "constative/performative binary" in his William James lecture (lectures later transcribed, edited, and collected by his students and posthumously published in 1955 as *How To Do Things with Words*). Interestingly, J. L. Austin himself abandoned his constative/performative hypothesis, noting that language does not work in such a neat contrasting way and that his formula ultimately failed to account for the contextual factors that determine meaning in everyday speech acts. Hence, he offered a revised hypothesis (the locution/illocutionary binary) to identify those complex aspects of sentences that highlight the thought and/or action expressed.

Whether we take his performative and/or locutionary model, neither proved fruitful for future generations of linguistic scholars that have been seriously pursuing an interest in understanding how language works, how the language faculty is acquired, and how rules and words combine to convey meaning.[13] And yet Austin's "performatives"—the name given to utterances that function in and of themselves as actions rather than as assertions—are employed again and again in theorizing the self. The reason, I suppose, is that Austin's notion plays nicely into the Derridean and Lacanian formulation of the subject as discursively constructed and of language (or "discourse") as perpetually self-referential. Since it is posited that discourse is performance and the subject is discourse, such a subject can only be a performative subject. And, by further extrapolation, race, sex, and gender are also performative discourses or acts, for bodies are never merely described, they are constituted in the very act of description. Thus, there is no truth or origin about anything, let alone race, sex, and gender—only performance and subjects produced in and through (discursive) performance.

From this point of view, if one decontextualizes normative race and/or gender identities through performance (Muñoz's reading of Carmelita Tropicana's drag performances that "disidentifies" heteronormative and racist discursive spaces), then one destabilizes oppressive heterosexist ideologies. It means that a theorist like Judith Butler can posit the performative *troubling* of originary and/or "primary" genders in parodic practices of "drag, cross-dressing, and the sexual stylization of butch/femme identities" (215). She continues, "If the anatomy of the performer is already distinct from the gender of the performer, and both of those are distinct from the gender of the performance, then the performance suggests a dissonance not only between sex and performance, but sex and gender, and gender performance" (215). Indeed, the idea that our everyday existence is a series of repetitions of behaviors (male and female, straight and queer, say) that are fictions (naturalized or not) within dominant hegemonic systems (not a central part of our identity) that can be destabilized through a parodic performance has been recognized as ineffectual by Butler herself, who has admitted that such a performativity cannot change the system. All it does is give the individual performer of such and such identity the possibility of creative play, as someone would do on stage; when the curtain falls, while the performance might have engaged its audience and even opened the public's eyes to certain social injustices, nothing will have changed in the real world of the real people that suffer daily from those injustices. (See also "The Professor of Parody: The Hip Defeatism of Judith Butler," wherein Martha Nussbaum locates Butler's theories more within theater arts than with Austin's analysis of the performative sentence.)

Whether we talk of Muñoz's "disidentifications," Butler's "performative," Derrida's "operators of generality" or "*différance*," Lacan's "Real," "Imaginary," or "Symbolic," we must ask do such ideas and categories actually help further our understanding of queer (borderland, postcolonial, or otherwise) subjectivity and how oppressive social conditions might be transformed? Can there be a slippage between the signifier and the signified? Is meaning really deferrable? Is the subject and the world experienced by the subject unstable and fragmented? If subject and world are linguistic constructs, then how can we account for the real stigmatization and real suffering and real pain that the ethnoqueer subject experiences in the real world "out there"?

In real everyday practical terms, if meaning were infinitely deferrable, then thinkers such as Derrida or Lacan would never be able to translate their work. And, even more basically, doesn't the fact that we can communicate (even if it is to communicate a tautology) indicate that there is finitude? Communication happens everyday and thus it is clearly not the case that meaning never touches its target; that it never *arrives,* as Derrida proposes. And, can we really write against and destabilize nation? Namely, is the nation really a signifying system (conceived as strings of signs in the Saussurean sense)? Is it the same as the cultural objects that fill up our world? Can we really conflate culture (so-called fantasized or imaginary communities) with real political, geographical, economic, and judicial structures that make up the nation in the real world? What does history tell us about counter-hegemonic resistance? Has social transformation taken place as a result of discursive destabilization of nation-states?

Stripped down, such theories lead to dead ends because even a cursory look at facts shows a different story about how social change is enacted and how real bodies experience the real pain involved in the lack of such change. So when theorists put forward the fantastical notion that only a performative identity has the strength to make at least a little room for play within the "prison house of language" (a "prison," by the way, of their own theoretical making), and that all a racialized, gendered, and/or sexualized subject can do is to enact a parodic performance within the master narrative structures of power, they are upholding not only a hugely pessimistic viewpoint but also an idiosyncratic hypothesis that is contradicted by all variety of historical and scientific evidence. And, to formulate a queer (borderland or postcolonial) resistant subjectivity and counter-nationalist discursivity that carries the same ontological weight as a political treaty, a mass social protest movement, or a revolutionary force—by identifying centers of power like the nation-state as discursive constructs—also appears to contradict what labor historians have shown: for social resistance and political change to take place, real sites of power must be targeted in order for the organization of masses of people acting on such sites to take place. Power is somewhere.

Imagined Sites of Power . . .

This is also where we might do well to question Foucault's theorizing of power as discursively constructed and devoid of a specific location. In *The History of Sexuality* Foucault states, "Sexuality must not be described as a stubborn drive, by nature alien and of necessity disobedient to a power which exhausts itself trying to subdue it and often fails to control it entirely. It appears rather as an especially dense transfer point for relations of power: between men and women, young people and old people, parents and offspring, teachers and students, priest and laity, an administration and a population" (103). If sexuality is the "dense transfer point" that forever fends off hegemonic control, it can both reveal "relations of power" and resist within networks of power. Thus, Foucault writes, "These points of resistance are present everywhere in the power networks. Hence there is no single locus of great Refusal, no soul of revolt, source of all rebellions, or pure law of the revolutionary. Instead there is a plurality of resistances, each of them a special case: resistances that are possible, necessary, improbable; others that are spontaneous, savage, solitary, concerted, rampant, or violent" (96). If power circulates in society through discourse—historically inflected ways of speaking, writing, and so on—then resistance to hegemonic power structures is simply the act of decoding the systematic articulation of power through discourse that controls and regulates what is desirable and undesirable. Namely, for Foucault, because power creates resistance in the instant it exerts force on desiring bodies, power is not simply a top-down, unidirectional force: capitalism's control and regulation of desire—the privileging of bourgeois heterosexuality, for example—de facto leads to its creation of a "reverse discourse" (101) that we might locate at the site of ethnoqueer sexuality. Such a formulation allows for the simultaneous critique of the discursive power articulations controlling desire—those cultural representations, judicial acts, and so on that prohibit queer desiring or racial subjectivity or both—and the use of such controlled desire as a "reverse discourse" to demand its legitimacy and denounce a dominant hegemony.[14]

Can, I ask, a Foucaultian decoding of a discursively constructed ethnoqueer sexuality really reveal the "contradictory transfers of power," hegemonic and counter-hegemonic, that *are* the nation?[15] Perhaps, this simply does the opposite of its intent: to erase the very real sites of power situated within the State apparatus, itself controlled by the real ruling class, to theorize out of existence the real exploitive and oppressive systems of capitalist and neocolonial heterosexist rule. The danger in such an approach seems obvious. To promote acts of transgressive pleasure (metropolitan, middle-class "shocking" sex) as politically subversive and as a strategy of "resistance" dangerously romanticizes the mutilation of bodies and simply goes against common sense: pleasure and sex (straight or queer, transgressive or vanilla) do not lead to social transformation. As labor historians have shown, such transformations over the last two hundred years have required a constant struggle by millions of people all over the world to force nations to establish, adopt, and maintain democratic and labor rights. (See Ellen Meiksins Wood's historical materialist analysis of global capitalism in *Empire of Capital* and *Democracy Against Capitalism*.)

...and Real Sites of Power

The economy and most of the political and social structures of postcolonial Third World countries are still overwhelmingly submitted to the dictates and the hard fists of the First World–controlled International Monetary Fund. And what is now fashionably termed the "process of globalization" is being experienced more and more patently as a global domination by First World countries, themselves becoming more and more subservient to American imperialist interests. So, wherever the rule of law has been challenged and weakened or destroyed, or a nation has been deeply dislocated, as in many countries once part of the Soviet Union, in some Eastern European countries (such as the former Yugoslavia), in most of Africa, and even in Latin America (for instance, Colombia and Argentina), a Mafia-styled warlordism has become rampant. So theorists who posit the diffusion of borders and the subversion of nation, while seemingly proposing a progressive, radical, left-wing policy, are actually favoring some of the most destructive and reactionary tendencies exhibited today by capitalism in its road to barbarism. There is nothing emancipatory and recuperative in the exploitation of women and men transferred from Eastern European countries to work (perform?) as sex workers in the West, including the United States, nor is there in the spread of dictatorships, patronage systems, racism and genocides, sexism, and fundamentalism all around the globe.

In today's specific state of corruption attained by capitalism as a world system, these and many other scourges are pandemic when the framework of nation is destroyed, as many theorists influenced directly and indirectly by Foucault, Derrida, and Lacan would ultimately have it. A clear example of this is the widely published news that half the territory of Argentina (*la cona sur,* or the southern part of the country) is envisioning the possibility of becoming an independent nation. This is the richest part of Argentina, the region where most agriculture, oil, gas, mines, water, and other important resources are located. And the secessionist option is a direct result of the policy applied in Argentina under the orders of the Bush (Jr.) administration and the International Monetary Fund, a policy that has been leading the Argentinean people to starvation and the country to a catastrophic dislocation as a nation.

This example shows that to theorize spaces of resistance (ethnoqueer or otherwise) that putatively exist between the lines of signification is to ignore the long history of struggles waged, with massive human loss, by working subaltern peoples within the borders of nations to impose upon the ruling and proprietary classes the rights that set limits to oppression and exploitation. As Marcial González states succinctly, "the problems emerge when critics interpret social ambivalence as the foundation for a counter-hegemonic cultural identity" ("A Marxist Critique of Borderlands Postmodernism," 280). Such "ambivalence" or inter-dicta resistance erases and fragments real sites of power and real forms of resistance and struggle; it also dangerously suggests that we destroy the very framework that allows for such struggles to continue. Because capitalism cannot do without its own foundational principle (the right to the means of production and distribution as private property and the right to put these in motion by using a labor force that produces more value than it receives in the form of wages), historically the bourgeoisie has had to accept the existence of laws generally, and in particular those that protect the laboring classes. Hence the importance today of the framework of the nation for subaltern (queer and straight) struggles worldwide, for it is nowadays the very political framework in which all the wage earners and the oppressed peoples of each country fight to obtain and preserve—even against the most violent opposition of the ruling classes—their democratic and labor rights.

As one can easily conclude then, for emancipation to happen for borderland and postcolonial subjects (queer and straight) all must join in the everyday struggle necessary to acquire and maintain the democratic rights of *all* to a decent job, to decent housing, to free access to education, health care, and public transportation, to freedom of speech, and to the right to organize in independent unions and political parties. The success of César Chávez and Dolores Huerta's pan–working-class unionizing and organizing is a case in point.

And, as Peter Drucker forcefully reminds of postcolonial Third World struggles, "true democratization will require mobilizing and organizing the poor majority, which in turn can set in motion fundamental social change" ("Reinventing Liberation," 213).

The stigmatization of queers of color has many causes that ultimately find their roots in our present social system based on exploitation and oppression. Therefore, for liberation to take place, we need to turn our attention to the basics: the advanced state of decomposition attained today by global capitalism, the leading role played in this respect by its American component, and the precise forms of resistance and struggle evinced in international and national proletarian political practice. Likewise, we need to understand capitalist hegemony in relation to, as Adam Katz contends, "the notion of social necessity (in the sense of the laws of motion of a social form) rather than in terms of contingent and unstable articulations" (101). This is not going to happen, as Donald Morton writes, with a "semiotic democracy" (7) in which people speak (only) for themselves and that gives credence to "a non-class, coalitionist, liberal politics" (7). Borderland and postcolonial queer-identified emancipation will only be realized within the framework of the collective struggle waged in every country to resist oppression and exploitation, to defend the democratic rights of all workers, and to overturn capitalist relations of production.

As queer-identified borderland and postcolonial theorists, we must always ask ourselves, What does this such and such theory entail in practical terms? If sexual orientation and gender is just a performative, then where is the material content to the assertion that one is a gay Latino? What does this translate to in terms of real positions in a real, materially constituted world. As queer-identifying borderland and postcolonial theorists, we might do well to avoid obscurantism and the deleterious confusion of concepts (linguistic and psychoanalytic, nation and narration, symbolic and real). We might do well to distinguish between the materiality of our real world (testing novel hypothesis and thought experiment with scrupulous observation and verification of data) and the study of such cultural phenomena as ethnoqueer literature and film. We might do well to choose carefully those tools (narratology, history, cognitive science, for example) that offer us great explanatory and predictive power.

To build a solid foundation for further inquiry aimed at obtaining a better understanding of borderland ethnoqueer subjectivities, we must be accountable for what we say and do in our scholarly pursuits. The confusion of nation with narration, speech act with political praxis, literature with the ontological facts that make up our reality, power with discourse, and the world with the text deviates from such a responsible accounting. Of course, we need to continue to defend the democratic rights of all citizens worldwide (queer and straight and of all hues) just as we need to continue to conduct research in history, language, and literature, to open eyes to a queer subaltern existence past and present, but in so doing we must keep in mind that ethnoqueer borderland and postcolonial theorizing in and of itself will never enact the kind of radical transformation of society required of millions of people.

Wrapping It Up

I end with a brief reiteration of my focus in *Brown on Brown:* the analyzing of each of the queer Chicano/a (by and about) narrative fictions according to the principles that govern fiction and film. That is, I wish to keep in mind centrally that my task here is not to study Chicano/a queer literature and film as a form of political activism, but rather as a way to shed light on how such queer Chicano/a narrative fictions engage and disengage readers. Paying attention to how Rechy, Islas, Castillo, Ortiz Taylor, Rodriguez, and Olmos organize theme and plot, texture character, and play with point of view, for example, is not to "sell out." It is to explore how such queer Chicano/a literature and film can challenge the expectations of the audience as well as open its eyes to new ways of thinking about, perceiving, and grasping the world. Such queer borderland fictions do reflect both critically and artistically on hegemonic patriarchal, heterosexist features of capitalist society, but do so according to the conventions of genre and storytelling styles that bracket off reality and invest each text with an aesthetic function.

This does not mean that the narrative fictions aren't inflected with history or politics; it simply means that such inflections are subordinate to aesthetic functions (style, play with chronology and point of view, characterization, and so on) that mimetically bracket off and reorder elements of reality that open up "the possibility of a new perspective on . . . reality" (Fluck, 88). In this bracketing and remaking process, such queer Chicano/a narrative fictions have the potential to open, as Heinz Ickstadt declares, "the particular toward something shared beyond the boundaries of difference" (272–273). Indeed, the power—and beauty—of queer borderland narrative fiction lies in its massive capacity to invent possible worlds, and not in its putative function as political doctrine. The only meaningful way in which borderland queer literature or film can have social value is precisely once we understand its aesthetic function—not as cut off from the world, but as an object organized according to its own unique conventions of communication that engage readers and audiences alike.

I end where I began: Rodriguez's texturing of a "bifocal" queer New World self. We read Rodriguez's fictionalized, highly stylized autobiography, *Brown,* not because of his straightforward presentation of fact. We are drawn to his writing because of the dominance of the aesthetic function (or "will to style") in *Brown*. We read *Brown* for his crafting of image through fresh and exciting new phraseology, and not because of the presence of a political harangue. We read *Brown* because it engages the imagination; in it we can discover a possible creative rendering of the complexity of the human condition without needing to conflate the text with radical social transformation. We read *Brown* because we can enter a world where our imagination opens to the pains and pleasures of his brown, queer identity and experience, and because we want to be touched by the sublimity of the act of literary creation. Finally, then, we read and interpret queer Chicano/a literature and film because it provides, as David Novitz argues of literature more generally, "new ways of constructing and making sense of the various happenings and events in our lives, and in doing so often furnishes us with new ways of thinking about ourselves" (233).

CHAPTER 2

John Rechy's Bending of Brown and White Canons

Outlining a Queer and Chicano Critical Frame

In 1963 John Rechy published his runaway bestseller *City of Night,* introducing the American critics and readers alike to a fictionalized American demimonde. As guide into America's cities at night, Rechy invented the unnamed, biracial (Mexican/Scottish) and bisexual protagonist from the bordertown El Paso. Since *City of Night,* Rechy has introduced his readers to dozens of other similar self-identifying characters. In spite of his long-standing emplotment of such ethnosexualized characters, however, Rechy has been traditionally identified as part of a Grove Press avant-garde—and not as a key player in the shaping of contemporary Chicano/a letters.

The identification of Rechy as author of "outlaw" (queer, bisexual, and straight) avant-garde fiction is not entirely the result of mainstream critical and scholarly reception. In a number of interviews, the biographical Rechy has sidestepped identification as a Chicano writer. In a 1995 interview with Debra Castillo ("Outlaw Aesthetics," 122), Rechy self-identifies as an "outlaw writer" and "literary saboteur" who writes novels that stretch the boundaries of "realism" (118), defy canons, and ultimately embrace all of the human experience—racial, sexual, and/or otherwise. And, in an interview in 2001 with Jonathan Kirsh (KCRW, November 28, 2001), Rechy discusses the fact that he'd always been "writing about Mexican Americans" but also expresses a "discomfort" with being "pigeonholed" in any one writerly category. He embraces instead the category that "transcends them all." So while Rechy understands that categories such as "gay writer" as well as "ethnic writer" have helped make his work visible, his sense of himself as an author is as one who writes outside a given category.

That he writes of the complex experiences of Chicano/a border-dwellers is reason enough to return to his fictions to acknowledge his position both within a literary avant-garde and a (queer) Chicano/a literary canon. Indeed, it is perhaps because of his sense of himself as a literary saboteur that he so powerfully imagines an otherwise essentialized and/or neglected queer Chicano/a identity and experience. Perhaps, it not a question of framing Rechy's narrative fictions as within an either/or paradigm. Perhaps, Rechy as literary saboteur can complexly re-imagine what it means to be Chicano/a precisely by employing avant-garde technique to bend genre and reconfigure world literary canons.

The value of Rechy's novels as a focus of study, then, is to explore how he employs a variety of narrative techniques and genres (for instance, the picaresque mode, Joycean stream of consciousness style, and/or the mixed media pastiche of a Dos Passos or Cortázar) as a plastic form that radically reframes traditional depictions of ethnosexualized characters. Rechy's value lies in our understanding how he makes memorable his protagonists' sexual/racial identity and experience in the world by employing and redeploying narrative technique and genre used by authors from all nations and from all literary periods. Here I focus on several of Rechy's early novels, *Numbers* (1967), *This Day's Death* (1969), *The Sexual Outlaw* (1977), and his more recent, *The Miraculous Day of Amalia Gómez* (1991).[1] How each novel variously conveys the psychological transformation of a number of different Chicano/a (straight, bisexual, and gay) characters emerges from exploration of both Rechy's use of narrative form (technique and genre) and his invention of story (theme, plot, and character), examples being the use of modernist interior monologue to convey Amalia's kinesis of consciousness and a postmodernist mixed-media pastiche that powerfully represents the fevered sexual self-exploration of his Jim.

Queer Chicano (Con)Texts

As mentioned above, even though many of Rechy's first novels had biracial (Mexican/Anglo) identifying protagonists, he was not taken readily into the Chicano/a literary fold. During the 1960s and early 1970s when his first novels were published and offered up as tour de force imaginings of U.S. demimondes, Chicano scholars were focused on making present those authors whose work more deliberately represented the racial and ethnic experience: Alurista and José Montoya's *causa* poetics and Rudolfo Anaya's narrative reclamation of Aztlán; Rolando Hinojosa and José Antonio Villarreal's more *straight*forward narratives of the everyday conflicts of the individual within *familia* and society. While this period of shaping a contemporary Chicano/a canon focused on those important themes and characterizations traditionally absent and/or stereotypically present in the literary mainstream, it had yet to turn its gaze to queer Chicano/a emplotted texts like those of Rechy. Indeed, it would not be until the end of the 1970s that such narratives would even be acknowledged by those within the Chicano/a scholarly community.

In 1979, a number of scholars of Chicano literature published a series of essays on John Rechy's *City of Night* in the journal *Minority Voices*. That the essays appeared in this journal known for its groundbreaking comparative analysis of U.S. ethnic literatures automatically contextualized his work within an racial frame. His novels were not just queer- and hustler-identified, but were now also Chicano. In "The Sexual Underworld of John Rechy," Charles Tatum read Rechy's work alongside that of James Baldwin, identifying their response to a shared experience of being gay and ostracized within their already racially marginalized group. For Tatum, Baldwin and Rechy are able to articulate a nonessentialist racial existence precisely because of their sexual outsiderness. Importantly, too, in Tatum's analysis we first see how the sexual confusions felt by the unnamed protagonist of *City of Night* are grounded in a like confusion over racial identification. Now, Rechy's protagonist was not just a queer urban denizen, but a protagonist ultimately forced into self-exile as a result of his conflictual racial (Mexican-Scottish, El Paso/Juárez) identification. And, in this same issue of *Minority Voices*, Carlos Zamora began to re-situate Rechy within world literature generally. In his essay "Odysseus in John Rechy's *City of Night*: The Epistemological Journey," Zamora reads *City of Night* not as "a salacious book about homosexual life" (53), but as a narrative that extends the line of the Ancient Greek epic: El Paso is the yearned-for homeland (Ithaca) for the exiled Odysseus-like protagonist whose journey through hostile worlds leads ultimately to deep wisdom and transformation of self. And, in another essay in this issue, "In Search of the Honest Outlaw: John Rechy," Juan Bruce-Novoa pays attention to content and form in *City of Night* and *The Sexual Outlaw* to identify how his narratives articulate a "Rechian dialectic" (37) that becomes the space for his protagonists to resolve their Dionysian/Apollonian struggle. In this special issue of *Minority Voices*, Tatum, Zamora, and Bruce-Novoa made the first steps towards positioning Rechy both within minor canons (Chicano/a and African American) as well as elevating him from the status of demimonde/cult-hustler writer to that of a serious writer concerned with his craft and extending the horizon of world literature generally.

While these early steps began to explore the complexities of Rechy's early novels, it is important to note that others during this period of canonization were not so expansive in their critical purview. Wittingly or not, many critics continued to identify his novels as having value only in their perversity. In a 1982 issue of *Southwest Review* Ben Satterfield, for example, at once celebrates Rechy for writing "outrageous" novels that reveal the hypocrisies of society and denigrates his work for its "terrifying" depiction of the "taunted and tortured, of the desperate and deviant" ("John Rechy's Tormented World," 78). Satterfield simply reproduces a critical sensibility that not only hyper-pathologizes the non-heteronormative but also restricts rather than expands Rechy's interpretive horizons.

While there was many a Satterfield during the early 1980s, there were also many gay/lesbian scholars and writers coming into their own. As with the renaissance of Chicano/a letters, this moment in the formation of a gay/lesbian literary landscape deepened further the complex understanding and theorization of Rechy's novels. For example, one of the preeminent scholars of gay/race/ethnic literature, Emmanuel S. Nelson, published an essay titled, "John Rechy, James Baldwin and the American Double Minority Literature." Nelson takes up the lead from Tatum, exploring more fully the relationship between Rechy and Baldwin as writers who not only hail from "ethnic and sexual minority groups" (70) but whose narratives express a different relationship to home. For Nelson, Rechy expresses both a simultaneous nostalgia for home and an "acute sense of homelessness" (73). Given the cult of machismo (active/bully vs. passive/sissy) that pervades Latino/a culture, it comes as no surprise to Nelson that Rechy's characters are conflicted about their racial identity; they feel both at home and estranged as biracial, Mexican/Anglo subjects. For Nelson, then, Rechy negotiates this "double minority alienation" (73) by inventing characters that often "operate outside the legal and moral boundaries of society and wander into the forbidden territories of human sexual experience" (73). Finally, in a move that greatly complicated the scholarly topography on Rechy, Nelson introduces the subject of gender and how Rechy's queer characters ultimately disrupt the otherwise "neat dichotomous categorization of sex roles" as defined by "standards of hypermasculinity" (72–73).

Rechy's texturing of a complex and multiform ethnoqueer sensibility continued as out-lesbian Chicana scholars and writers like Gloria Anzaldúa and Cherríe Moraga became a force within and outside the academy. Their unsentimental portraits of the Chicano community destabilized *raza*-identified binaries such as Anglo vs. brown, male vs. female, queer vs. straight, clearing the way for other scholars to embrace a wider range of Chicano/a voices. During this period, Rechy began to appear in reference books on gay and Latino/Chicano literature in which race and sexuality were no longer seen in opposition, but as composites of a whole experience. In one such book, *Chicano Literature: A Reference Guide,* for example, John Chávez identifies Rechy's characters' desperate search "for communion with others" as a result of being ostracized sexually (323). And Juan Bruce-Novoa, whose prodigious scholarly output had now made him visible as one of the key scholarly voices in the shaping of the Chicano/a letters, published an essay titled, "Homosexuality and the Chicano Novel" in the journal *Confluencia* (and re-printed in *European Perspectives on Hispanic Literature of the United States*). Bruce-Novoa not only solidified the union of "gay" with "Chicano" vis-à-vis Rechy, but also situated his work within a greater continuum of Chicano/a fiction that to varying degrees textured a gay and/or lesbian Chicano/a identity and experience. Rechy now sat alongside authors like Sheila Ortiz Taylor and Arturo Islas, as well as some rather unexpected authors like José Antonio Villarreal and Floyd Salas. Bruce-Novoa extended the gay Chicano/a literary purview by exploring the representation of gay characters with others (like the pachucos) who live their lives "between societal categories" and that manifest "an intercultural synthesis of binary opposites, perhaps never fully secure and thus always dynamic and exciting" (100). Not only is Rechy identified as a formative element in Chicano/a letters, but his novels that resist any "static order" (101) become for Bruce-Novoa the apotheosis of the "in-between zone of constant shifting and flux" (102) that characterizes the Chicano/a literary sensibility generally. With this in mind, Bruce-Novoa proclaims, "If the novel gives us an accurate reading of the Chicano community—a question in itself debatable—we can say that our community is less sexually repressive than we might expect. If nothing else, among Chicano novelists there are varying attitudes and a willingness to address the topic. This makes the Chicano novel a progressive space of dialogue, an appropriate space in and through which a more androgynous and humane Chicano identity may be forged" (105). By the mid- to late 1980s, Rechy's novels had come to embody the raison d'être of Chicano/a letters.

This climate of a Chicano/a writerly and scholarly gay/lesbian inclusiveness paved the way for the arrival of a new generation of critical reception and scholarly edification vis-à-vis Rechy's ever-expanding list of novels.[2] Many such essays aimed to think beyond the traditional perimeters of literary analysis and instead to ask bigger questions of epistemology. In this analytical turn, Rechy's novels became repositories of cultural critique. For example, in a 1992 published essay titled, "Desire and Death: The Early Fiction of John Rechy," Laurence Birken explores how Rechy's ethnosexual "Tex/Mex" characters reveal a mainstream "culture of impersonal consumption" that dominates a "dying culture of production" (237). For Birken, questions of race and sexuality in Rechy transmogrify into larger explorations of how his narratives "reflect a late-capitalist global economy of closed circuits of desire. Where racial differences exist not as political categories but as fetishes" (241). Rechy's characters who indulge in non-productive/non-work activities (body building, sex-hunting and so on) come to be read as working against and in resistance to a capitalist economy of consumption. Birkin now locates Rechy's value in his constructing of a "sexless sex" (241) that offers a counter-discourse to a late-capitalist culture of consumption. And in his essay, "Sexuality Degree Zero: Pleasure and Power in the Novels of John Rechy, Arturo Islas, and Michael Nava," Ricardo Ortiz identifies Rechy's queer Chicano characters as experiencing a Lacanian formulated trauma of fragmented subjectivity. In this early 1990s critical turn we see Rechy's novels become sounding boards for various epistemological formulations of resistance to and intervention in discourses of heteronormative capitalist containment.

The poststructuralist turn in Rechy's scholarly canonization appeared in various forms and permutations. In "The Place of Gay Male Chicano Literature in Queer Chicana/o Cultural Work," Antonio Viego attends also to questions of epistemology, but as manifest by the inclusive/exclusive divisions that define queer Latino critical studies. To disentangle from traditional gay/Latino-studies epistemological knots, Viego remaps a gay male Chicano literary discourse that is to be seen not as a site of either failure and/or success, but as an in-between space that is elastic enough to include both racially "closeted" texts like those of Rechy and queer reticent texts like Arturo Islas's *The Rain God*. And another scholar, Karen Christian, provides a Butlerean analysis of Rechy's novels in her book, *Show and Tell: Identity and Performance in U.S. Latina/o Fiction*. For Christian, Rechy invents character's that perform an "excess" (31) of sexual, racial, and gender identities and therefore subvert dominant constructions of identity that restrict and/or oppress. Such performative acts—the "unrestricted pursuit of sexual pleasure through homosexual encounters, cross-dressing, sado-masochism" (41)—are sites of resistance to heteronormative constructions of masculinity and femininity and they texture, as Christian writes, "the constant slippage between identities that makes gay Latino subjectivity readable" (53).

This sketch of the scholarship that has gravitated around Rechy's novels aims to briefly map the many twists and turns in his scholarly emplotment. Certainly, such a mapping of a critical genealogy is important to better understand how Rechy's novels *Numbers, This Day's Death, Sexual Outlaw,* and *The Miraculous Day of Amalia Gómez* engage then *disengage* different literary conventions and racial, sexual, and cultural figurations. We've certainly reached a place on this map where we no longer have to question whether Rechy should be included within the Chicano/a critical fold. As David William Foster nicely sums up, "It is no longer possible to say that Rechy's fiction is not really Chicano-marked, which was always a reason to exclude him from the canon of Chicano literature of the 1960s and 1970s" ("John Rechy," 197). However, I wonder if this is also the point in the road when we can take a critical pause and read his fictions as literature, not necessarily in a step back to the kind of reading seen in Bruce-Novoa and Zamora's early essays on Rechy, but in ways that might shed light on how his narratives work as fiction to engage, and possibly transform, the imagination of his readers. Perhaps we can now interpret Rechy's novels on their own terms: queer-Chicano and as highly organized aesthetic entities. It is with this in mind that I will now turn to an exploration of Rechy's more sexually explicit *Numbers* and *Sexual Outlaw*, as well as his more racially explicit *This Day's Death* and *The Miraculous Day of Amalia Gómez*.

More than *Numbers*

John Rechy's interest in creatively texturing queer/*mexicanidad*/borderland themes and characterizations was not skin-deep. Even before his turn to novels, he had long been writing pieces on the Mexican question for *The Nation* and other popular publications. In one of his early short stories, "El Paso del Norte" (published in *Evergreen Review* in 1958 and the seed for *City of Night*), he invents the first of a long line of borderland characters whose acute sense of being a racial outsider interweaves with a sense of sexual ostracism. Here, Rechy's narrator describes the racialized subjects as in-between figures much like the "band of fairies" who inhabit a crossroads between the United States and Mexico and also between "the hot Eastcoast and the cool Westcoast (fuzz-wise, vice-wise)" (131).[3] Rechy's narrative imagining of various border subjects is more fully realized in the 1967 publication of *Numbers*, the first novel published after his best-selling *City of Night*. Here, Rechy continues to texture an ethnoqueer borderland, but emphasizes more, at least at first glance, the queer aspect of his character's identity and experience. While the narrative introduces us to a biracially identified protagonist, Johnny Rio, as the story unfolds, it focuses more on his chaotic quest to find a new sense of sexual self and less on his experiences as a racialized subject. And yet, the more Rio sex-hunts, the more the reader has the sense that his identification as biracial does powerfully inform his sense of sexual self. Attending to how Rio's journey is textured as well as to pivotal psychological moments will reveal how race and sexuality complexly intersect in *Numbers*.

Rechy uses the conventions of the road-novel genre (a modern-day avatar of the picaresque) to frame Rio's seemingly chaotic and purposeless journey. Even before entering the storyworld proper, an extratextual blurb (first edition, 1967) identifies the novel as depicting the "grubby, lonely, nearly psychotic underside of such a life." And another blurb tells the reader that Rechy has "great comic and tragic talent." Together, they form an extratextual frame—comic, grubby, and showing the underside of life—that positions the novel within the genre of the picaresque. That is, the reader has a preview of the readerly contract that will follow: To engage with Rio's story, the reader is not to expect the character arcs and grand moments of awareness of the *Bildungsroman*, but rather the episodic story of a character who changes little and whose journey reveals the underbelly of society. And, Rechy's inclusion of a foreword where he describes how he wrote *Numbers* while on the road (one hand on the steering wheel while driving from L.A. to El Paso) further spells out this readerly contract: We are not to expect great transformations nor a clearly resolved end. Not surprisingly, when his narrator begins the story, it is in medias res and with the protagonist on the road: "He left Phoenix in the morning, in the early dawning moments . . ." (9). Much like the narrator of *Don Quixote* and other more-Chicano picaresque narratives, like Acosta's *The Autobiography of a Brown Buffalo* and Manny Martinez's *Drift*, Rechy's narrator uses a self-reflexive technique to call attention to the artifice of the narrative as an invented story and to hold up a fun-house mirror to society. Once inside the fictional world, the reader realizes that this isn't the picaresque road narrative of an Acosta or even a Jack Kerouac where episodic adventuring characters find pause in moments of heteronormative abandon, but rather one that will engage readers by texturing "the sexual frenzy" (2) of its outlawed queer protagonist, all while revealing the underbelly of a puritanical U.S. society.

As we might deduce from the narratives position within the picaresque tradition, Johnny Rio is invested with an insatiable appetite and a sense of delight in the corporeal that characterize the *pícaro*. The difference is that Rechy's *pícaro* is queer and his episodic adventuring turns upside down heteronormative rules and regulations. With the introduction of a queer *pícaro*, Rechy engages and disengages this storytelling mode by flattening out the otherwise exaggerated style that typifies such paradigm picaresque narratives as *Don Quixote*, *Tom Jones*, and *Candide*, to name a few. We see Rechy return to the picaresque again and again, including in his recent *The Life and Adventures of Lyle Clemens*, where in an epigraph he quotes Fielding's *The History of Tom Jones*: "It is well remarked by one (and perhaps by more) that misfortunes do not come single." Rechy's re-forming of style—the narrator tells the story in a straightforward, realistic voice sans hyperbole—functions much like the narrator's description of Rio's self-sculpting: it is not done to exaggerate and deform the body ("rigid grotesques with coconut muscles") for a hyperbolic or parodic exaggerated effect, but "to keep lithe and hard" (17) and natural looking. Much like the descriptions of Rio's lithe, hard body, so too does the narrator's style ask the reader to encounter the *pícaro* Rio as hard and direct. The queer subject is to be taken seriously and at face value and not as playful performer. Moreover, it is Rio as *pícaro* that the reader identifies as the character most aligned with the third-person narrative. Rio's worldview—episodic and subversive—is identified as the main filterer of the events. When the narrator first introduces Rio, it is as if he were sitting on the narrator's shoulders; there is nothing to distinguish between their different takes on the world: "Once again, Johnny can slash the desert in his speeding new car, as he has done from Texas to New Mexico, in to Arizona—the country he has traveled from Laredo, through the burned desert, the level lands leprously spotted with dried bushes; and he's rushing to Los Angeles for a reason he does not know: knowing only that he's returning for ten days" (10). And the more the narrative descriptions accumulate as the story unfolds, the more the reader aligns the narrator with Rio's point of view. The storyworld becomes an amalgam of the omniscient descriptions of the third-person narrator and the point of view of the biracial, bisexual Rio. In the reader's mind, the disembodied (conventional narrator) and embodied (queer Rio) voices create a shape-shifting and subversive composite worldview.

Numbers brings together protagonist and narrator as the narrative unfolds in its rhythmic ebbs and flows. Rio's movement along the freeways of L.A. mirrors the movement from the narrator's describing scenes in a slow and/or fast tempo. For example, there's the lulling, slow description that begins the novel as Rio sets out on the road, noticing that "the world is purple" and seeing on the highway "bands of spectral birds clustered on the pavement searching for God knows what—certainly not food, not on the bare highway and so near the sleeping city" (9). Then there is Rio on the road: "Expecting them to take flight quickly, he did not reduce his speed" (9). Or the slow/fast descriptions of Rio in L.A.: Rio enters a sex haunt, the grotto in Griffith Park, that is described as "An opening of branches before the grotto like hollow reveals the awesome spectacle of the rest of the park as it yawns in lazy sunny stretches for miles" (116). And the narrative moves forward more quickly when describing Rio's frenetic sexual encounter: "The blond youngman, who is moving along the path, has fixed his cock so that its head protrudes over the bikini, and he's stroking it. Fiercely, Johnny turns away, resenting him deeply. . . . Frantically he faces the dark one, who, finally encouraged, moves swiftly into the grotto, touches Johnny between the legs—ignoring the blond youngman approaching" (117). Again, we see how Rio and the narrator solidify into one, projecting a non-heteronormative picaresque spirit of subversion. Rio's sexual adventures are episodic, but with no grand romantic goal in mind; his encounters come with great risk (violent LAPD's vice squads, courts, and incarceration), but they are not those of Quixote's battles with marauding windmills nor Tom Jones's hetero-conquests.

The narrative pushes forward through a series of slow- and fast-paced plot and descriptive configurations that texture Rio's delaying of sexual gratification—he feels most alive while "at the edge of release" (81)—and postpone the reader's own gratification. The narrative moves forward in this slow/fast pulsating descriptive rhythm, keeping the reader in that state of intensified expectation. The narrative striptease delays that Barthean readerly *jouissance.* As a result, the reader is reminded of the text as fictional construct: one that controls how information seduces and rejects, entices and holds at bay; one that keeps us at that edge of transforming the narrative from picaresque novel to queer erotica. Not surprisingly, Rechy ends the novel sans climax; and the novel ends sans resolution—the narrator describes Johnny *in media fellatio,* then Rio announces, *"Thirty Seven"* (256). Rio reaches sexual conquest number thirty-seven, but it could have been any number as he never stated a goal. Finally, there's the overwhelming sense that this is merely one glimpse of a much longer narrative that will never reach its end. Rio will simply continue sex-hunting ad nauseam without any kinesis of consciousness. With a turn of the last page the reader is denied that final sense of *jouissance.*

While Rio's encounters often lack content (psychological and/or romantic), they do provide the reader certain in-roads into his queer, biracial interiorscape. When we first meet Rio, he is a hermetically self-contained subject that's all smooth, surface veneer and all body. Rio's Mexican and Irish genealogy, when identified and described as separate elements, locate his racialization in another space and time (the border and his parents). The Mexican element is identified with his mother and the border, a place far from L.A. that is never given narrative dimension; the Irish element, with an absent father. However, the biracial elements do come together when the narrator aesthetizes Rio's body: "Each summer his skin becomes like brown velvet" (18). Rio's connection to his racial sense of self is aesthetic. It is also auto-erotic. On one occasion the narrator describes Rio touching his sweaty glistening body then, after licking his own sweat, "feeling excitement burgeoning between his legs. He spread his knees, arches his body" (14). This is certainly not a character whose experiences in the world have led to an immediate sense of an Us vs. Them racialization. This is a character whose biracial identification becomes an expression of an in-between desiring and fetishizing of the self as Other. As Ricardo Ortiz discusses, Johnny's last name, "Rio," is significant in that it directs us to an identification of him as existing in-between U.S. and Mexican cultural and racial spaces. Ortiz reads Rio as failing finally to fully occupy such an in-between space because he cuts short the exploration of the "Mexican side of his own psyche" (115). Perhaps, however, it is precisely Johnny Rio's aestheticizing of his Mexican/Irish biracial identity that allows him to inhabit such a state of radical in-betweenness.

Numbers ends with Rio en route in an amorphous L.A., in between conquests number thirty-seven and thirty-eight, and between a past and a future. At the novel's close, the narrative reminds the reader that it is the process of

Rio's journey that allows him to come to terms with his past: "unpleasant memories" (22) of growing up in El Paso and of his mother's dying. Rio is a modern-day *pícaro* whose sense of racial and sexual self is strategically aesthetic and radically innocent, allowing him to move more freely along those in-between routes within his panoptically contained world.

Reclaiming *This Day's Death*

This Day's Death departs from *Numbers* in several ways. Its story follows more the formal conventions of *Bildungsroman* psychological realism than the conventions of the picaresque. As such, the narrative delves more deeply into the psychological workings of its protagonist, Jim Girard. Not a strategic reflective surface of biracial/bisexual identity, the narrative provides the reader with different windows into the messy entanglements of race and sexuality. (Perhaps, this messy race/sexuality tangle was a little too close to home for Rechy and the reason why he disowned *This Day's Death*. See his 1984 "Foreword" to *Numbers* and Debra Castillo's interview with Rechy in *Diacritics* [1995].)

Even before the narrative unfolds, it begins to weigh heavy with psychological complexity. On the 1969 paperback edition, the *Los Angeles Times* extratextual blurb celebrates its successful ability to get "the reader to share the agony." Other mainstream critics highlighted the narrative's powerful texturing of the dark and guilt-ridden mother/son relationship. Academic scholars also emphasized the mother/son relationship, focusing more on this as an allegory of Jim's sense of entrapment within a heteronormative society. For example, Ben Satterfield analyzes the mother's dying and diseased body as a symbol of the "pathogenic world" in which Jim exists (82). And Jim's flashbacks to El Paso and his mother that fill out the story with temporal dimension are, according to Juan Bruce-Novoa, "two sides of the same coin: the judge and the mother are figureheads of the two-headed social order and enforcers of the necessary repression of instinctual behavior" ("In Search of the Honest Outlaw," 40). As the story, packed tightly with psychological detail, unfolds and Jim travels back and forth between L.A., where he is being tried for sexual "misconduct," and El Paso, where his mother is dying, he morphs from bisexual to a more fixed gay sexual identity. By the novel's end, Jim has learned to negotiate both a suffocating motherly presence and a heteronormative socio-judicial system and comes to identify with a more liberated sense of racial and sexual self.

Much like Joyce's *A Portrait of an Artist as a Young Man*, the novel moves seamlessly between different temporalities (past and present) and follows the experiences of a culturally marginalized protagonist (the central filterer of the third-person narration) who struggles with memories of a dying Catholic mother. Distant and proximate memories of Jim's Mexican mother constantly overwhelm the narrative present; he struggles to hold back an ever-present assault of images of his sick mother (described ominously as breathing oxygen with the clank clank of a machine and wearing an "eyeless mask" [100], for example), as well as reimagined (often in the form of nightmarish dreams) bedside conversations filled with guilt and oppressive love. On one occasion, the narrator describes how in a silent dream "she had come to him after her death, her wasted body within its loose brown graveclothes giving off an odor of wax and rosewood . . . A bowl of white china had stood beside her deathbed holding the green sluggish bile which she had torn up from her rotting liver by fits of loud groaning vomiting" (5). Jim, like Joyce's Stephen, must also discard a sexually restrictive identity (both the moralism of Catholicism and heteronormative society generally) to exist more freely. And both stories speak what it is like for an individual (straight and/or queer) to choose a different path to the norm as they work through conflicts of life and death, guilt and outrage. Indeed, we see here how Rechy absorbs and transforms the Joycean *Bildungsroman* by infusing into the form a racialized Mexican and bisexual/gay subjectivity. Here, as the narrative thickens with flashbacks (that *mexicanidad* associated with Jim's experience of the domestic within a racial borderland world), we see Rechy using the form of the *Bildungsroman* to texture yet another response to racial and sexual identity. Unlike, of course, Johnny Rio in *Numbers,* Jim's connection to his *mexicanidad*—his mother and the Texas/Mexican border—is both more complex and less emancipating.

As the story unfolds, the reader sees how Jim's transformation of self is an interlocking two-fold process: to come to terms with the "riot of memories" (23) of his dying mother (his racial subjectivity) and to come to terms with his same-sex desires. Jim's relationship to his mother and his sexuality are powerfully linked when the narrative descriptions collapse both worlds. On one occasion, for example, the narrator describes Jim's confusing of memories of the sounds made by the mother "pulling her body" along and making an "awful tapping of her cane" with the sounds that fill up his present tense situation: the sounds of the jail doors clanging closed after being caught having sex with another man in a Griffith Park grotto. Past and present merge in the readers mind as sound-images of jail and the mother collapse images of racialized (childhood) and sexualized (adulthood) surveillance. This continues as the narrative imagery used to describe his childhood—memories of the "cold beam" (12) of his mother's flashlight penetrating the dark hallways of his home—recurs in the imagery of being surveilled by the menacing lights of police cars and helicopters that hunt him down as a sexual outlaw in L.A.

Jim's self-transformation takes place only once he learns how to renegotiate *both* his brownness (to determine anew a healthy relationship to his *mexicanidad*) and his sexual desire (to determine anew a healthy relationship to his same-sex sexuality). This begins with his learning to identify positively with his ethnic matrilineage. The narrative characterizes the mother as the repository of both a Spanish and mestiza *mexicanidad*: her name, Guadalupe, or "Lupe" (also the name of Rechy's mother), acts as an identifying marker of this hybrid *mexicanidad,* calling forth the religiously syncretic figure of *la virgen de guadalupe,* who is a composite of pre-Columbian, European, and mestiza Mexican. She is the Catholic Virgin Mary, the pre-Columbian princess Iztaccihuatl, and the *indígena* figure who appeared at Tepeyac to Juan Diego. The narrative describes Lupe as dark and Indian featured, but with green eyes. In the novel, then, Lupe comes to represent a *mexicanidad* that is both culturally and biologically hybrid. As the narrative unfolds and Jim reflects on his past, the reader learns, along with Jim, that her "orthodox" Catholicism in practice is also syncretic. On one telling occasion, she prays for salvation while being healed by a local *curandera.* That the narrative always identifies her as inhabiting an in-between space (life and death, as well as U.S./El Paso and Mexico/Juárez) further emphasizes this hybrid existence and sensibility. Indeed, the more Jim moves away from a static understanding of the maternal matrix with its concomitant imagery of darkness, decay, and suffering, the more he can come into a new, more pleasurable sense of his own *mestizaje.* Those dark and oppressive images (the mother's wheezing sounds, breathing masks, her rosary beads, and so on) shift to images of the ocean and light.

Jim's sense of racialized subjectivity is codified not just in his relationship to his mother, but also in the absence of his French-identified father, whose presence in Jim's life was only ever that of a static image: an "austere and stern" (18) photographic portrait or a tableau of his father's acts of "black rage" (64) frozen in his memory. Again, Jim's understanding of himself is tied to how he relates to biological lineage. Here, it is less his sense of opening to a more hybrid cultural/racial identity as seen with the mother, Lupe, and more his ability to reread his father as weak and impotent and not as omnipotent tyrant. He de-couples the static and oppressive image of father and learns to live without fear and to experience, as the narrator describes, "for the first time a hint of fulfillment" (242). For Jim, finally, this opens him up to a new way of engaging with the world sexually; it no longer has to be violent and filled with "rage and anger" (73). Jim's coming into a more liberated sense of himself sexually goes hand in hand, then, with his complicating of a static and oppressive image of Euro-Anglo patriarchy and his hybridizing of a Mexican matrilineage.

Jim comes into a new relationality to father (violence associated with European conquest) and mother (static repository of violence) within a topsy-turvy contemporary Los Angeles. Prima facie, L.A. might not appear to be the most conducive of places to foster such a transformation. On one occasion, the narrator describes it as a "smoggy tangle of gray" (158); on another, it is filled with insomniac exiles described variously as "haunted," "hunting," and "lost" (31). It is described as a city where such lost souls are swallowed up by its freeways and its tangles of "overpasses," "underpasses," and "on ramps" (222). This is a vision of L.A. that describes more a place that would deepen Jim's alienation and estrangement and less a place for a positive transformation of his racial/sexual sense of self. Perhaps, however, Rechy's vision of an apocalyptic L.A. (and we see this in many of his novels) is both degenerative and regenerative. Within such a space of chaos and destruction, a character like Jim can rise again from the ashes. We can read the novel's end—Jim speeding along the freeways to return home to, the narrator describes, "the edge of the city, El Paso" (244)—as just such a rebirth. The narrator uses images of movement and freedom to describe his return home where he will, as the narrative suggests, write down the story of his coming to terms with his biracial and bisexual sense of self.

In or *Out* of the Law?

Nearly a decade after Stonewall and during the flourishing of a late-1970s queer/lesbian sex scene in places like New York, San Francisco, and L.A., John Rechy published his experimental novel *The Sexual Outlaw: A Documentary* (1977). To creatively capture this period when, in the words of Jonathan Dollimore, "sexual radicalisms paved the way for those at margins of society to be seen as resistant force that exists outside dominant hegemonic paradigm" (*Sexual Dissidence*, 213), Rechy departs from his earlier, more linear and singularly emplotted narrative style. Here, he combines a number of different voices—interview, journalistic reportage, and third-person gritty realism—to provide a kaleidoscopic vision of a contemporary L.A. that follows a moment in the life of the biracial queer protagonist, Jim. Rechy's collage of narrative styles along with his many deliberate moments of fictionalizing fact de-essentialize racial and sexual subjectivity, embodying, as Dollimer further delineates, a "restless search ever further outward in search of new marginal extremes of being" (214). The form and content of *The Sexual Outlaw*, then, take the reader less along those trajectories already seen with Rechy's *Bildungsroman* and picaresque stories and provide instead a series of mutually interacting and reciprocating voices (straight and queer, white and brown) that texture, as Rafael Pérez-Torres states, "a demimonde beyond the horizon of heterosocial vision" ("The Ambiguous Outlaw," 205). Indeed, as the narrative unfolds and the voices dialogically collide, the narrative reveals both the contradictions of heteronormativity as well as how an outlawed sexuality can itself become oppressive.

This pastiche narrative form contains a number of differently tagged voices, some more explicit and dogmatic than others. For example, when the narrative cuts in the so-identified "Voice Over" sections, the narrator might state something like, "The promiscuous homosexual is a sexual revolutionary" (28); or it might announce, "Promiscuity is the righteous form of revolution" (31). In the "Mixed Media" sections, the narrative takes the shape of news reportage, often describing heterosexual rape and "perverse" same-sex sexual acts in the same breath. However, such voices along with others are organized in such a way as to provide a complete worldview—a narrative gestalt that tells the reader to read this as a novel organized according to aesthetic structures to convey such a view of the world. That is, while the voices taken individually represent stark ideological positions, as a whole they convey a complex and contradictory racialized and sexualized Los Angeles. Rechy's collage storytelling technique calls attention to its artifice as fictional construct, reminding its reader that, for example, Jim's S&M encounters are not to be taken as a real politics of resistance.[4] The novel's self-reflexive and playful form importantly solidifies in the reader's mind the role of the literary text to capture such a world and, at best, to open eyes to the experiences of the biracial queer character, Jim; at the same time its technique and characterization also reveal the role of real forms of power, located in the state apparatus and executed by a real ruling class, that dominate and exploit ethnoqueer subaltern subjects through police force, legislation, and judicial institutions.

As the novel unfolds and the different voices increasingly intercut into the narrative flow (Jim's story), Rechy situates *The Sexual Outlaw* within a storytelling tradition that can be traced back to François Rabelais's *Gargantua and Pantagruel*. Like Rabelais's narrative extravaganza, *The Sexual Outlaw* also juxtaposes voices to create, as Mikhail Bakhtin writes of such narratives generally, "a florid milieu of admixtures and recombinations" (*Rabelais and His World*, 157). Moreover, it sets up the terms of the readerly contract: it is to be read as a playful recombination and interanimation of voices that destabilize monologic narratives. It is a novel that continues to stretch that genealogy of storytelling we also see in John Dos Passos's *U.S.A. Trilogy* and Julio Cortázar's *Hopscotch*. With this in mind, the reader will understand that Rechy's narrative aims to convey a multiform representation of the many lives and voices that make up a total vision of a city—a technique used, for example, by Dos Passos with his "camera eye" (more poetic), "newsreel" (more straightforwardly journalistic), and biographical (stories of important historical figures) styles. Just as Dos Passos used juxtaposition of style and voice to find the form to represent New York City in all its complexity, so too, then, does Rechy juxtapose styles to create a multilayered montage gestalt of his L.A. However, of course, Rechy's novel re-forms this technique considerably when he uses his "Voice Over," "Mixed Media," and so on to map territories of the hustlers, cruisers, and the sexual racial "exile" generally (*Sexual Outlaw*, 23). As the story unfolds, Rechy uses the collage effect to engage, then disengage with the conventions that characterize this storytelling mode.

The repository for this disengaging sensibility is Jim. In much the same style seen in *Numbers* and *This Day's Death*, Rechy uses a straightforward narrative style to plot Jim's story, but with an increased presence of freeze-frame descriptions that have more of startling effect: "Jim's body contracts! Pulls forward like a gun! Death is challenged. Cocks explode! Jim's cock shoots in the ass. The tall man shoots into his lover's mouth, the other shoots a gliding arc of sperm into the air" (106). The stark narration here reflects the confidence of Jim; he is not the sexually confused character of Rechy's earlier novels, but rather a practiced sex hunter. The use of the tableaux style mirrors Rechy's invention of a character who isn't trying to renegotiate his relationship to his sexual and racial self (past and present), but a character who has already arrived. For Jim, as the narrator describes, "each moment bears its total reality in his hunting existence—*now*. The past evaporates" (138). Jim wants to clear the space for a sexual utopia. Jim is a character driven by his huge appetite for sex. There's no pathologizing (ironic or not) of a biracial queer identity here. Rechy's Jim is a perfectly contained character that provides no psychological depth in order to reflect on a polished surface the contradictions of his social world.

This isn't to say that such a hermetically sealed and all-surface character doesn't reflect. Ironically, at the moment of absolute self-assurance comes a reminder of his own fragility: his body's natural process of decay. To exist only as surface (by embracing an identity based solely on his quick and psychologically meaningless sexual encounters), his surface must remain attractive: his body must remain youthful and desirable. Yet, as the narrative unfolds, he becomes desperately aware of this impossibility. So, while Jim seeks to strip physical intimacy of its ideological dressing (heterosexual codes of courting and romance), he finds himself contained by a similarly restrictive belief in the youthful body. The narrative continually reminds the reader of this contradiction—that for sexual outlawry to take place, it must conform to common (straight and queer) principles of desire. Not only is the narrative replete with Jim's noticing various "shriveled" and "skeletal" (73) bodies that cause revulsion, but this is contrasted with his obsessive need to work out to maintain that tight, sculpted look of a body in its prime (22, 43, 48). More than a struggle against heteronormativity, he's fighting biology to prolong the inevitable: to be "loose-fleshed," "abandoned and desperate and alone" (114). The novel ends with Jim experiencing a hallucinatory vision of an old man wearing dark sunglasses and holding "a color-tipped white cane tap-tap tapping on the dry sidewalk" (306). As the narrator describes, "Jim realizes that the strange night creature is advancing toward his car with the cane flailing fiercely. Jim puts his car in reverse, U-turns, and drives away" (306). His dramatic response reflects less a character in control of himself and more one who reflects on a different level the ultimate fragility of existence. No matter how perfectly contained and complete a character such as Jim, there will be something that will destabilize.

Feelings of death and decay not only appear in the form of haunting old men figures, but also in the omnipresence of an apocalyptic L.A. In *Writing the Apocalypse*, Lois Parkinson Zamora not only identifies this narrative genre as focusing less on the "psychological interaction" of characters than on the complex historical and/or cosmic forces in whose crosscurrent those characters are caught (3). It is a genre that seeks to render visible larger cultural and historical contexts within which characters behave and move; it is a narrative filtered through the point of view of a narrator "radically opposed to existing spiritual and political practices" and who exists "outside the cultural and political mainstream," awaiting the arrival of "a new and transcendent realm" (2). *The Sexual Outlaw* clearly employs such apocalyptic conventions. However, unlike the Judeo-Christian promise of a God-like cleansing, redemption, and harmonious reintegration, Rechy's L.A. relishes the now of the apocalyptic in-betweenness: it is real and present and surreal and in transition; it is disintegrating and integrating at once. Moreover, Jim's sex-hunting and quest to transgress heteronormativity is made impotent when police car headlights like a "wrathful white sun" or the "strange glare . . . from a demonic cop helicopter" light up and "freeze the sexhunters" (52).[5] So in spite of the utopic impulse, Jim is forced to move in the shadows of a city that is itself in decay. Jim's L.A. is framed by fires that create an apocalyptic effect when, as the narrator describes, "the noon sun attempted powerfully to penetrate the clouds of smoke, the city turned fiercer orange" (35); again, in the narrator's words, the "California sun scorches coldly white" behind thick layers of smog (147). It is a city that constantly threatens to swallow Jim with its natural disasters that lead to impenetrable orange skies and mudslides. The narrator describes him standing in its "white sun" thinking that "the palmtreed city would explode before he reached his car" (241). However, L.A. is also a city at the edge of massive transformation. The narrator describes "thousands of gay men and women riding a tide of pent-up rage released at last" (183) to suggest their own cleansing and redeeming of those who so easily hurl epithets like "faggot," "nigger," "chink," "kike," and "spic" (232).

Perhaps Rechy's *The Sexual Outlaw* ultimately offers a new way of understanding queer (ethnic or otherwise) sexuality not so much in the characterization of Jim, but in the presence of the fiction itself. Namely, that it is the reader's engagement with textualization of these oppositions—racial/ethnic versus queer identity, beauty/youth versus ugliness/decay, and so on—that offers a glimpse of the new relationality Jim seeks, found not in bodies and selves and "hard cocks" that "strain in isolation" (65) and that ultimately lead to "Nothing. Nothing" (65) but in the act of reading the novel. Accordingly, Lois Parkinson Zamora describes how apocalyptic narratives generally "dramatize the decisive moment when an old world discovers a believable new world and either reacts against the old system or incorporates it into its new design. In contemporary fiction, that new design may be the literary work itself" (177). *The Sexual Outlaw* dramatizes the rising of the new against the old sexual and racial paradigms in a narrative of novel hybrid design.

Ethnic (Post) Modernism

The 1980s witnessed the coming into their own of Chicana writers such as Ana Castillo, Denise Chávez, Sandra Cisneros, Gloria Anzaldúa, Cherríe Morgan, and Helena Maria Viramontes, who made visible to their Chicano counterparts and to a mainstream readership those figures otherwise left out of Chicano and mainstream letters. It was also a time of pause after a decade of mainstream hysteria fanned up around AIDS. Gay and lesbian authors could begin to be seen once again as human and as not monstrously perverse and threats to civilization. (For more on this historical moment, see David Román's essay, "Fierce Love and Fierce Response: Intervening in the Cultural Politics of Race, Sexuality, and AIDS.") With the 1980s conservative backlash diminishing somewhat, Rechy published his more Chicano/a-identified novel *The Miraculous Day of Amalia Gómez* (1991; paperback edition 1993), which textured issues of race and gender more than his earlier novels had. Rechy invents as the novel's central protagonist—and sometime filterer of events—the straight Chicana Amalia, who must come to terms with her own implicit participation in the violent homophobia and racism that pervades her contemporary, post-AIDS L.A. Gender, race, and sexuality are intimately interlinked. As he states more directly in an interview with Debra Castillo, "I believe that the basis of anti-homosexuality lies in antiwoman attitudes" ("Outlaw Aesthetics," 115).

When the novel first appeared, many critics were taken aback with Rechy's fleshing out of a Chicana (not his usual queer, biracial) protagonist. As with other "ethnic" novels that appeared during this period, many mainstream critics simply identified it as a kind of ethnographic text that documented a hot and spicy Chicano/a way of life. For example, a reviewer for *Publishers Weekly* writes how Rechy "scorchingly evokes the prejudice faced by Mexican Americans and other minorities, the poverty, gang warfare, illegal border crossings and visions of salvation amid hopelessness" (87). And in a review for *Library Journal,* Mary Molinaro describes how the novel gives readers a glimpse into "the motivations and challenges of *barrio* life" (147). Rechy had moved his biracial sexual "outlaws" to the side and center-staged a day in the life of an East L.A. Chicana, providing his reviewers another form of an insider track: this time into a barrio life *exotica.*

The publication of *The Miraculous Day* also meant that he could be more fully taken into a more gender- and queer-inclusive post-1980s Chicano/a literary fold. Indeed, as the story unfolds (mostly through a series of flashbacks) not only are readers given a sense of the ups and downs of the straight Chicana Amalia, but also of how her life intimately intersects with sexual "outlaws" that include her gay hustler son, Juan. The story reveals a contemporary L.A. filled with xenophobes and homophobes but where a true understanding of self requires the embracing of all the complexities of being queer and straight, male and female, old and young.

The novel's reception by several Chicano/a and Latino/a scholars traces its complex texturings of race, sexuality, and gender. In "Sexuality Degree Zero," for example, Ricardo Ortiz chooses to read the novel as a document that manifests Rechy's own anxiety about being "out" as a racialized subject. Desire, Ortiz contends, "plays more often against than with itself in the construction of a subject at once libidinally and ideologically 'free'" (113). And, in a review of *The Advocate,* "Less than a Miracle," Eric Gutierrez sees Rechy's radical departure from his earlier, more queer-focused novels filled with "valor and truth" (86) as a complete failure. For Gutierrez, Rechy's attempt to texture Chicano life in L.A. is told "imperfectly" (86) because of his distant remove from his material and subject; this results less in the writing of a complex novel about race, sexuality, and gender than in the mainstreaming of L.A. barrio life for a Geraldo television audience. Gutierrez concludes, "In trying to tell the story of Mexican Americans in Los Angeles, he has told no one's in particular, at least not Amalia Gómez's" (86). In a more laudatory fashion and one that focuses more on race than sexuality, Carl Gutiérrez-Jones's critical review essay explores how the novel critiques the cultural constitution of "illegality"; by this he means the judicial rhetoric that leads to discursive and real containment of Latinos in the United States. For Gutiérrez-Jones, Amalia's quest leads to her discovery of a space for the free "expression of sexuality not bound by violence, exploitation, or humiliation" ("Desiring B/orders," 106); it is also a narrative that ultimately takes its readers on a journey that provides a "critical stance toward consensual ideologies that keep people like Amalia herself fixated upon the supposedly empowering exercise of often limited, even deranged, choices" (106). And Luis León applauds the narrative for its poetic use of a revised Catholicism (invested with Aztec and Nahuatl Amerindian myth and iconography) that helps the socially marginalized like Amalia overcome an everyday world filled with racism and sexism. León writes, for instance, about how Rechy's invention of Amalia "brings into relief religion from oppression by inscribing a human face on the poetic *uses* of religion in a postcolonial context, demonstrating how Amalia rewrites her social script by reordering her symbolic cosmos, connection cognition and action: practice" ("The Poetic Uses of Religion in '*The Miraculous Day of Amalia Gómez*,'" 221–222). Finally, in *Border Matters*, José David Saldívar interprets the novel as a radical expansion of a "borderland consciousness" (108) that is more inclusive of a queer Chicano subjectivity. Here, Rechy's use of a surrealist narrative technique destabilizes those discourses that make "real" and "natural" the denigration of those like Amalia and "Rechy himself" (119).

The Miraculous Day of Amalia Gómez is a story that couches within its pages a deep anxiety about being "out" racially and sexually. Amalia is a character who has been the victim of racism and heterosexism and responds accordingly by existing in denial. Yet, in the characterization of Amalia, the story finally delights in her being out as a Chicana who discards her heavy veils of denial, accepting her son as gay and finally standing up to the abuse of her daughter within her own household. And, she's a character much like Rechy's Johnny Rio, Jim Girard, and Jim. In spite of her traumatic experiences with men and sex, for example, she continues to enjoy her own body's form. And, much of her attraction to Catholicism stems from its sensuality: at one point she's drawn to Christ's "loincloth revealing sinews over his groin" (150–151).

Of course, there is more to the story than Amalia's sensual proclivities. It is a story that opens its readers' eyes to the experiences of a Chicana character (single mother of three) living in an L.A. filled with everyday racist and sexist violence. It is a story about how being identified as Chicana or Chicano within a xenophobic mainstream can lead to different silences: Amalia and her mother's silence regarding familial abuse, for one. It is also a story that culminates in a religious "epiphany," an epiphany that takes place within the secular, hyper-capitalist space of a Beverly Hills shopping mall. Indeed, in a discussion of Rechy's work, David William Foster extends the definition of epiphany to describe that moment of "discovering not what one *is*, but what one *has become*" ("Homoerotic Writing and Chicano Authors," 49). It is precisely this sense of *becoming* that pervades all of his novels and that is central to the Rechian narrator worldview. As Foster concludes, "Rechy's view of social instability, not as the curse of a degraded world but as part of a lived experience that is constantly renewing itself, is eminently queer insofar as it refutes the fixed, frozen, or immutable (and, therefore, dead-end) categories of straight ideology" (49). Finally, then, Rechy employs a number of different storytelling modes such as the modernist identified stream of consciousness to radically emplace Amalia's subjective experience and impression of this topsy-turvy world.

Indeed, though *The Miraculous Day* is largely governed by a stream of consciousness narration, Rechy uses a number of other styles, including straightforward realism. The novel's opening in medias res and with a third-person point of view readily reveals just such a mixture:

> When Amalia Gómez woke up, a half hour later than on other Saturdays because last night she had had three beers instead of her usual weekend two, she looked out, startled by God knows what, past the screenless iron-barred window of her stucco bungalow unit in one of the many decaying neighborhoods that sprouts off the shabbiest part of Hollywood Boulevard; and she saw a large silver cross in the otherwise clear sky.

(3)

This straightforward, third-person realist description, however, swiftly shifts to the more subjective narrative as filtered through Amalia's point of view: the reader is never sure if this "cross" is a miraculous appearance, a "filmy cloud," or a streak of smoke caused by "a sky writing airplane" (3). The line between real and imagined increasingly blurs also as the narrative fills up with Amalia's internal monologues and her re-memory of her early life in El Paso, Texas. Of course, though the narrative is predominantly filtered through Amalia's experience and (mis)interpretation of her world, Rechy uses a number of other styles here. As he mentions on one occasion, he also uses what he calls a "Mexican–Catholic-Church style" (Debra Castillo, "Outlaw Aesthetics," 118), a "rich, ripe" writing style that, he states, "comes from an early exposure to blood-drenched statues of saints writhing in exhibitionistic agony in churches; statues real and artificial at the same time (like the best art); exposure to grand melodrama of the journey to Calvary, performed by gorgeous agonized creatures" (118).

It is precisely this "Mexican-Catholic-Church style" that reinvests a Chicano presence into this narrative modeled after *Ulysses*. Rechy provides us with more than style and technique to attune his readers to his Chicano revising of a British/Irish literary modernist tradition. The initial narrative cues are as follows: The novel begins with Amalia waking up on a Saturday morning to begin her journey through Los Angeles; though it is a Thursday and in a Dublin of 1904, Joyce's Leopold Bloom also wakes up to journey through his city. Both Amalia, a Chicana who distances herself from her mother's internalized racist, *criollo* values, and Bloom, a converso-Jew who delights in "grilled mutton kidneys" (55), are at the ethno-racial margins of society. Both live in their imaginations: Bloom through imagined romantic forays as Henry Flower Esq. with his pen-pal Martha, and Amalia through her Maria Felix *telenovela* fixation. Both walk around their cities with letters in their pocket: Bloom with the letter from Martha and Amalia with two letters in her pocket, one from the public attorney saying her son Juan was caught hustling his body and another from her son Manny, who recently committed suicide.[6] Both are silenced: Bloom by Molly and Amalia by her patriarchal and racist environs—after she is raped, she wanted to scream, "but couldn't form the words" (59). Both are betrayed: Bloom by his wife and Amalia by each of her three husbands. Both wake up feeling hopeless—physically and emotionally impotent.[7] In addition to the affiliation with Bloom, Amalia reveals a strong connection to the Irish-Catholic Stephen Dedalus: though Amalia is more Catholic than Stephen, both are postcolonial subaltern subjects who struggle with absent fathers and oppressive memories of their mothers. And, like Stephen, Amalia sees her life as a procession of unactualized possibilities. Amalia is part Molly Bloom: both of them struggle with memories of a lost son—Amalia's guilt is over her son Manny's suicide (murder)—and both ultimately come into a positive vision of themselves and the world at the close of their stories. Molly announces the deeply affirming "yes, yes, yes . . ." and Amalia exclaims, "Yes! . . . I am sure!" (206). Finally, when we first meet Amalia, we learn that she has had three beers the night before, has been divorced three times, and has had three children, including Manny, who committed suicide.[8] That the number three works as a leitmotiv in *The Miraculous Day* further solidifies its connection to Joyce's *Ulysses*, a novel divided into three main sections that reflect the three elements of the Trinity (and syllogistic rhetorical form generally) that lead to the perfect, unified essence.

While much of the narrative of *The Miraculous Day* progresses through a series of internal monologues that give shape to Amalia's past, her journey through L.A. largely follows that of Bloom's through Dublin and unfolds as follows:

- Amalia sets out on her journey and first encounters death. The narrator describes how "the new sights of the city accosted her. Hollywood Boulevard, just a block away from here, was the worst, at times like a graveyard for the walking dead, so many of them young, dazed, hollow-eyed" (115). In episode 3 ("Proteus"), Stephen sees a dead dog and muses on the return to primal matter.
- Amalia encounters Protestant zealots. In the face of this assaulting presence, she declares, "I was born Catholic and I'm gonna *die* Catholic!" (117).

This is both an affirmation of her religious faith, and also her identity as Mexican American. In episode 1 ("Telemachus"), Stephen embraces his Irishness and rejects the British Protestant Haines's overtures of friendship.

- Amalia stops off at Carl Jr.'s for a bite to eat. However, her wish to eat breakfast is swiftly dashed when she's told it's no longer being served. She orders a special hamburger meal instead, mostly to get the promised free pair of "shades" (120). When her meal arrives, its an "undercooked bloody burger" (122) that she cannot eat. (The emphasis on "shades" and not sunglasses here also directs us to Bloom's encounter of the shades, statues of the dead, in episode 6, "Hades.") The waitress rejects Amalia's request to change the food. This is also when Amalia begins to think of Reynaldo and her daughter Gloria. In episode 8 ("Lestrygonians"), Bloom is disgusted by the sight of men shoveling all sorts of food down their gullets in the Burton restaurant Davy Byrne's Pub. The episode is characterized by images of peristalsis, indigestion, and rejection. Bloom remembers Molly and his dead son; he then narrowly escapes an encounter with his archrival Blazes Boylan by ducking into the National Museum.
- Amalia encounters a man rushing at her announcing the end of the world and whose "presence was so terrifying that everyone nearby dodged away except Amalia. She could not move" (129). She says "No" to the terrifying figure, and moves on. In episode 6 ("Hades") Bloom's encounter with death is filled with references to cannibalism (171).
- Amalia takes pause in her journey to sip a "frothy orange drink" (132). In episode 4 ("Calypso"), Molly awaits her morning tea in bed; the dominant color in this episode is orange.
- Amalia stops at a Mexican bakery (136) that also sells lottery tickets; then she moves on to El Bar & Grill. Here, Amalia recalls the night when her date with love-interest Angel turns from romantic interlude to a violent and degrading assault on her body. She also remembers her son Manny's death. In episode 11 ("Sirens"), Bloom visits the Ormond Hotel, where he sees Molly's lover Blazes Boylan and contemplates defeat, rejection, and defection. Here he also recalls the death of his son Rudy.
- Amalia enters a church and remarks on the presence of "a cadaver in black, so terrifying in her display of sorrow and pain." (148). This again triggers memories of Manny's funeral. Here, Amalia also confesses to a priest who needs to hear her story in "precise words" to identify "precise sins" (156). She wonders afterwards if he needed these details to masturbate. This has a strong parallel with episode 6 ("Hades") in the focus on death (Paddy Dignam's funeral), as well as episode 11 ("Sirens"), with its images of tumescence and masturbation.

- Amalia encounters Anglo environmentalists who hurl racist epithets at her when she refuses to sign their petition. Afterwards, she visits a *curandero*: "A small peep-door opened. An eye looked out" (164). Unlike the *curandero* who sees the world myopically, Amalia begins to see her world stereoscopically and with more complexity. (She becomes more understanding of her son Juan's sexuality, for example.) This has a parallel with episode 12 ("Cyclops") when Bloom enters Barney Kiernan's Bar; here, he encounters grotesque chauvinism and racism. The pub-goers only see the world narrowly and seemingly myopically. Bloom also has greater insight and sees the world more complexly.
- Amalia ends her journey at a Beverly Hills shopping mall, which leads to her being taken hostage, the misfiring of a bullet, and the shattering of the shopping mall's glass atrium. She has a vision of the Virgen de Guadalupe. In episode 15 ("Circe") Bloom meets Stephen at a brothel in "nighttown" and the narrative spins into a series of phantasmagoric episodes that play out Stephen's feelings of rejection and guilt toward his dead mother (she visits him as a ghostly aberration) and describes his smashing of the chandelier with an ashplant and crying, "Nothung!" (583). (This act has been identified by critics like Malcolm Bradbury as the end of history.) Bloom and Stephen leave the brothel and find themselves on the streets of an apocalyptic Dublin: "brimstone fires spring up. Dense clouds roll past. . . . Whores screech. Foghorns hoot. . . . The midnight sun is darkened. The earth trembles. . . . A chasm opens with a noiseless yawn" (598). Notably, too, Rechy's narrator describes the day Amalia first arrives in L.A. as "eerie" and when the "Santa Ana winds blew in from the hot desert and fires blazed along the horizon" (4). On the day that Amalia sets out on her journey, she remarks on the "heated winds" and the fierce fire that "raged and coated the sun with a veil of smoke," as well as "the red, yellow, and green of traffic lights [that] glowed strangely out of the film of ashes" (38). On yet another occasion, L.A. is described as a "pit of madness" (130).

The Miraculous Day crescendos with the scene of shattering glass in the Beverly Hills shopping mall. Amalia has an epiphany, discussed as the convergence of "ethno-racial formation, homosexuality, and maybe even queer theory" by José David Saldívar in *Border Matters* (122). Saldívar concludes that Rechy's "displaced fable" is a critique of "conventionally understood class liberation that ignores gender, sexuality, and ethno-race" (122). Amalia's epiphany is about her seeing the world clearly—her coming out of a deep denial about her racial, sexual, and gendered self. It is also an epiphany that expands the boundaries of the novel. It announces the novel's allegiance with other modernists, like Yeats and Woolf. Just before Amalia has her epiphany the narrator describes her thinking, "The world is coming apart . . . I am coming apart" (188). This is more than the narrator detailing her response to the news that her son Juan is queer and the revelation of her daughter Gloria's abuse by the stepfather figure. It is this, as well as Rechy alluding directly to Yeats's "Second Coming" (1920). And, at the beginning of the novel, Amalia sights the "cross" and wonders if it is a "filmy cloud" or "a sky writing airplane" (3), a direct allusion to the recurring image and motif of Virginia Woolf's *Mrs. Dalloway* that is similarly constructed as a series of internal monologues that unfold in and through a city (London). This is Rechy's solidifying of the bond between his narrative fiction and that of either a British woman writer like Woolf or Irish modernists like Yeats and Joyce. Like these writers, Rechy, too, is an author writing from outside a dominant/dominating (Anglo, heterosexual) world. Like the modernists, Rechy is a writer disillusioned by his world filled with death and destruction. Like his predecessors, Rechy, too, is concerned with giving texture to the subjective experience of a reality that is increasingly uncertain and uncontrollable. Of course, where modernists like Joyce and Yeats had Heisenberg's Uncertainty Principle, the destruction of civilization as witnessed by the WWI and the British colonization of Ireland, and a world reinterpreted by Marx, Freud, and Darwin, Rechy had contemporary racist anti-immigration (the U.S./Mexico border-patrol war) and a "gay-plague" homophobic society that exposed him to meaninglessness and the destruction of any traditional sense of the wholeness of individual character. It would seem almost obvious, then, that he would choose a modernist like Joyce as his model in the writing of *The Miraculous Day of Amalia Gómez*.

When I refer to modernist, I do not refer to the "high modernist" technique of self-reflexivity and abstraction that makes for a distant and removed narrative, but merely those techniques used by Joyce and others that break with convention to give the reader a glimpse into the unfamiliar and chaotic underside of everyday life; it is Rechy's giving texture and life to Amalia, who lives under the chaotic freeway: "On the sidewalk and just a few feet from her bedroom window was a sign that said TO HOLLYWOOD FREEWAY" (110). Rechy is a "barriological writer" (see Raúl Villa's *Barrio-Logos*) who reinhabits "reified spaces of dominant urban planning" (Villa, 155) in a redeployment of the modernist form and a texturing of a Chicana subject. He uses a postcolonial modernist writer like Joyce to texture the everyday struggles of Amalia to survive in a world filled with a long legacy of conquest and colonialism. Just as Joyce's Irish character Stephen sees the British history of colonization of Ireland as "a nightmare from which I am trying to wake" (*Ulysses*, 34) that leads to his shattering of the chandelier in a Dublin brothel and declaring: "Nothung!" (583), so, too, does the shattering of glass in the shopping mall

(*The Miraculous Day*, 191) function as an epiphany for Amalia: the shattering of the glass emits a "translucent brightness" (201) and for the first time she feels alive (206).

Concluding Remarks

John Rechy certainly invents narratives that set up a complex relationship between Chicano identification and experience and that queer sexuality. Perhaps, however, what is interesting about Rechy's novels is not how much of ingredient A and B make for more or less Chicanoness and/or more or less queerness. Perhaps we're finally at a stage of Chicano/a criticism that can take these aspects of his writing as a given and can focus on how he engages and disengages with a variety of genres and narrative techniques to both seduce and then open his readers' eyes to complex and creative formulations of racial, sexual, and gendered identity. His characters, such as Jim Girard in *This Day's Death* and Johnny Rio in *Numbers,* come into a more fluid sense of racial and sexual self as they travel freeways between El Paso (a birthplace filled with Catholic guilt and associated with brown Mother) and Los Angeles (freedom of sexual play and associated with white Father). Moreover, Rechy's engagement with the closet metaphor is complicated in the fleshing out of a Chicana protagonist in *The Miraculous Day of Amalia Gómez.* Here, Rechy's redeployment of *Ulysses* as narrative container demonstrates how queered Chicano/a texts can engage, then disengage a high-aesthetic modernism to texture the lives of those at the U.S. social margins. Finally, John Rechy's novels are queer and Chicano, and much more, in their texturing of the complex contours of race and sexuality as engaged with world literary themes and genres.

Arturo Islas's and Richard Rodriguez's Ethnosexual Re-architexturing of Metropolitan Space

In *La Mollie and the King of Tears* and *Days of Obligation* respectively, novelist Arturo Islas and journalist Richard Rodriguez pen homographic texts that queer the contemporary Chicano/a and mainstream U.S. textual landscape. Islas and Rodriguez create first-person narrating subjects—a smooth-talking pachuco, Louie Mendoza, for Islas and a hesitantly vulnerable yet penetratingly bold self-as-narrator for Rodriguez—who journey through world cityscapes to destabilize zones of racial and sexual control, then reinhabit such zones sans a North vs. South, straight vs. bent oppositionality. The authors Rodriguez and Islas engage and disengage with narrative convention in their fictionalizing of metropolitan spaces and emplotting of complexly textured queer Chicano subjectivities.

This move to locate Chicano/a subjectivities (queer or otherwise) in the contemporary U.S. metroplex doesn't originate with Islas and Rodriguez. Speaking to the rise of urban Chicano novels generally, critic Juan Bruce-Novoa claimed,

> if the novel gives us an accurate reading of the Chicano community . . .
> we can say that our community is less sexually repressive than we might
> expect. . . . This makes the Chicano [urban] novel a progressive space for
> dialogue, an appropriate space in and through which a more androgynous
> and humane Chicano identity may be forged.
>
> ("HOMOSEXUALITY AND THE CHICANO NOVEL," 105)

Since the early 1970s, Chicano/a textscapes have looked increasingly to the formation of the Chicano/a in the city.[1] Nonetheless, these early cityscape texts mostly turned to urban centers to foreground an Us/Them struggle between the brown characters and the Euro-Anglo powers that be. Chicano writers like Rudolfo Anaya and Ron Arias painted cities heavily scratched with the grit and grime of racial oppression while thickening the sepia-toned layers that describe Chicanos in the Aztlánified countryside—a space that sanctions the hardened Chicano phallus while denigrating the Chicana *panocha*. And when writers complicated the characters' sense of self/Other in the city (as with Oscar "Zeta" Acosta's massively ingestive narrator-as-self, who metastasizes all of mainstream and marginal culture), they often reproduced restrictive heteronormative paradigms: Chicanas are either virgins or whores (*Chingadalupes/malinchistes*); queers are either invisible or hypergenitilized half-men. As more Chicana-authored texts made it to print—those of Isabella Rios, Lucha Corpi, Cherríe Moraga, Gloria Anzaldúa, Alma Luz Villanueva, to name a few—the cityscaped text (set in Tijuana, San Francisco, Los Angeles, for example) was radically revised and constructed as a space to disrupt age-old heteronormative fictional narratives.

Writers Arturo Islas in *La Mollie and the King of Tears*[2] and Rodriguez in *Days of Obligation* turn to the metropolis to invent coexisting subjects that inhabit palimpsestic cityspaces that enfold race, sexuality, class, and gender.[3] For example, while Rodriguez-as-narrator *comes out* in the telling of his life in San Francisco's Castro, he inhabits a simultaneously soft/hard queerness that destabilizes heteronormative constructions of the masculine and feminine. And while Islas invents a straight protagonist to narrate *La Mollie*, Louie comes into a *bent* re-visioning of straight/queer self and city. Both authors re-architexture queer and straight spaces, creating characters that float somewhere in a tangible in-between space that complicates the representation of Chicano/a identity and experience.

Not surprisingly, the texts that Arturo Islas and Richard Rodriguez build to house their coexisting metroplexed characters destabilize conventional genre and storytelling technique. For example, in *La Mollie* Islas shifts gears from his other mythopoetically narrated, pastorally set dynastic novels—*The Rain God* and its sequel, *Migrant Souls*—and uses the narrative technique and fast-paced tempo readers associate with noir; there's a mystery to solve, and Islas's Louie uses short, quick Dashiell Hammett–styled sentences to unfurl it. And in *Days of Obligation* Rodriguez's narrator uses an investigative journalist voice (snappy openers, short and to-the-point paragraphs, and an in-the-crack probing eye/I) to describe Mexico City, San Diego, Tijuana, and the reconstructed California missions. However, neither author uses conventional forms simply to house a narrating subject. Each de-forms a genre. Islas's noir is revised as the storytelling frame shifts from the white, hetero-masculine subject à la Raymond Chandler to the pachuco, caló-speaking and -troping Louie Mendoza. Likewise, Rodriguez's narrator doesn't simply factualize to provide an entry into the national journal of record (the *Los Angeles Times*, for example); his narrator's detailed offerings of the socio-material reveal often contradictory narrating selves. *Days of Obligation* turns out to be not exactly objective. His writing often makes issues like AIDS visible and personal, for example.

Rodriguez and Islas confuse narrative form as their narrating protagonists move through the metroplex. For example, Rodriguez's narrator employs quick-tempo journalese and the autobiographic confession to detail his alienation as a Chicano who can't speak Spanish in Mexico City. He opens the first chapter, "I am on my knees, my mouth over the mouth of the toilet, waiting to heave" (xv). Islas's Louie begins, "I shoulda told la Mollie I'd be back to her place right after the gig" (1996, 3; 1987 MS, 1). As the narrative progresses, the hip, noir slang moves increasingly to the background as Louie's Chicanismos emerge. Louie's hybrid Chicano caló and noir-speak thus re-situate the narrative frame.

Hybridizing form for Islas and Rodriguez is not just about performing Euro-canonically high / low coded genres (pulp fiction and autobiography, objective journalism and the subjective essay). Their fusion of forms works also to displace expected moments of heteronormative textual *jouissance. La Mollie* (manuscript and published novel) ends sans conclusion; the reader never discovers whether or not the hospitalized and near-death la Mollie will live. In *Days of Obligation* the narrator's voice—a style *Kirkus Review* identifies as "disarmingly baroque" (1115)—consistently inverts and collapses back on itself through a series of syntactic and wordplay acrobatics. For all of Louie's hard-edged noir/pachuco stylization, the novel's *coming* denouement finally hangs limp; and Rodriguez's narrator's inverting sentences cruise forward through a paradoxical series of double takes. Both open up the textual space Roland Barthes calls a "site of bliss" either by defying the coming expectation (adding a softness to Louie's hardness) or by syntactic double takes that engage the reader's cruising gaze just long enough to delight in "the perverse bliss of words" (*The Pleasure of the Text*, 18, 35). Finally, both engage and disengage with a variety of genres and styles to invent cityspaces and narrator-protagonists that texture plural ethnoqueer identities and experiences.

Rodriguez's Hol(e)y Logos

As mentioned already, in *Days of Obligation* Rodriguez-as-narrator (distinct from the textualized, arguably fictionalized Rodriguez and the biographical Rodriguez) first cruises, then forces a double take to make the reader "see" such cities as Mexico City, Tijuana, and San Francisco. While his cruising remaps otherwise tightly surveilled urban spaces—turning upside down the U.S. popular imagining that restricts San Francisco's Castro district to queers and

Mexico City to the hypergenitalized, uncivil Other—he does so while he himself is located in both the metroplex and the familial home. The narrator comes out while a writer living in San Francisco, and such a coming out is still, he reminds, "predicated upon family laundry, dirty linen, skeletons" (30). Indeed, "to grow up homosexual is to live with secrets and within secrets. In no other place are those secrets more closely guarded than within the family home" (30). Yet the home's urban location allows him to gain the requisite distance to re-memory the hetero-familial space. He can then reinhabit his past domestic space, and newly inhabit the present, tangible space of the Castro's erstwhile hetero-occupied Victorian houses. Such houses were traditionally, writes Rodriguez caustically, "the reward for heterosexuality, with all its selfless tasks and burdens" (35). The hetero-inscribed homes of the present and past coexist with his present queer subjectivity and inform his homographesis.

Indeed, Rodriguez-as-narrator's simultaneous present/past, straight/bent self-locating allow him to turn topsy-turvy the readerly scripts that have aligned Mexican and U.S. national identity with the masculine and feminine. Namely, as the narrator moves through his homes (the Castro and the Sacramento of his childhood) and through various cities north and south of the tortilla curtain, he confuses and realigns masculine/feminine coded spaces. For Rodriguez-as-narrator, the mother (traditionally coded as passive, soft) and the father (traditionally coded as macho, active, hard) switch places. The mother is the figure who is hard and assertive in the public domain; she uses English to earn higher wages and fight for her family's rights, concluding, "because of my mother there is movement" (203). Rodriguez locates the mother's ability to come into a hardness with her non-nostalgic approach to life; she doesn't position the lost homeland—Mexico—in a glorified, static past. Conversely, the father becomes paralyzed north of the tortilla curtain.

Rodriguez-as-narrator also redraws the blueprint for gender hierarchies (feminine = soft and masculine = hard) naturalized within the home. As he dismantles his familial space from a new queer Castro perspective, he announces, "I was born at the destination," and that destination, as he identifies earlier, is indeed San Francisco (208; 202). The process of selecting information to present as he sits and writes from within a queer space allows his life story to appear to come full circle: he's back where he began. However, this time he emerges with a bent writerly voice that penetrates and destabilizes the narrating of the self as a whole. The text taken as a whole, then, envelops Rodriguez within the core of the story and creates a line of angled penetration that moves frictively in and out of the reader's sense of self as whole. So, while the narrator packages himself and his text to be consumed as a whole by the reader, his coming into a sense of a penetrative vulnerability— an influxing (w)hole—resists the reader's attempt to fully penetrate, control, and contain the Rodriguez-as-narrator while he re-creates a sense himself within a Home.

The Impure within the Pure

Rodriguez-as-narrator's simultaneous holer/holed penetrative/vulnerable narration splits open and interrogates his *activo/pasivo*-coded Euro-colonial legacy. Here, the traditional Euro-hetero-macho construction of Self-as-*activo* (the holer) and *indio*-as-*pasivo* (the holed) is re-visioned while in Mexico City. Coming into contact with his mestizo-ness replays through inversion (he's invested with the power to move and penetrate spaces) the conquistador's forced penetration of the New World subject:

> I am on my knees, my mouth over the mouth of the toilet, waiting to heave. It comes up with a bark. All the badly pronounced Spanish words I have forced myself to sound during the day, bits and pieces of Mexico spew from my mouth, warm, half-understood, nostalgic reds and greens dangle from long strands of saliva.
>
> (xv)

As Spanish (the language of the Euro-father) forces its way inside, he bends over and performs the Euro-*hispano* father's construction of the *indio*-as-*pasivo* (subordinate). Here, the Euro-father-as-bully sissyfies Rodriguez, forcing him to react by spewing his "warm" pieces from his mouth. However, subordination swiftly turns into resistance as Rodriguez actively locates himself within a history of an *indio* subjectivity that can penetrate back. He comes to inhabit a contradictory space of simultaneously being sissy and bully to perform a Chicano identity that is not-quite macho *hispano* (his Euro-Spaniard bloodline coded as *activo*) and not-quite Mexican (his mestizo bloodline coded as *pasivo*). On another occasion, he writes,

> I had a dream about Mexico City, a *conquistadore*'s dream. I was lost and late and twisted in my sheet. . . . I dreamed sheets, entanglements, bunting, hanging *larvaelike* from open windows, *distended* from balconies and from lines thrown over the stress.
>
> (21; EMPHASIS MINE)

Here, he is both conquistador (*activo* and penetrating) and the *indio* (*pasivo*) who dreams. Rodriguez is both the one impregnated (*pasivo*) and the one about to give birth (*activo*); he is both the circularity of the flowing dream and the hard-strung lines that hold the linen. Rodriguez re-visions himself neither simply as *activo* nor *pasivo*, *gringo* nor *hispano*, Chicano nor *indio*—but as a confluence of coexisting identities.

Rodriguez-as-narrator reveals the clashes and confusions (*indio*-as-sissy vs. Euro-father-as-bully) that continue to inform the contemporary Mexico City metroplex. Ironically, for Rodriguez it is the very exaggerated belief in the colonial sissy/bully model that leads this city into a space of *indio*/queer emancipation. Indeed, because of Mexico City's extreme need to separate bully from sissy, *indio* from *hispano*, it has become "centuries more modern than racially pure, provincial Tokyo" (87). Namely, in its excessiveness Mexico City can't help itself; it will spill over into impurity where the *activo* and *pasivo* invert and coexist as holer and holed. He continues to refine his definition of Mexico City, writing, "in its male, in its public, in its city aspect, Mexico is an arch-transvestite [that] doesn't even bother to shave her mustachios. Swords and rifles and spurs and bags of money clink and clatter beneath her skirts" (61–62). Rodriguez-as-narrator's city becomes such an exaggerated society of the spectacle that it spectacularizes and denaturalizes the scaffolding that holds in place racial, gender, and sexual hierarchies. In Mexico City the Euro-gazing and light-skinned *hispano* becomes so hyperbolically macho that he becomes a parody of himself, exposing (unwittingly) the fragility of the sissy/bully relational paradigm. Finally, however, Rodriguez-as-narrator doesn't uncritically represent his desire to inhabit such an unbounded space. He still "fears being lost" (96) in the impure womb-space of the city where the traditionally hard, Euro-Western–identified ideologies soften and enfold.

It is Rodriguez-as-narrator's slanted vision that lets him see Mexico City as looking simultaneously forward (postmodern) and backward (colonial legacy), allowing the "impure" and "pure" to coexist and, in their frictive rubbing up and down, constantly reinvent themselves. Yet, while he wants to inhabit such a space, he also "fears being lost" in it. It reflects too accurately his own sense of co-being, threatening to swallow him up and not provide an outside anchor to his consciousness. Rather, it is the space of the United States that offers up just such an anchor: an antithetical position that allows him to maintain an identity that is brown and of Mexico and that coexists with, yet isn't synthesized by, such chaotic environs. For example, he identifies the Anglo-American space as pure and oriented toward individuation and self-creation, writing how it functions as the site "long imagined [as] clean, crew-cut, ingenious" (91). Moreover, he settles into an age-old Manichean duality, opposing the space of the United States (he identifies himself as gringo, writing, "*we* are an odorless, colorless, accentless, orderly people") with the space of Mexico (Mexicans are "carriers of chaos [with] diarrhea, leprosy, brown water") (91).

Rodriguez doesn't keep clear the lines between U.S.-as-individualizing-center and Mexico-as-miscegenational-chaos. Just when it seems possible to pin-point Rodriguez, who appears to celebrate the assimilatory, individualist space of the United States, he (con)fuses U.S. and Mexican (North/South, macho/sissy) spaces. We see this in the aforementioned dreamscape sequence and in his celebration of Mexico City as a multi-layered ethnosocial space. Later he comes to celebrate such "impure" spaces as Tijuana not as a chaotic dystopia that threatens to swallow his identity, but rather as a city that exists in a fully miscegenational present—a space that is already "here" (106). Rodriguez seeks to empresence himself in the chaotic space of Tijuana, inhabiting, at least in fictionalized form, a world-city positionality that destabilizes traditional binaries.

Church as Homotopia

Rodriguez's fictive inhabitation of an in-flux subjectivity destabilizes not only readerly scripts of Mexican-U.S. spaces but also spaces of the church. Unlike his asexualized construction of self in *Hunger of Memory* (1982), *Days of Obligation* locates specific sites of spatialized pleasure. Architextualized spaces of the Catholic church, perhaps oddly, become sites of an eroticized re-memory for Rodriguez. On one occasion, as the adult narrator enters into a California mission, he remembers Brother Michael from his parochial school days: "passionate, athletic, sarcastic, the stuff of crushes" (178–179). Not only does Rodriguez come to see Brother Michael through an ethnoqueer lens, but he realizes that Brother Michael first awakened his same-sex desire and inspired him to become a writer. The queer erotic and his double-voiced writing (the soft/hard style I discussed earlier) conflate in Rodriguez's mind as he stands physically within the walls of the mission church. The church, then, acts as the glue that holds the two identities—public writer and private queer—together.

Yet, while Catholic space opens up an ecstatic same-sex–desiring space for Rodriguez (he eroticizes both Brother Michael and Larry Faherty, whose hair, he recalls with delight, descended like a woman's "over his collar"), Catholic space also acts as the space coded as *pasivo* and feminine. He rejects the Catholic church because of its association with the passive and feminine, turning to Protestant spaces where "in its purest mold [the episteme] is male" (181). Rodriguez isn't so much interested in the Protestant doctrine here, however. Rather he's drawn to its "call to manhood, a call to responsibility" (182). For Rodriguez it represents that space he identifies with the United States generally as *activo* and where, he writes, "I feel a masculine call to action" (188).

However, he emplaces himself in an in-between U.S./Mexico space, remarking with an ambiguity that blurs the boundary between his choice of desired object (men, especially Larry Faherty) and his choice of religious faith, "I will always be attracted [to men and both faiths], for the same reason I will never become" (179). Rodriguez inhabits a space in between the two circumscribed faiths, both feminine- and masculine-coded, that allows him to exist, at least fictionally, within a constant state of non-normative erotic becoming.

San Francisco as Homotopia

Rodriguez-as-narrator's third-space/queer vision not only destabilizes restrictive national and theological epistemic spaces that traditionally encode hetero-gazed race and gender hierarchies of difference, his acts of narration re-vision a traditionally white/brown, queer/straight surveilled San Francisco cityspace. Here Rodriguez-as-narrator's cut voice (soft/hard) seeks to complicate queer spaces, setting up the Castro, for example, not as de facto resistant to, but rather as coexistent with mainstream hetero-erect spaces. Notably, queer- and straight-coded places are separated in a time/space palimpsest. Typically straight- and queer-identified spaces crisscross and overlay one another through time. For example, the Miesian hetero-erect phallus of today— found in Market Street's financial district and Union Square's department store monoliths—was the seminal space for alfresco cruising and bathhouse transgression during San Francisco's Gilded Age.

In Rodriguez-as-narrator's most homographic chapter, "Late Victorians," he superimposes constructions of what he defines as the "human infused," "playful," and "carnivalesque" Castro with the white, hetero-moneyed "interests of downtown" (37). Here, within the lived space of the spectacle—defined by Guy Debord as "*capital* accumulated to the point where it becomes image"(12)—queer neighborhoods and straight, hetero-identified spaces exist side by side in a late-capitalist society. For Rodriguez-as-narrator the queer subject, himself especially, doesn't necessarily inhabit a bent space of capitalist resistance. Indeed, the celebration of his queer homespace spins out of the middle-class process of gentrifying unwanted (mostly) ethnic enclaves. He lives in a re-visioned Victorian—a structure that he emphasizes was symbolic of the hetero-erect, middle-class gender divided household of yesteryear. So while he identifies the queer reclaiming of heterospace—transforming the Victorian's vertically hard, hetero space into a set of free-floating apartments coexisting horizontally and housing "four single men" (30)—his inhabitation and remapping are middle-class dependent. Those without the means—racialized Others without the dollar incomes to rise up to the Twin Peaks heights—were swallowed up by middle-class *activos*. For example, when Rodriguez locates this queer transformation of space with details of his hallway's various disguises (it was "repainted to resemble an eighteenth-century French foyer," then later transformed by a "baroque mirror" and the laying of a "black-and-white marble" floor and painting of "faux masonry" walls), he describes participating within the faux-making enterprise of the society of the spectacle (31). His metaphoric "glory hole" where single men could float in and out of horizontally coded communal spaces is swept into the commodity machine and becomes a decadent reconstruction of an 18th-century foyer (33).

This spectacle-making process extends beyond the domestic and into Rodriguez's sense of queer public spaces. For example, he describes the local gym's mirrored interior and its all-glass walls that separate the street from the bodies inside as both "a closet of privacy and an exhibition gallery" (39). The gym, like his glory-hole-cum-decadent-French-foyer, creatively represents the space of socioeconomic privilege. It exists as a queer space and is therefore marginalized in the heterosexual scheme of things, yet it also acts as a place for privileged bodies who have the power to exhibit and make public a commodity-culture–oriented, "aesthetized" look. Of course, Rodriguez-as-narrator's cut and lean re-visioning of queer space leads to his critique of a hetero-inscribing queer subject that in its "architectural preoccupation" demonstrates "a parody of labor, a useless accumulation of the laborer's build and strength" (39). For Rodriguez, the built queer body doesn't so much make visible a subject traditionally invisible in heterospaces as refashion the body into an armored object that only desires to consume. Rodriguez concludes, "The effect of the overdeveloped body is the miniaturization of the sexual organs—of no function beyond wit" (39).

Finally, while queer and mainstream spaces are traditionally surveyed by a heteronormative public-policy making apparatus, Rodriguez destabilizes both spaces (straight spills into queer and queer into straight). Rodriguez's Castro with, as he defines, its "human infused," "playful," and "carnivalesque" spirit (37), is overlaid by the urban grid of hetero-spectacle making. However, his narrator does open the reader's eyes to ways of reshaping this space. As he explains of his own redecorating impulse, it "is not to create but to re-create, to sham, to convert, to sauce, to rouge, to fragrance, to prettify. No effect is too small or too ephemeral to be snatched away from nature, to be ushered toward the perfection of artificiality" (33). He works within the frame that governs the hetero-spectacle, but from an ethnosexually queer angle that stylizes and parodies architextured bodies.

Islas's Queering of Straight World-City Spaces

In *La Mollie and the King of Tears,* Arturo Islas's first-person narrator and protagonist, Louie Mendoza, coexists with other sociosexually emplaced subjects
while physically traveling *across* a 1973 San Francisco metroplex. (To reiterate,
while I will be quoting from Islas's posthumously published novel edited by
Paul Skenazy, the plot and style differ little from Islas's June 1987 manuscript.
I will identify in parenthesis where changes were made.) We first meet Louie
telling an unnamed academic with a tape recorder in hand his experiences
during the last twelve-plus hours. It is here, in the absolute present tense of the
story while Louie sits at his love-interest's hospital bed, that he remembers the
immediate past of his journey through San Francisco's ex-centric spaces:
Haight-Ashbury, the Castro, South of Market Tenderloin, and the Mission.
The act of telling provides the fluid container for him to re-experience the
many spatialized identities that coexist palimpsestically and come to inform
the Louie-as-narrating-subject. Louie doesn't experience the sort of epiphany
that traditionally identifies a character's dialectical synthesis of the encoun-
tered Other, but rather he comes to coexist as a straight, thirty-something
pachuco with a vision that queers segregated urban spaces. For queer author
Arturo Islas, then, straight Louie's *queer* remapping of traditionally white, het-
ero-controlled ethnosexualized ex-centric spaces makes room for a straight-
inclusive queerspace imaginary.

As I mentioned earlier, *La Mollie* is a fictional narrative that doesn't so
much fuse different genres as allow them to speak in and through one another.
The testimonial-like novel speaks through 1950s noir that speaks through the
loose-ended, episodic picaresque; genres traditionally coded masculine and
hard, like gritty realistic detective fiction, coexist with those coded feminine
and soft, such as the romance. For example, Louie's storytelling technique is
simultaneously hard, as with tough-guy, pachuco slang and take-no-shit posturing, and soft, as he aches for that sappy, *telenovela*-styled romance. Louie's
act of narrating through multiple generic registers takes place as he moves
through San Francisco's ex-centric spaces. Louie's multiple-voiced storytelling mode and the narratives de-forming of genre foreground Islas's invention of such a fictionalized interstitial Chicano subjectivity.

Louie learns from an early age that multiple speech acts can permeate
racially inscribed border zones. He grows up in El Paso, Texas, a place that
constructs borders between subjects according to skin color and language. For
example, Louie recalls attempting the crossover, as a bilingual caló-speaking
subject, into an English-only school space. However, when Louie's Euro-
Anglo school teacher overhears his code-switch into Spanish, he's punished

and locked in a closet. So when the adult-narrator Louie uses the multiple linguistic registers that characterize caló, he dares to cross a language border.

Much like his linguistic code-switches that destabilize dominant/subordinate linguistic hierarchies, Louie confuses the traditional borders between highbrow and lowbrow aesthetic culture. For example, he recalls reading *Hamlet* in high school not as a great European tragedy, but as "Shakespeare's version of *High Noon* with a big swordout instead of a shootout at the end" (1996, 9; 1987 MS, 9, reads "instead a shootout"). He mingles the high and low aesthetic in a mode typical of Chicano *rasquachismo*. To be *rasquache*, Tomás Ybarra-Frausto writes, "is to posit a bawdy, spunky consciousness, to seek to subvert and turn ruling paradigms upside down" (155). Louie is a self-described "eclectic man" who takes "from here and from there whatever works" (1996, 45; 1987 MS, 51), turning the "ruling paradigms" that naturalize linguistic, racial, and aesthetic difference "upside down." Louie's re-signifying *rasquache* sensibility and slanted vision congeal and become the site of pleasure as he becomes both the object and subject of surveillance.

Louie's multiple inhabitation of language spaces is informed by his movement into and out of marginal city spaces. For example, when he enters the Latino enclave of the Mission district, he transforms the urban barrio space, coded in the white imaginary as dangerous and savage, into a place of quiet refuge. This is the place that Louie associates with his Latin jazz/salsa playing and where he re-signifies temporality. Time, he informs, becomes "nothing to me except a beat for my sax" (1992, 45; 1987 MS, 53, reads "got no meaning for me except when I'm playing my sax and have to follow a beat"). As he enters into a space traditionally controlled by residuals of the brown-as-savage/white-as-civilizer colonial narrative, he emplaces the Chicano-as-subject.

Yet, even Louie doesn't slip into a *raza* romanticism that ends up containing the brown subject. Rather, his place of refuge (utopia) exists within a larger, more omnipresent space of white, moneyed heteronormativity that objectifies and oppresses women of color. He describes, for example, how the brown women walk "up and down the street in crotch-length miniskirts, their tits playing peekaboo with the dudes driving by in their limos and giving em the once over" (1996, 82; 1987 MS, 111, reads "dudes driving slowly by"). Louie doesn't sepia-hue his reinhabitations of space. Rather, he reveals how ethnosocial subjects can create a small corner of stillness within white, hetero-sexist hegemonic urban griddings of marginal space. Louie coexists within spaces that oppress/repress and those that emancipate. For example, he is an El Paso–born, working-class Chicano living with a white, upper-middle-class, self-assured cosmopolite, la Mollie. Louie reveals la Mollie to be oppressive—

even, in her politically correct way, a racist and homophobe—and her apartment, suffocating. La Mollie tells him on more than one occasion that he's "a
dumb Mexican"(1996, 25; 1987 MS, 27), for example. The street, on the other
hand, provides Louie with a cure-all to the hetero-middle-class space of the
apartment. When he leaves the apartment at two o'clock in the afternoon—fed
up with her manipulations of his emotion and desire—he delights in the car-
nivalizing of space and desire the street offers.

An Erotics of Remembered Space

Louie's "pure San Francisco" (1996, 37; 1987 MS, 41) gravitates around his
transformation of space into place—the city's abstract, white gridded spaces
becoming the place of ethnosocial infused memory. In *Space and Place*, Yi-Fu
Tuan defines the process of transforming space into place as the following:
"The ideas 'space' and 'place' require each other for definition. . . . Furthermore, if we think of space as that which allows movement, then place is pause;
each pause in movement makes it possible for location to be transformed into
place" (6). For example, as Louie passes children playing in Hayes Valley low-
income projects, he recalls being a kid in El Paso afraid of *cucuys*—Mexican
bogeymen. The movement in space triggers a memory that anchors Louie
within his Chicano imaginary. Louie transforms abstract space into the place
of felt ethnic heritage.[4] And, when he moves through the Mission district's
streets, he remembers his first love-interest, Sonia, who "was pure Chicana"
(1996, 47; 1987 MS, 56). Sonia's memories of her parents make him "thinka my
own parents. They have that Indian way, man—silent, proud, all-knowing"
(1996, 27; 1987 MS, 56), firmly anchoring him within his mestizo heritage.

Space is not only transformed into a variety of racialized zones (hetero-
romancings with Sonia, and the *cucuys* of his El Paso childhood), but also into
the place of macho hetero-romance. As Louie walks through Golden Gate
Park he pauses at the arboretum, a place that triggers memories of the first time
he met the white, middle-class, Ph.D. anthropology student la Mollie "during
a love-in while the Dead were wailing away" (1996, 46; 1987 MS, 54, reads "during a love-in right on that very spot while the Dead were wailing away"). Also
from this stretch of grass, he sees the Kezar Stadium, reminding him that all
stadiums, from the moment he met la Mollie forward, make him "think of one
thing and one thing only. Vaginas." (1996, 59; "thinka one thing only. Vaginas."
in 1987 MS, 72). The racial and heterosexual recallings of space aren't so un-
connected. La Mollie, he recalls, expressed interest in him only because he
proved a good ethnic-object specimen of study. As he walks the undifferenti-
ated street spaces, then, certain built objects and/or bodies in space (brown and

black children playing) trigger a re-memory process that transforms spaces into, at this point, simultaneously heterosexualized and positively racialized places.

This isn't to say that Louie uncritically reproduces delimiting heterosexist, racialized paradigms. His exaggeration of such Chicano phallic transformations of these spaces—the stadium as vagina, for example—into differentiated racial/sexual places destabilizes those scripts that inform such spaces. For example, during his walk he recalls his best friend Virgil Spears's father. He was a "Jack Daniels poppa did all kindsa things to make a man outta him and make sure he wasn't no momma's boy on his way to being queer" (1996, 73; 1987 MS, 98, reads "Jack Daniels ex-Marine poppa . . ."). After Louie describes with horror the father's forcing Virgil (arguably his long unrequited love) to shoot some puppies to make a man out of him, we begin to see how Louie further destabilizes such heterosexualized scripts, here demonstrating the male heterosexual fear of dissolution into a female subject constructed as the dark abyss.

While Louie identifies as straight, he goes to great lengths to spectacularize that heterosexualized identity. For example, when he travels through street-spaces and a memory of la Mollie is triggered, it's often filtered through an exaggerated silver-screened imagination. On one occasion he'll recall how he keeps his "Bogart cool" (1996, 24; 1987 MS, 26) when she glares at him "like Bette Davis at Joseph Cotten" (1992, 24; 1987 MS, 26). Katharine Hepburn, Olivia de Havilland, Rita Hayworth, Rock Hudson, Spencer Tracy, Montgomery Clift, James Dean, and Marlon Brando, among others, stand in at different moments to describe his interaction with la Mollie (all mentioned, and more, in the manuscript). Jack Babuscio identifies such a reimagination of Hollywood icons as the main ingredient to the camp aesthetic. Babuscio writes about how the focus "on the outward appearances of role, implies that roles, and, in particular sex roles, are superficial—a matter of style. Indeed, life itself is role and theater, appearance, and impersonation" (24). Of course, camp isn't about mere imitation, it's about exaggerating the imitation: mouths super-red-lipsticked gape and caked-on facial powder accentuates facial hair to exaggerate the feminine Look. While Louie doesn't put on the red lipstick when he filters his relationship with la Mollie through the Hollywood silver screen, he recycles an otherwise wasted mode of white, heterosexual cultural production to destabilize Euro-Anglo, hetero-cultural icons and meaning. As a Chicano (albeit straight) character, Louie is also denied access to mainstream heterosexual iconographic representations.

As Louie spectacularizes "masculinity" and "femininity," he sidesteps a heterosexual descriptive authority that assumes all places he inhabits are heterosexual. For example, even when he fleetingly mentions meeting his first partner, Sonia, he identifies the locale as a "unisex bar on the edge of Pacific Heights" (1996, 27; 1987 MS, 44). And when he stumbles on a homeless person while walking in the Haight, he thinks of the progenitor of homogenic love, the poet Walt Whitman, whom Islas quotes in the novel's epigraph: "Who goes there? hankering, gross, mystical, nude . . ." (1996, 2; 1987 MS, n.p.). Not only do the multiple references to Whitman resonate loudly with his homographesis, but they anchor the reference to Gold Rush San Francisco — an era when male-male relations and desire dominated this cityspace. Les Wright comments of Gold Rush–crazed San Francisco (circa 1848–49),

> The first Anglo-American migrants, predominantly from Puritan New England, engaged in homosexual activity and created homosocial spaces within the liminal moral and social spaces created by San Francisco's vast geographic remove from the structured moral spaces of the urban and even rural communities of mid-nineteenth-century America.
>
> ("SAN FRANCISCO," 164)

Often, too, Louie mentions rainbows, Judy Garland singing "Over the Rainbow," and Dorothy and the yellow Brick road (same in manuscript). During the 1950s conservative era, when many gays were forced into the proverbial closet and used coded language to communicate, "Are you a friend of Dorothy's?" became a universally recognized code. As Les Wright comments, "Garland became the most beloved camp idol to several post-war generations of homosexual men. San Francisco became the land of Oz, the Technicolor world over the rainbow where gays would finally find a home" (173). Louie's space/place re-memory teeters between the straight and queer, taking neither as the only way of existing sexually.

If Louie's choice of references betray a homographic sensibility, then his admiration and hero making of queer characters brings this home. Indeed, not only does Louie admire Virgil Spears (based loosely on Islas's partner, Jay Spears, who died of AIDS in the mid-1980s) for his pool game and his take-no-shit butch-daddy attitude, he also sees him as a masterful guide into San Francisco's inferno-esque other worlds. For Louie, Virgil is the holder of an alternate way of seeing the world. He recalls, "It was Virgil Spears taught me about queers, man, I ain't ashamed to tell you" (1996, 72; 1987 MS, 97, reads "But the first guy who ever beat me up was queer, man, I ain't ashamed to tell you"; the setting up of Virgil as teacher-of-queerness remains the same). For example, it is Louie's boyhood friendship with Virgil that stands in as an alternate possibility of desiring in the world. After Louie is made to feel abnormal by his peers for masturbating en masse with other boys in a basement, it is Virgil who de-pathologizes these formative experiences. On another occasion, when Louie slips into a heterosexual mindset, asking Virgil if he's queer because of his abusive upbringing, Virgil responds matter-of-factly,

> look at me and tell me exactly when you decided to be straight. I wanna know the moment you looked down at your crotch and your brain told your dick it was only gonna be interested in pussy for the rest of its life. . . . You see, you can't tell me. Cause it's not something you decide with your head. Hell, if that was how it worked, I'd decide to be straight in a second. You sons-of-bitches have the whole world at your fucking feet and nobody minds you screwing as long as you keep away from the real little girls.
>
> (*LA MOLLIE* 1996, 76; 1987 MS, 102, READS THE SAME,
> ADDING "YOU KNOW WHAT I MEAN, BEAN BREATH?"
> AFTER THE SECOND SENTENCE)

Thanks to Virgil, Louie comes to understand that the line between straight and queer is not so clear cut. (To really drive home the point, Islas expands this Virgil-educating-Louie scene in the original manuscript.) Moreover, in de-pathologizing queer desire, Virgil makes it apparent that this isn't simply a fashionable *look* ("Hell, if that was how it worked, I'd *decide* to be straight in a second"), but rather a permanent reality with very real consequences.

As Louie moves back and forth through present (San Francisco) and past (El Paso) time/places, he floats into an in-between straight/queer space. Ironically, it is when Louie is most assaulted by the queer gaze that he slips most into a queer sensibility. For example, while looking for his brother Tomás at an S&M club called The Mine Shaft, he is quick to remind his interviewer, "Like I told you, man, I can't even think about sex without tits around. Real soft ones" (1996, 138; 1987 MS, 187). Yet, it is right after his entering into this place of male-male erotica that he comments, "I still don't know what it was that got in my skin about that place, but it had me stuck there in the alley so's I couldn't of moved if Sherman's army'd showed up" (Islas 1996, 146).[5] On occasion, however, this amorphous something under his skin gels into a tangible quantity. For example, in the same bar where he spots Sonia, his attention shifts away from heterosexualized love object to "the cute little waiter" (1996, 48; 1987 MS, 58). And while Louie doesn't slip entirely into a male-male desiring libidinal economy, he does edge up against a semiformed bisexuality.

Indeed, Louie's frictive moving in and out of queerspaces happens during the night—that time most associated with the transgressive and with subconscious desire. For example, when Louie arrives in the Castro he recalls,

> When I got there, all them guys were flexing their pecs on their fire escape like they were putting the make on the sun, which was setting behind them

buildings. It's the saddest part of the day for me, man, when the light's starting to change from day to night and the dark's coming on like a big wet heavy wool blanket all smothering.

(1996, 69; 1987 MS, 92)

Then later, he informs, "I can't figure out why, man, but it's getting dark that gets me" (69).[6] Of course, it's not that Louie comes into a straight/queer identity at night, but that this is when the struggle manifests itself. So even when the hetero-panic snaps into place—"I try not to pay no attention to the way the guys walking up to Castro Street keep looking at my crotch and then at my face the way straight dudes look at girls' asses and legs behind their backs" (1996, 72; 1987 MS, 97, "guys" reads "gays" in manuscript)—it is expressed in such a way that Louie actually reveals why heterosexuals fear the queer gaze: not because the man stands in for the woman as object ("the way straight dudes look at girls' asses"), but because his role as active penetrator is subverted. But there's more to Louie's "looking away" from the queer gaze. He looks away yet knows he's being objectified like a woman. He fears and desires the male-male encounter as a point of reordering hetero-masculinity-as-active (one that gazes, shapes, and evaluates reality) to open up the space for his own desire to *actively receive* the sexual Other. Arturo Islas's fictional narrative creatively remaps San Francisco as a palimpsest queer/straight space; as the reader follows Louie's movements through San Francisco's cityspace we also follow his move away from straight/queer oppositionalities into a more fluid understanding of queer and straight Chicano identity and experience.

Gay Chicano writers Richard Rodriguez and Arturo Islas thus invent narrator-protagonists that exist within in-between city and ethnosexual spaces. Such world-city protagonists "queer" the socio-metroplex experience and open their readers' eyes to those Us vs. Them paradigms that delimit the Chicano/a experience.

CHAPTER 4

Ana Castillo's and Sheila Ortiz Taylor's Bent Chicana Textualities

Chicana Mainstreams and Tributaries

U.S.-dwelling Chicana authors have come into their belle lettres own. Since the 1980s, names like Ana Castillo, Lorna Dee Cervantes, Denise Chávez, Sandra Cisneros, Lucha Corpi, Pat Mora, Cecile Pineda, Mary Helen Ponce, and Helena María Viramontes, to mention a few, have become regular sights at mainstream bookstores like Borders and Barnes & Noble across the country. This is not a result of some deus ex machina intervention. Increased visibility is the result of much thumping on the doors of corporate book editors and mainstream agents by Chicana, Nuyorican, Cuban, and Dominican women writers for decades prior to their renaissance in the mid- to late 1980s. It is the result of massive civil rights struggles that eventually led to the increased numbers of Chicanas and Latinas entering universities; it is the result of years of our predecessors struggling to pave a way for us to acquire the skills for better-paying jobs (academic or otherwise) than those available to our forefathers and foremothers. It is the result of eventual growth of an ethnic-identified middle-class in the 1980s, hungry for stories other than those of the Brett Easton Ellis or Donna Tart variety. It is the result of a wave of newly minted Chicano/a and Latino/a PhDs who entered the academy to reshape the humanities and university curricula, setting ablaze what has become known as the late-1980s "culture wars." It is the result of those creative writers working within the academy—Norma Cantú, Cherríe Moraga, Pat Mora, Lucha Corpi, Alicia Gaspar de Alba, and Gloria Anzaldúa, for example—who forced open doors for Other voices to enter into a literary scene dominated by Euro-Anglo authors.

Although initiated in 1981 with the publication of *This Bridge Called My Back,* edited by Moraga and Anzaldúa, not until the late 1980s and early 1990s would a Xicana feminist theory take hold within the academy, and outside (albeit to a lesser degree).[1] This new wave of Chicana critics sought to identify a Chicana borderland aesthetic that expressed, as Carmen Cáliz-Montoro states, "a battleground of identities" and "a crossfire between camps" (14). With the dust settled, a crystallizing Xicana feminism identified the border as the site to critique the triple oppression of Chicanas (race, gender, and sexual orientation) and also as a space for intervention, resistance, and affirmation. Gloria Anzaldúa's 1987 publication of *Borderlands/La Frontera*— a hybrid mix of poetry, prose, and metaphysical inquiry—best represents this move away from fixed notions of Chicano/a identity and experience. While *Borderlands/ La Frontera* experimented with genre, it was not to be confused with a contemporary, Anglo-identified postmodernist disaffection. For Anzaldúa, playing with language and form aimed to unfix heterosexist and racist texts. Just as Anzaldúa celebrated a queer/straight Chicano/a subjectivity, so too did other Chicana feminists, among them Norma Alarcón, Mary Pat Brady, Deena González, Angie Chabrám, Cordelia Candelaria, Teresa McKenna, Cherríe Moraga, Emma Pérez, Sonia Saldívar-Hull, Tey Diana Rebolledo, Martha and Rosaura Sánchez, Chela Sandoval, Carla Trujillo, Yvonne Yarbro-Bejarano, and María Herrera-Sobek. They have expanded the traditionally male-dominated Chicano literary canon to include straight and queer Chicanas. For example, Norma Alarcón theorizes the mestiza subject's "provisional identities" as a form of intervention into "dominant Chicano and U.S. Anglo-European discourses of power" (135). And others like Sonia Saldívar-Hull formulate a "New Mestiza consciousness" (172) to articulate a "feminism on the border" that makes visible the sexism, homophobia, and economic exploitation within and outside Chicano communities (34).

Certainly, the 1980s proved a hugely transformative moment in Chicana authorship. Much of this change can be attributed to socioeconomic shifts within ethnic groups in the United States and the hard-won struggles of the Chicano/a intelligentsia and artist communities. However, much was also about dollar profits. Mainstream publishing conglomerates are not interested in the social well-being of the people nor in academic protest—unless there are dollars to be made. As Rosaura Sánchez points out, "Interest in this literature had undoubtedly been fueled by the vogue of multiculturalism and the growing market for ethnic and women's literature both in the academy and more generally throughout the nation and even abroad" (52). Indeed, with increased demand for "ethnic" American culture by Anglos and people of color alike in the 1980s, mainstream publishing houses were making money moving books authored by Chicanas, Latinas, African Americans, Asian Americans, and Native Americans. Little wonder, then, that publishing house titans like Doubleday would buy from *Bilingual Review* the rights to Castillo's American Book Award–winning *The Mixquiahuala Letters* (1986). After giving this novel in verse a glossy, Maya-encrypted makeover, Doubleday quickly secured the rights to all her past, present, and future work: *Sapagonia: A Novel in 3/8* (1990), *So Far from God* (1993), her collection of short stories, *Loverboys* (1996), and *Peel My Love Like an Onion* (1999). (For more on this, see Samuel Baker's "Ana Castillo: The Protest Poet Goes Mainstream.") Castillo's reader base stretched much wider than under distribution of her works by Arte Público Press, and her mainstream visibility certainly increased after her move to Doubleday. For example, just before *Loverboys* was published, *USA Weekend* ran a story on Castillo that reached forty million readers and thus forty million potential buyers/readers of her books. Her move also brought huge profits to Doubleday.

Ana Castillo wasn't the only one swept up in the fanfare. Random House stepped in on Arte Público to take over the rights to Sandra Cisneros's *House on Mango Street* (1983), giving it a glossy, barrio-look makeover in their 1991 reissue. After Random House repackaged *House on Mango Street* and Cisneros's "author-look" (the author photo has her in a rebozo, weighed down with Mexican folk jewelry, and wearing dark eyeliner and red lipstick), the book brought in profits from the sale of over 1.2 million copies. Random House went on to publish her short story collection *Woman Hollering Creek* (1991), which also sold well, and later her novel *Caramelo* (2002). Afraid to miss out on the multicultural boom, Farrar Strauss & Giroux caught Denise Chávez in their net, offering her a large-dollar incentive—and national distribution—to break her contract with Arte Público, which had published her novel *Last of the Menu Girls* (1984). In 1994 Farrar Strauss & Giroux published her novel *Face of an Angel* (which caught the eye of Robert Houston, who described it as a "spicy Southwestern stew of anecdotes" in *The New York Times Book Review*) and then her novel *Loving Pedro Infante: A Novel* (2001). (For more on the marketplace and Chicana/Latina fiction, see Ellen McCracken's *New Latina Narrative: The Feminine Space of Postmodern Ethnicity*, as well as Eliana Orteaga and Nancy Sternbach's essay, "At the Threshold of the Unnamed: Latina Literary Discourse in the Eighties.") And with the Latino purchasing power massively expanding—to half a trillion dollars according to current estimates—several publishers have established Latino-focused imprints, like HarperCollins's Rayo Press.

Many such Latina/Chicana writers that have appeared in the last two-plus decades have both complicated and/or one-dimensionally "tropicalized" contemporary literary canons. In terms of the latter, I think of an Isabel Allende or an Himlice Novas who uses formulaic writing to invent exotic, hypersexualized Latinas. Of the former, I think of Norma Cantú, Terri de la Peña, Sheila Ortiz Taylor, Emma Pérez, and Alicia Gaspar de Alba, whose writing defies convention and whose representations are radical and complex. It is clear that authors that challenge their readers are less likely to get the backing of big publishers and less likely to appear in bookstores across the country. In *Extinct Lands, Temporal Geographies,* Mary Pat Brady reads Terri de La Peña's dedications to fellow Chicana authors in her novel *Margins* (published by the small Seal Press) as a sign of the "fragility" (97) and "anonymity" (98) of these writers who shun formula and challenge mainstream literary expectation.

So what are we to make of writers like Ana Castillo and Sandra Cisneros who defy storytelling expectation, give flesh to lesbian Chicana characters, and who cross over?[2] What does a Cisneros or a Castillo do that a Gaspar de Alba or a Sheila Ortiz Taylor doesn't do? Is there some magical recipe for an author to both engage then disengage readers generally? Is it simply that authors such as Ortiz Taylor, Cherríe Moraga, and Terri de La Peña, for example, prefer to publish with smaller presses? In an interview, Moraga discusses how her Chicana lesbian-themed plays have a hard time getting production money, as well as how her essays and poetry find little "mainstream interest." She attributes this to both her mixing of genres and a mainstream publishing world that either shows no interest, or when it does, ends up controlling too much how her work should look. As she states, "The few times I've attempted to go that route, I've turned back to those presses that have never hassled me and that make sure my work stays in print. Of course, I don't make lots of money from these presses, but I figure it's the quality of the production and the lasting power that best serves me in the end" (Moraga interview in my forthcoming *Contemporary Chicano/a Arts and Letters: Mapped by Interview*). For others who emplot Chicana feminist protagonists, like Lucha Corpi, to publish with a smaller house is a question of loyalty and a sense of their commitment: "I feel that no matter what we have to somehow support our institutions. They've always been there for me—right from the beginning. And so now I'm giving back. . . . I want my books to live long after I'm gone and Arte Público is dedicated to making sure Latino writers continue to be read" (Corpi interview in *Contemporary Chicano/a Arts and Letters,* forthcoming). And, even once a Chicana author has published with a mainstream press, this doesn't always guarantee publication of subsequent work. Pat Mora not only had a hard time breaking into the mainstream market, but still receives rejections: "Now that I'm well published. . . . It continues to be an unending struggle—even a relentless struggle" (ibid., Mora interview in *Contemporary Chicano/a Arts and Letters,* forthcoming). What is clear from conversations with many such Chicana writers is that they want to maintain their creative independence and also have as many people as possible engage with their work. However, they know that, while the mainstream press offers wider circulation (and the possibility of greater monetary support), it also delimits creativity—especially when it comes to Chicana lesbian-inhabited storyworlds. This is to say, while Moraga, Ortiz Taylor, and others are writers with like writerly ambitions (to create freely, engage many, and make a living from writing), one way or another the mainstream literary marketplace continues to exclude the more radically experimental and non-heteronormative narratives.

While supply and demand marketplace economics have certainly added "color" to an otherwise monochromatic contemporary American literary canon, Chicana authors—especially lesbian ones—continue to face a deeply prejudiced book publishing industry. This is largely the result of a predominance of nonethnic, Ivy League–trained editors who, once they've caught their token "ethnic" writer that guarantees a dollar profit, no longer actively reach out to other writers. So, within a globalizing late-capitalist system, we've witnessed an increased number of Chicana writers being published by New York's titans, followed by a decrease in the number of actual Chicana voices represented. For example, Cisneros is in every Borders bookstore, but you would be hard pressed to find Cherríe Moraga's more explicit mestiza lesbian-themed collections of poems, essays, and plays. Those like Castillo, Chávez, and Cisneros, then, are grist for a publishing mill that, in order to maximize profits and satisfy stock-market goals, carefully determines which group of readers is willing to spend the most money on what kind of book; once authors who reach these profit-margin goals are identified, publishers need not look for other authors. And this is precisely how capitalism works: first by heterogenizing and then by homogenizing cultural phenomena. So although formerly marginalized voices and cultural forms have experienced heightened visibility in today's literary marketplace, this is simply the capitalist system's way of covering over exclusionary practices that continue to operate in the politics of cultural representation.

Does a crossover writer like Castillo textualize a lesbian identity and experience differently than the more marginal Sheila Ortiz Taylor? Is it a question of the politics of representation at work: that Castillo is publicly straight (privately bisexual) and that Sheila Ortiz Taylor is publicly lesbian? Is it that their fictions are unapologetically lesbian and Chicana feminist? To begin to answer this, I explore how Sheila Ortiz Taylor and Ana Castillo variously invent fictions that engage with (straight) Chicano and mainstream literary techniques and genres to disengage their readers. I first analyze how Castillo's *So Far from God* (1991), *Loverboys* (1996), and *Peel My Love Like an Onion* (1999) variously use conventional narrative techniques and readily identifiable genres to engage, seduce, then radically disengage mainstream readers by texturing a Xicana border-erotic that ruptures oppressive white and brown heteronormative canons. I next look at Sheila Ortiz Taylor's hybrid-pastiche novel, *Coachella* (1998), to begin to explore the politics of representation and how a writer's choice of narrative technique and genre as well as degree of lesbian / Chicana explicitness determine degree of exposure (mainstream readership or otherwise). Ultimately, then, while a Castillo and an Ortiz Taylor are read differently and are circulated within different readership communities, I argue that both types of authors create fictions that destabilize heterosexist patriarchal narratives (brown and white) naturalized in Euro-Anglo– and Chicano-authored texts that tend to normalize the representation of brown female bodies (straight and bent) as consumable exotic objects.

Castillo's Bent Frames

Given that the mainstream publishers set out to promote writers who often make the Chicana identity and experience an easily swallowed pill, should we dismiss a writer like Ana Castillo as a sellout? Or is it possible that such a writer can engage with certain readily accessible genres—magical realism in *So Far from God* or that of the romance in *Peel My Love Like an Onion*—to disengage and challenge mainstream readers? Can a writer like Ana Castillo write narrative fictions that work within the recognizable literary conventions that the mainstream might identify with the "exotic" tale while simultaneously de-forming such conventions to open her readers' eyes to different ways of experiencing the world?

Since the publication of the hugely successful *One Hundred Years of Solitude*, magical realism as a storytelling mode has been widely used by U.S. Latino/a authors. However, as the last several decades have proved, very often writers like Isabel Allende, Himlice Novas, Sandra Benítez, and María Amparo Escandón, to name a few, employ magical realism in an extremely formulaic way to serve up, as already mentioned, caricatures of Latinas. This use of magical realism does little to engage and disengage the reader's imagination, instead providing a prepackaged exotic form of Latina identity and experience. However, an author like Ana Castillo engages with magical realism in a non-formulaic manner (what I identify as a "rebellious mimetics" in *Postethnic Narrative Criticism*) that powerfully *disengages* her readers from their everyday understanding to offer fresh new insight into the world. We see this especially in her novel *So Far from God*, where she re-forms the mode into a self-reflexive story that plots the character Caridad's coming into a lesbian sexuality and Xicana mestiza sensibility.

Ana Castillo employs the magical realist (or magicorealism) mode to complicate novels that one-dimensionalize Latina characters like Himlice Novas's Latina who even orgasms while eating tropical fruit. She uses the mode to complicate those Latin American novels that focus on patrilineage and that sweep the women figures to the hypersexualized or domesticated narrative margins to complicate Chicano magicorealist fiction (such as that of Rudolfo Anaya, Oscar Zeta Acosta, and Ron Arías, among others), where the Chicana characters are usually figured as a body in need of domestic and sexual containment. Moreover, Castillo uses magicorealism in *So Far from God* to critique this very process of gendered containment by inventing the lesbian/ Chicana-identifying Caridad and her various encounters with a heterosexist socio-sexual economy.

The character's experiences make visible the misogynistic and racist violence that a society of the spectacle otherwise seeks to normalize. The narrator describes how Caridad finds herself in a gutter, having been mysteriously attacked by "a thing both tangible and amorphous [that] was pure force" (77). However, when the reader learns that this mysterious "pure force" was responsible for her violation and disfigurement, along with the fact that she was out with a man the night of the attack, the narrator is careful not to leave the mysterious event as only mysterious: Caridad's "nipples had been bitten off. She had also been scourged with something, branded like a cattle. Worst of all, a tracheotomy was performed because she had also been stabbed in the throat" (33). The mysterious is the violence of a society of the spectacle that covers over the "pure force" of a sexist and racist hegemony. Caridad's society of the spectacle brands, maims, and disfigures gendered bodily sites—and it silences.

Feminist critics have expressed an uneasiness with Castillo's *So Far from God* and its spicy flavorings, which some see as diminishing the gravity of Caridad's rape, for example. And critic Ellen McCracken is critical of Castillo's introducing of Caridad's lesbian desire as if "it were a natural and expected component of the narrative," yet finally leaving her story "increasingly muddled," "closeted," and without a sense of completion (37). Within the narrative logic of the story, where all the characters are "flat" (as per the picaresque genre it participates in) and appear and disappear, perhaps such an analysis is a little off the mark. Rather, as Rosaura Sánchez writes, it is a "kaleidoscope of flat narratives that serve here to challenge traditional representations of women" (58). Sánchez concludes, "In calling attentions to itself as narrative—and as pastiche—with its inclusion in its narrative soup of every conceivable stereotype in the book, it does in fact elicit a hilarious reading of a multitude of differences and essentialisms and, in the end, provokes a desire for a critically produced construct of collectivity that considers the interconnection of gender, class, ethnicity, and sexuality" (58). Castillo's use of hyperbole and magicorealism, then, is both a critique of racial/sexual/gender essentialism and a self-reflexive emplotting of the story of Caridad (as well as her mother, Sofia, and her three sisters, La Loca, Esperanza, and Fe) as they exist within a late-20th-century world dominated by capitalism that naturalizes as normal the estrangement these characters feel in an increasingly spectacularized society. It is also a narrative that self-reflexively clears a space for the story of a Xicana lesbian border-erotic to unfold.

In this self-reflexive fictional texturing of Caridad's coming into her same-sex subjectivity, the narrator offers a fictional counterpoint: the character Maria, who is the static, "exotic" caricature. This is a character who self-identifies Chicana but relates to her culture from a distant remove. As Maria tells her Greek love-interest Helena, she's never kept in touch with her "relatives in Truchas" (129). However, because she's fed up with the banality of her everyday life in L.A., she returns to New Mexico not to find meaning but to appropriate her "own" culture's folkloric past. The narrator uses her characteristic parodic voice to describe how "upon arriving at the great abandoned [Anazasi] ruins described them in her journal like this: 'It was as if the Great Cosmic Mother had tossed her broken pottery to the ground'" (121). Maria comes to stand in for the dangers of fetishizing a mestiza-ness; she's a character devoid of deep engagement with her mestiza roots, only knowing how to appropriate as she drives across her ancestral homeland. As a contrast to Caridad, Maria objectifies and appropriates, never willing to leave anything behind—including "books on healing arts . . . and the CD player" (124)—to learn from the new culture. The parodic technique the narrator employs is critical of her coopting of her own culture as a way to "authenticate" and give substance to her middle-class, lesbian identity as a lifestyle. On the other hand, Caridad's relationship to her New Mexican heritage (Mexican, Spanish, and Amerindian) is represented as a clear counterpoint. The narrator spends time fleshing out Caridad's character and her eventual crossing over of straight/queer borders.

When we first meet Caridad, the narrator immediately distinguishes her from her three sisters: Esperanza, a Gulf War frontline anchorwoman; Fe, an activist turned Yuppie; and La Loca, a precocious cross-dressing curandera who performs at-home abortions on her sisters. Caridad doesn't share their distinctively "flat butt of the Pueblo blood" (26). The narrator, however, is careful not to uncritically reproduce stereotypes: to be Xicana you have to assume a certain biologically determined shape. Rather, Caridad's lack of the defining characteristic of the Pueblo Indian doesn't preclude her from having a "right" to claim her *indígena* roots—that place (symbolically figured when she flies off the cliffs at the Acoma Pueblo) where she discovers absolute unity as a Chicana and a lesbian.

It isn't by chance that Caridad's rape, by that spectacularized "thing both tangible and amorphous" (77), occurs at the beginning of the novel. Caridad experiences an oppressive, psychologically disturbed patriarchal society in the most brutally hegemonic form—she's discursively and physically raped and disfigured: her nipples are bitten off, she is scourged with something, branded like cattle, and stabbed in the throat (33). Her throat and breasts are the sites for her disfigurement—she is silenced and must breathe through an artificial hole in the neck, and the physical parts that threaten and mark difference are violently mutilated. Western medicine's answer to the violent act is to "half repair" her, "tubes through her throat, bandages over skin that was gone, surgery piecing together flesh that was once [Caridad's] breasts" (38). Importantly, here the narrator describes how Western medicine does a messy job of healing her.

Within the realm of fiction, this acts as a plot device: the fact that Western medicine could not heal her allows Caridad the opportunity to self-heal and then re-create herself. That Western medicine does not heal her offers her the opportunity to become the agent in shaping her life and reveals how her identity works within a frame of male-dominated Chicano culture. In heterosexual relationships she's the object to be acted upon. The narrator tells us on one occasion that "Caridad had a somewhat pronounced ass that men were inclined to show their unappreciated appreciation for everywhere she went" (26) and, before she experiences the life-changing event that leads to her self-repair, she's described as hung up on her high-school sweetheart, Memo, who leaves her for the apotheosis of the ultimate in patriarchal institutions, the Marines. At this point, early in the story, the narrator foregrounds Caridad's preconscious, mestiza lesbian identity; she's described as a victim and without agency: "three abortions later and with her weakness for shots of Royal Crown with beer chasers after work at the hospital where she was an orderly, Caridad no longer discriminated between giving her love to Memo and only to Memo whenever he wanted it and loving anyone she met at the bars who vaguely resembled Memo" (27). She's described as lost and dispossessed of any identity.

Caridad's crossing over into a same-sex borderland space begins after her rape and disfigurement. The narrative more than suggests that Caridad must pass through death to be re-born as a mestiza lesbian. Castillo's narrator, then, counteracts the hyper-heteromasculinist violence that leaves Caridad mutilated in a gutter by creating a new narrative. In a move that could only happen in fiction, Caridad self-heals. Here, the narrator describes the mother, Sofia, stepping back when she saw "not what had been left of her daughter, half repaired by modern medical technology, tubes through her throat, bandages over skin that was gone, surgery piecing together flesh that was once her daughter's breasts, but Caridad as she was before" (33). This is part of Caridad's rite of passage from straight to lesbian mestiza identity; however, as the parodic narrator reminds the reader, that this rite of passage takes place in and through her rape by a "thing most intangible" is not to be judged according to the same values we might use to judge ontological fact; this is a narrator describing a fictional world, and not condoning rape as a process for coming into a lesbian subjectivity in the world beyond the text. Caridad passes through a physical and psychic death, then passes into a lesbian, Xicanista consciousness—her "Holy Restoration"—that takes place over the course of a year. She reconstructs her body, making herself "whole and once again beautiful" (37), in an act of "pure will" (55). Within the organization of the narrative, it takes this process for her to become conscious of, then discard those destructive heteronormative structures that deaden her experience of the world.

As she physically reconstructs herself, she also becomes more in tune with her intuitive faculties, discovering her ability to predict upcoming events in her dream quests. Not surprisingly, Caridad moves out of her mother's home in order to begin self-scribing new boundaries of home: papier-maché skeletons, an "authentic" wooden trunk made by some *indios* in Chihuahua, a single futon bed, and a "three-dimensional picture of La Virgen de Guadalupe, San Martin Caballero, and El Santo Niño on the wall" (114). The value she places in these folk objects, however, acts as an obstacle she must overcome in order to access more genuinely her *"fronterista"* sensibility (Saldívar-Hull 62). In fact, it's only when they're removed that she can learn how to heal others as a *curandera.* She trains under doña Felicia, who, mixing French, Spanish, and English in everyday speech and practicing a Catholic/indigenous-based medicine, epitomizes the mestiza identity. Now, the narrator tells us, "her dreams were not hits and misses no more like in the beginning, but very clear messages which, with the help of her mentor, doña Felicia, she became adept at interpreting" (118). The more she learns and shares and the less she appropriates, the closer she comes to crossing over sexually to *el otro lado.*

Before she can come into her own, she must get over this process of objectifying according to masculinist codes, and that includes her lesbian love-interest. When she first sees her, she's "sitting on the adobe wall that surrounds the sanctuary" (75), symbolic of her placement between the sacred and ideologically restrictive (the Catholic Church) and the expansive possibility of a world on the other side. Caridad objectifies her, naming her the "Woman-on-the-wall." Romanticized and objectified, Woman-on-the-wall functions superficially as an icon of the other to be appropriated. We enter Caridad's point of view: "In and of herself there was nothing about her that was unusually striking. She was dark. Indian or Mexican. Black, black hair. Big sturdy thighs. She could tell that because the woman was wearing cutoffs" (79). Desire is constructed around the gaze at the dark Other, which is a little too much for her, and "suddenly [she] got up and without a word to doña Felicia began to wander about in search of her because she knew that she could not bear the thought of living without the woman" (79). Interestingly, the process of objectifying the dark Other gives way to desiring intimacy with, as we discover later, someone who looks similar. The Woman-on-the-wall, now as speaking subject, says to her in a later encounter, "I just thought you were someone I had seen at Chimayo last year, but I guess I was wrong. . . . Anyway, you looked so much like a cousin of mine that I ain't seen since we were girls. She's Pueblo, like me"(93). The Woman-on-the-wall moves their relationship outside of a desire dynamic of gazer-gazed, into a familial matrix of communal interaction. In addition, she's given substance—she's the one who speaks and gives meaning to the event at the sanctuary. This moment goes hand in hand with the deromanticizing of Woman-on-the-wall. Caridad thinks to herself, "But she could not possibly be la Woman-on-the-wall-later-on-a-hill that had obsessed her to such an extreme that she had all but abandoned life itself . . . could she?" (92). The Woman-on-the-wall becomes more than just a one-dimensional object to be consumed.

Significantly, just before Caridad's crossover happens, the narrator tells us "Caridad's own obsession was . . . Woman-on-the-wall-later-attendant-at-Ojo-Caliente, who inadvertently had caught Caridad's snarelike heart and who finally got a name" (204). In the process of discovering that her love interest is an individual, she can now completely and mythologically pass over into her lesbian identity. The narrator explicitly activates the mythic dimension in order to give old meaning new dimension. The final crescendo comes: "*Tsichtinako* was calling! . . . The Acoma people heard it and knew it was the voice of the Invisible One . . . although no one had heard it in a long time and some had never heard it before. But all still knew who It was" (211). The narrator here alludes to the Aztec worldview of Ometeotl, the genderless generative force that is invisible and intangible, dialoguing the crossover moment in a less differentiated mythic tradition in this contemporary reenactment. The narrator makes it clear that it is a creative force inherent within the indigenous consciousness—even those who have never heard it before know what "It" is. Though they have the innate capacity to hear, they aren't given the privilege of experiencing this state of non-dichotomized gender existence. Not surprisingly, the narrative's allusion to Ometeotl replaces the Judeo-Christian, patriarchal creationist story with that of a *fronterista*, feminist source. Ometeotl, the narrator states, is the god "which had nourished the first two humans, who were also both female" (211). Caridad in touch with her Amerindian, *fronteriza* self can now make the final crossover. The narrator describes Esmeralda flying "off the mesa like a broken-winged moth and holding tight to her hand was Caridad, more kite than woman billowing through midair . . . [guiding them] back, not out toward the sun's rays or up to the clouds but down, deep within the soft, moist dark earth where [they] could be safe and live forever" (211). Caridad comes into a lesbian mestiza self enlivened by generative mythologies that are same-sex inflected: the communal space of the Amerindian Acoma Pueblo (matrilocal) and the Aztec Ometeotl gender-less generative forces (see M. A. Jaimes-Guerrero's discussion of the Acoma Pueblo in New Mexico in "Native Womanism"). It is within this woman-centered, "geomythological" (see Jaimes-Guerrero) social and cultural matrix that Caridad finally experiences an existence free of the spectacle. The Acoma Pueblo villagers hear the thunderous voice of Tsichtinako, a god the narrator describes as "the Invisible One who had nourished the first two humans, who were also both female" (211). So, when Caridad and Esperanza take a leap off the mesa cliff, they do not fall to their death but magically disappear into the earth; they magically return to an indigenous- and feminist-empowered origin. To this end, the narrator describes their flight not as "out toward the sun's rays or up to the clouds" (211)—which a reader might confuse with the more patriarchal and Western Icarus myth—but as a flight that leads them "down, deep within the soft, moist dark earth where [they] could be safe and live forever" (211). In the magicoreal world of Castillo's fiction, the god Tsichtinako calls and Caridad and Esperanza enter a non-gendered mythological space.

With and Against Mainstreams

Although written during the period when Castillo was living in Albuquerque and writing her novel *So Far from God,* the twenty-three short stories that make up the collection *Loverboys* employ very different narrative techniques and styles. Here, Castillo shifts narrative gears to use the concision of the short-story form along with a number of different styles (those that characterize, for example, the *cuentista* tale, first-person gritty realism, and third-person sentimental fiction), and she inflects each with a self-reflexive dimension that calls attention to the fictionality of her character's various racialized and sexualized identities and experiences.

Many critics have failed to appreciate Castillo's use of different narrative techniques to resist penning narratives that exoticize ethnosexual characters. Whereas in *The Review of Contemporary Fiction* Brian Evanson recognized Castillo's envisioning of a "fluid" sexual, cultural and social identity in *Loverboys* (201), a reviewer for *Publishers Weekly* wrote of the "earthy eroticism and zesty humor" in its depiction of "hot-blooded characters" (73). Indeed, more often than not, critics failed to see how Castillo uses a variety of techniques to destabilize an exoticizing mainstream reader's gaze.

Just as many of Castillo's characters move between different sexual identities (some less easily than others), so, too, do the narratives call attention to the construction of a racially motivated voyeuristic impulse. In the stories, we see this often in Castillo's emplotting of a protagonist that defies heteronormative sexual behavior but objectifies racially his/her love object. For example, the title story "Loverboys" begins in media res: "Two boys are making out in the booth across from me. I ain't got nothing else to do, I watch them" (11). At first, Castillo resists identifying the narrator's gender, which in this case allows the reader room for a flexible sexual identification and a variety of sexual engagements with the event: two boys making out. Then Castillo identifies the narrator as bisexual and Chicana, solidifying as fluid her sexual axis of desire as well as providing the reader with a guide to how they might align their sexual desire. As a reader, we can have pleasure in a variety of heterosexual and non-heterosexual encounters—all while the narrative calls attention to its own (straight and queer) objectification of racial Otherness. For example, the bisexual Chicana narrator fixes her sights on a patron she describes as having "Indian smooth skin like glazed clay" with the "offhanded manner of a chile alegre" (13) and "obsidian eyes" (14). Here, Castillo builds into her narrative a self-reflexivity that calls attention to how sexual emancipation doesn't necessarily lead to a non-essentialist racialization. So, while the narrator and reader might experience a certain pleasure in their fluid pleasuring of bodies and texts, the narrative self-reflexively reminds of a not-so-utopian racial gaze. We also see this double-identity configuration in the story "Crawfish Love," where the protagonist Vanessa confesses, "I'm ashamed to admit it but on that first official visit I, too, thought of Catalina only as a fine little waitress" (133). While Vanessa's axis of desire is non-heteronormative, it is nonetheless racialized. These are only a few stories of the many that Castillo invents to both make visible a more fluid hetero/queer desiring subjectivity and also to self-reflexively foreground a not-so-emancipatory sexual gaze (protagonist and reader) that racializes and contains the Chicana subject.

The stories that make up *Loverboys* are populated with other such sexual/racial-identified characters that have been forced to inhabit society's margins. That Castillo chooses the short story form is not surprising. It has long been seen as the genre most appropriate for texturing such denizens of the fringe. This is partly due to its physical length—much shorter than a novel and therefore more likely for an unknown author to publish; even today, the forum for the short story is the magazine or journal and not the book as most book publishers tend not to take "risks" with new writers working in this already marginalized genre within the book marketplace. The short story's traditional appearance in the magazine or journal has been an especially important venue for authors of color to publish their creative work. Faced with a long history of racial prejudice in the publishing world, Chicanas like early-20th-century fiction writer Christina Mena published their work in magazines and journals, and the short story came to function as a way for Chicano/a writers to represent their experiences and community. As Mary Louise Pratt writes of the short story, it proved vital in "establishing a basic literary identity for a region or group, laying out descriptive parameters, character types, social and economic settings, [and] principal points of conflict for an audience unfamiliar either with the region itself or with seeing that region in print" ("The Short Story," 187–188). Castillo extends this tradition of representing and making familiar what is unfamiliar (to her mainstream readers)—queer, bisexual, and straight Chicanos/as inhabiting different socioeconomic-inscribed spaces of the United States. And, in keeping with the genre's tradition of experimenting with form to introduce, as Pratt writes, "possibly stigmatized subject matters into the literary arena" (187), Castillo's narrators variously revise the Joycean epiphany—traditionally focused on a male character (albeit an outsider, like the prepubescent Irish character in "Araby")—by self-reflexively emplotting the epiphanies of Chicana/o characters and their non-heteronormative sexual experiences that lead to moments of life-changing awareness.

Castillo's revision of the epiphany in her short stories also speaks generally to the powerful way her narrators capture experience, spiritual and otherwise. Sexual desires and experiences in the stories lead not necessarily to spiritual epiphanies in the form of religious visions, say, but, as Samuel Baker comments, to "aesthetic fulfillments" (60). For Castillo's characters, the spiritual and aesthetic are also bound up in the sexual—and not always a "sexual" figured as corporeal. For example, in "Ghost Talk" the first-person Chicana-identified narrator comments, "We are talking about friendship, that has its own tenets so we are not talking about romantic/love/sex capture of another soul but the true captivation of another's spirit, which happens between people of the same sex sometimes" (*Loverboys*, 47). Accordingly, in her interview with Samuel Baker, Castillo states that for her "spirituality is a manifestation of one's energy, and that energy includes who you are as a total being—including your sexuality" (Baker, 60). Of course, such a sexual/spiritual configuration isn't expressed as a static, unified whole in the narratives. In fact, none of the characters reaches this place; instead, the stories follow a volatile path that does not lead to sexual/racial utopias, but rather to a place of discomfort for the reader—a place that resists sexual and racial fixity. Namely, Castillo's various narrators resist romanticizing a queer Chicana/o identity as the articulation of a counter-hegemonic, resistant subjectivity. Too, while the characters do experience moments of epiphany, they do so only suggestively, holding at bay a reader's impulse to know all and therefore to contain these sensually figured, ex-centric characters.

As the stories in *Loverboys* unfold, the narrators also texture a deeply tense and contradictory social milieu (mainstream and Chicano/a). We see this especially in the story "Again, Like Before," where the first-person, lesbian-identified narrator portrays the explicit and more subtle forms of homophobia present in her world. Within this homophobic society, however, she notices its deep contradictions. Although she's the target of heterosexist epithets, her topics of conversation tantalize straight eavesdroppers. And, on another occasion, she notes that while her girlfriend's "straight" brother threatens to beat her if he found out that she was "like *that*" (84), it is this same brother that the narrator discovers romantically interested in a married man, sleeping with him in the "spoon position on the floor every night" (85). It is this narrator's ability to *see* these contradictions that acts as a source of empowerment. And, in the title-story "Loverboys," the narrator/protagonist ultimately finds her own self-worth as a bisexual subject in a heterosexually governed world that divides rather than unifies peoples. Much like Castillo's narrators who crisscross otherwise bounded sexual and racial identities, Cecilia Rosales identifies *chueco* as the ultimate border identity, defining it as "that which is not straight or aligned; that is, anything bent, curved, angular, twisted, or distorted[. It] also refers to the practice of the transvestite passing as a woman" (27). Castillo's narrators inhabit this *chueco* ("crooked") sensibility that crosses borders of identity and at the same time acknowledges the powerful presence of such borders that restrict their movement.

Castillo's stories flesh out a variety of racial and sexual identifying characters; she uses a variety of techniques to innovatively emplot such characters' experiences and grand epiphanies. Taken as a whole, the stories are a testament to the power of an author who innovatively and creatively critiques the many different manifestations of homophobia, racism, and sexism experienced by and/or reproduced by her many characters. *Loverboys* makes memorable everyday experiences of sexual emancipation (queer and straight), of loves lost and won (queer and straight), and of racial identification. The first-person narrator and protagonist of the story "Again, Like Before" captures such an experience when she states with simplicity: "I left you because I simply did not love you. I left you because your money was a nuisance in my life. Above all, summer had ended and I left because that is when I said I would leave, and I did" (88). Perhaps, it is Castillo's ability to make memorable all aspects (good and bad) of everyday experiences of gay, lesbian, bisexual, and straight Chicanas/os that prompted queer Chicana author Terri de la Peña to give *Loverboys* her seal of approval in a review for *Lambda Book Report*, calling it "her most appealing fiction yet" (15).

Textual Peelings

In 1999, Ana Castillo published her novel *Peel My Love Like an Onion*. Yet again, she demonstrated her determination to move from one genre to another, from one storytelling mode to another, to find the right voice and generic frame to present yet another character and yet another story. In this case, she turned to the *Kunstlerroman*—the novel that typically gravitates around the (male) protagonist's development as an artist. Here, however, she engages this form traditionally associated with a mostly European and/or Anglo-American male character to reinscribe at its narrative center the formation of a Chicana artist: the crippled flamenco dancer Carmen. Again, as the title already hints, Castillo invents a first-person narrator who exaggerates cliché to self-reflexively call attention to the narrative's own play with exotic rhetoric usually used to contain the Latina as ethnic-object specimen to anticipate (wittingly or not) the type of language used by many a critic upon its publication. For example, Margot Mifflin in her review for the *New York Times Book Review* describes the novel as "fiery" and filled with "hot chili peppers" (31). And, in a like-exoticist reading, Renee Shea writes how Castillo "flamencoed into a novel about the Chicano and gypsy cultures of Chicago" (38). Indeed, Castillo's Chicana-inflected *Kunstlerroman* proves that an author can engage certain storytelling conventions, not to flaunt the brown woman as exotic, but to self-reflexively invigorate, complicate, and disengage such an identity and its experiences within polymorphously ethnosexual Chicago metropolitan space.

The novel immediately identifies its self-reflexive impulse. As the first chapter begins, the reader first encounters a title—"Chapter 1. Uno: I remember him dark"—and then the narrative opens thus: "I remember him dark" (1). (This kind of repetition is used to open all the rest of the novel's chapters.) Here, Castillo de-forms the storytelling convention that maintains a separation between discourse and story. The chapter heading becomes the narrator's first line and therefore storyworld and the paratext bleed into one another, a device that functions as a mirror that reminds the reader of its organization as an aesthetic. Castillo engages with other self-reflexive narrative devices, such as the direct address to remind the reader of the story's fictionality. She invents a narrator that punctuates a colloquial storytelling style (and one that tends to laundry-list descriptive details) with the direct address: "What's the expression? Water, water everywhere . . . I was full—a vessel, a huge pre-Columbian pot, a copal-burning brassier, a funeral urn, a well, Jill's bucket up and down, a bruja's kettle simmering over the fire" (1). The tangent, excessive accumulation of detail, and the direct address, position the novel within the self-reflexive picaresque and Rabelaisian storytelling mode—a mode that is not only employed by authors to reveal otherwise unseen parts of society, but also works self-consciously to remind the reader of the fictional status of the narrative.

Though the narrator reminds the reader of the story's own artifice, this does not disengage the reader completely. The narrator/protagonist Carmen describes, and we enter her Chicago storyworld. In her present-tense experiences and those of a recollected past, the narrative fills out a sexually layered metropolitan space with all its attendant pleasures and pains. For example, as Carmen's leg throbs with pain, she describes the experience of a "sudden sinking feeling that my life has been ripped from under me, a generation has gone and my city at night is no longer exciting and grand but now a veritable battle front" (95). The adult Carmen is faced with the pain of her crippled leg that returns as she grows older: "Ever since I began to experience all the pain that I had not felt in so long and never thought I would again because I was strong and smart and young and could dance my way through it, I've been trying to figure out an escape from the little ice box that is my body's ongoing agony" (152). To escape the pain, she finds herself escaping more and more into memories to find refuge. On one occasion, while thinking about her mother dying in a hospital bed and her best friend Vicky's brother Virgil struggling with AIDS, she thinks, "you remember the night you slept with him when you were not in love and neither was he, a long time ago" (2). And, on yet another occasion, she recalls losing her virginity in a threesome with Vicky and Virgil: "Anyway I dug the brother, but I really liked Vicky too . . . then, next thing I know Vicky and I were making out naked in front of her brother" (46–47). She returns again to this formative experience, recalling "Vicky made love to me like a man and Virgil like a woman, or put another way, I lost my virginity to my best friend Vicky" (111). Carmen's re-memory of the past offers her mind and body a place to repose within a present filled with sharp pains from her crippled leg. It also allows the reader access to a more complex Carmen whose past and present provide a narrative gestalt of a character with a fuller sense of her fluid sexual self-identification.

Such a world of fluid sexual experience and identity is squashed in her present-day, adult life. Not only is she aware of the dangers of AIDS, but her sense of herself sexually is forced to conform and harden. Though she imagines herself as hermaphroditic and androgynous (91), the men she ends up with channel her desire toward heterosexuality and restrict her freedom sexually. Her pleasure, for example in female ejaculation—the "gush" (82) that she embraces, a "wet birth like a calf in a barn born just before light" (82)—is turned into the pains of dealing with a lover like Agustín, who dichotomizes and restricts; he sanctifies the image of his wife who takes care of his children in Spain (coded as the Virgin and the Old World) and denigrates Carmen (coded as the whore and *la malinche* of the New World). Instead of fluidity and ecstasy, Carmen is forced to abide by patriarchal, racist rules. She's increasingly repulsed by the "callused, clammy, worn-out brusque hand of a man that reaches out of habit and horniness for your tired breast in the dark" (65). Castillo emphasizes Carmen's heterosexist and racist containment when the narrator details Carmen's non-choice of being with her love-interest, Manolo.

She is forced to give up Manolo because he abides by the patriarchal system of *compadrismo*—he refuses to see her because she "belongs" to Agustín. The story makes clear that Carmen's sense of herself sexually intersects with her sense of racial self. Her sense of not feeling at "home" in Chicago is only a small part of a much stronger and pervasive feeling of not belonging anywhere. She states, "You never feel right saying that—*my country*. For some reason looking Mexican means you can't be American" (3). Not able to feel at home and with a strong sense of being deformed—she was born with a mangled leg that she describes as "bald and featherless, a limp dead heron fallen from its nest . . . a dead gnarled limb" (12–13)—she is drawn to the gypsy lifestyle of the flamenco dancer. At the elementary school for "cripples, retards, the deaf and dumb" (12) she attends, it is her teacher, Miss Dorotea, who celebrates Carmen's body, calling it that of a "beautiful gypsy girl" (14); this sparks her desire to learn flamenco and to lose her crutches on the dance floor. Dancing offers her a reprieve from a domestic-fixated mother ("Jefita") who is stuck in reveries of the homeland and the *telenovelas* that take place in Mexico City—a place she's never been but, Carmen informs, "she feels it is a lot closer to home than Chicago, even though she's lived in this town for over four decades" (27). It is during her career as a dancer that she meets Chichi, the transvestite who wears size-eleven pumps (46) with "mostly muscle beneath the satin miniskirt, garter and bra cut to expose the nipples" (45). She states, "I learned a lot about being a woman from Chichi, who was a lot of woman for being a man" (45). It also gives her a sense of freedom and empowerment as a Chicana who doesn't fit the ideals of Mexican beauty reproduced by the mainstream media: "thin-nose beauties with stick-on nails and their cavalier Euro-Latin lovers" (128). Instead, she assumes the performance name of Carmen "La Coja" (the cripple) Santos as an act of self-empowerment. Self-naming and learning the art of dancing—much like Frida Kahlo, whom she invokes—allow her to overcome feelings of estrangement and ultimately allow for a new expressive way of existing as a freely moving mestiza: "Ultimately you find that existence is nothing, the void. But to achieve the void is everything, the very essence of existence" (191). Finally, Carmen learns to live with her pains and pleasures that fill her present experience; as she expresses at the end of her story: "In our own skin we can be reincarnated. You don't have to have a baby, reproduce yourself for a new and improved you. You don't have to die first. You don't have to die at all" (197).

Bent Visions in Sheila Ortiz Taylor's *Coachella Valley*

In her 1998-published novel *Coachella* (sections of which first appeared in the important Latino/a journal *Americas Review* in 1996), Sheila Ortiz Taylor takes her readers into a Palm Springs desert community populated with straight, gay/lesbian, conservative and liberal Anglos, Chicanos, and American Indian characters. *Coachella* is a story that explores the range of pleasures and pains of these characters' manifold experiences of their bodies and desires in the world. It is a polyphonic novel that uses a number of different storytelling modes, such as the diary entry and that of the mystery/suspense narrative, to extend and expand her earlier, more lesbian-centered, less race-focused novels *Faultline* (1982) and *Spring Forward/Fall Back* (1985).

Although Sheila Ortiz Taylor has always strongly identified as lesbian and Chicana (as she clearly states in her preface to *Faultline*), she, like the author John Rechy, was not included in the Chicano letters fold until four years after publication of her first novel (*Faultline*). Again, as with Rechy, it was Juan Bruce-Novoa who forcefully opened the doors to her. In his essay "Homosexuality and the Chicano Novel," first published in *Confluencia* in 1986, he locates Ortiz Taylor within a contemporary Chicano literary canon that includes authors such as José Antonio Villarreal, John Rechy, Floyd Salas, and Arturo Islas. As Bruce-Novoa already discerned, her novels *Faultline* and *Spring Forward/Fall Back* do indeed make up an important part of the Chicano/a literary topography.

In spite of Bruce-Novoa's championing of Ortiz Taylor's "borderland narratives" that offer readers "alternative" possibilities for representations of love and desire within the Chicano community, her fictions continued to pass largely unnoticed. In *Show and Tell*, Karen Christian suggests that this is largely the result of her defying those easily identifiable categories used by critics to identify her either as the author of lesbian narratives or the author of ethnic fiction, but not as a writer who collapses both categories.

Sheila Ortiz Taylor is an author who destabilizes preconceived notions that exclude those Chicana voices deemed inauthentic. Her fictions certainly give more play to lesbian characters, but not to the exclusion of her texturing a racialized experience within a mainstream Anglo-American culture. She is a lesbian Chicana author who uses a number of different storytelling styles to invent characters whose experience of both race and sexuality is simultaneous and mutually inclusive.

Indeed, Ortiz Taylor's *Coachella* defies categorization, not only in terms of its ethnosexual queer content, but also in form. It experiments with storytelling form (first- and third-person narration, diary and epistolary entry, for example) to present as total a vision of this Palm Springs desert community as possible; it experiments with form also to engage and then present to the reader a harsh new vision of a post-AIDS straight and queer community. Even before submerging her readers into this world, the text juxtaposes two different genres: the identification of the book as a "novel" (fiction) on the jacket cover contrasts with the information provided in the epigraph (fact). The epigraph is a quote from a verifiable source of fact, *The Desert Sun* newspaper, and describes the "real" HIV contamination of a blood bank in Coachella Valley that, for eight years, left "a path of infection [that] remained mostly open for the AIDS virus." Mixing the conventions that announce fiction (the paratextual "novel") with that of fact (the newspaper quote) works as a self-reflexive device to remind the reader of the difference between fictional narrative and "real" ontological fact; it reminds the reader that this is a complexly organized aesthetic narrative whose characters powerfully suggest that *all* people (straight or queer) are responsible for and susceptible to diseases like AIDS; it is not a disease only confined to the "dark," hypersexualized spaces (urban) of the Other. Contrary to the comment by one character—that "lady boys" carry "this sickness with them, putting everybody at risk, regular people who have never done anything to anybody" (102)—AIDS is a problem for all.

With the novel's readerly frame set up (the self-reflexive juxtaposition of fact with fiction), the story proper begins. And, as the first line suggests, it will be a story that unfolds, though not completely, as a series of diary entries. The novel begins "February 15, 1983" and closes "June 1, 1983." With the epigraph having identified the setting (Coachella Valley), we now have an established place and finite period of time for the narrative to unfold. Moreover, the initiating of the narrative as a diary entry places the novel within a long history of women authors who used the diary and epistolary form. (I think here of Susanna Haswell Rowson's *Charlotte Temple*, 1791, Webster Foster's *The Coquette*, 1797, and Judith Sargent Murray's *The Story of Margaretta*, 1798, for example.) Once sanctioned by a patriarchal publishing world that deemed the realist novel too sophisticated a mode for women to employ, the diary form is used by Sheila Ortiz Taylor to express proto-feminist values. In *Coachella*, as the diary entries accumulate and the story unfolds, we discover that it is not only a vehicle for expressing a feminist point of view, but that of a Chicana lesbian, Yolanda. Her diary entries destabilize stereotypes of Chicanas as only open receptors to male domination, texturing instead the experiences bad (abuse and abandonment, for example) and good (interracial queer love) that inform this Chicana character's experiences and memories.

While Yolanda Ramírez's diary entries begin and end the novel and thus most align her point of view with the story's worldview (that which seeks to cut through clouds of prejudice and ignorance to reveal truths about the human condition), Ortiz Taylor also fills in the space between diary (and epistolary) entries with a number of first-person and third-person narrations. So while the narrative frame in toto is provided by Yolanda's point of view, the narrative gives way to narratives not filtered through her worldview. The net effect: the narrative makes room for other characters to speak; in the case of the third-person narratives, it also allows all the characters that fill out the Coachella storyworld, including Yolanda ("Yo"), to be seen and judged by an omniscient narrator: a presence that has the power to see beyond the closed door and into the interiority of characters, a power that Yo, for example, lacks. As a character within the story, she isn't privy to other characters' thoughts, nor can she see everything; the omniscient narrator fills out omissions in Yo's narratives and allows the reader to imagine this world more fully. The narrator also functions to foreground the narrative's central thrust: the line between diseased/non-diseased, private and public, individual and communal is blurred. That ultimately the narrator can see behind this community's closed doors emphasizes the general thematic thrust of the novel: those straight characters who consider themselves most self-contained and safe from a gay/lesbian HIV-identified world are actually just as much a part of this public sphere as anyone else. In the end, the boundary between that sanctified as a safe space (coded as Anglo, middle-class, and private) and that deemed chaotic and unsafe (coded as gay/lesbian, working class and public) blurs in a world filled with disease.

Diary, epistolary, and admixture of first- and third-person narrations make for a polyphonic novel that represents the often complex and contradictory lives of its characters. "Yo," for example, is not just a nurse with empathetic traits, but one who defies an oft-encountered dichotomy: the traditional doctor-as-civilized (mind) vs. nurse-as-primitive (body). The narrator describes her as "knowing [the patients'] names and ages, the relationship and occupations of their survivors, sometimes what they died of, their faces floating into her imagination like drowned bodies rising" (15). However, that she does not hold herself at a distant remove from her patients is a necessary narrative device; it leads to them pouring forth their otherwise closeted problems (domestic abuse, gendered self-esteem issues, at-home machismo that denies illness), which allows the narrative to unfold in her project of researching medical records and hemoglobin counts to sleuth out and solve the mysterious deaths of characters (straight and queer, brown and white, male and female). Their deaths, she discovers, are indeed caused by HIV-contaminated blood transfusions. In contrast, the narrator describes the money-hungry hospital administrator telling Yo, "I wonder if you couldn't invest just a little trust and confidence in men infinitely more qualified than you to alert this community in the event of real danger. I hardly think this hospital should cease to function because each lab technician with an AA degree from the local junior collage says the blood supply is tainted" (123). Indeed, she combines logic, research skills, and empathy to prove the doctors ignorant. She is the character invested with the intuitive and logical capacity necessary to reveal the scientific truth.

We also learn that Yo is on her own personal journey. As a Chicana without the presence of a mother and only a shadowed father figure, she finds a sense of place in embracing her lesbian sexuality and ethnic heritage. Yo is in touch with ethnic roots—for example, the third-person narrator describes her invoking the names of Coatlicue, Malintzin, Tonantzin, and Guadalupe, and she knows to walk "into one of the Indian Canyons" (56) to find balance and to cleanse herself—but Sheila Ortiz Taylor is careful not to romanticize her by freezing her sense of Chicanidad in some static sense of an Amerindian identity. To this end, the narrator describes her driving her "Red-spirit," her much loved Camaro (a word the narrator playfully associates with the Spanish, *camará*, or "girlfriend"). And, once deep into her hemoglobin count research, she even turns from considering "blood" as only a metaphor for her mixed-race ethnic heritage to seeing it clearly as an object for scientific analysis: "Blood was blood. Describable, quantifiable, essential, compelling life fluid" (66).

The narrative not only complicates preconceptions (class, gender, sexuality, and ethnicity) vis-à-vis Yolanda, but also other characters, like Eliana Townsend, the middle-class, light-skinned Chicana. We learn that her insecurities spin out of her being abandoned by her mother—*morena* (dark) and a migrant farm worker—when she was five years old; we learn that her bodily insecurities are fed by a society (including her racist, Anglo husband, George) that circulates only certain images of women (Anglo, thin, and so forth); and we learn, too, that middle-class means provide the time for Eliana to fixate and internalize a "white"-coded, glamour magazine morphology that's simply "unnatural" for her to conform to. We also learn that with time and money she can willy-nilly surgically transform her body. In her quest to alter her body into the "ideal" image/shape of Woman (white and emaciated), she tragically comes to embody this very unreal possibility. Her contracting of the HIV virus through a post-liposuction blood transfusion leaves the reader feeling the bitter taste of her ironic and deeply tragic end. At one point, the narrator describes powerfully how "ugliness is moving into her body, *lo feo*, a process that has somehow speeded up now that her attention is elsewhere, fixed on this invader who has taken up residence inside herself, consuming all her energy" (41). The character most obsessed with transforming her body into an image of Woman as constructed by the mainstream media is the one who most dramatically self-destructs: the narrator carefully details her swift emaciation and death.

While the narrator primarily locates this internalizing of the spectacle of Woman-ness within a Chicana, middle-class subjectivity, the narrator also invests a working-class Anglo character, Biscuit Reed, with this same destructive impulse. Biscuit Reed is fixated on her maintaining her youthful look. She waxes nostalgic about those days when she "weighed only ninety-eight pounds and had a little bitsy waist" (13). Much like Eliana, her HIV infection from a tummy-tuck operation adds tragic irony to her nostalgia for a youthful, lithe body. As she learns rapidly, thinness is a sign not always of health, but also of death. Although both women are from different ethnosocial backgrounds, their characterization powerfully speaks to the destructive effects of one's internalizing of spectacularized images of the self perpetuated by mass-media iconography.

In contrast to the characters Eliana and Biscuit, the narrator also breathes life into the lives of gay characters such as the Cahuilla-Indian–identified Gil. Gil's contraction of HIV is not about revealing the tragic hypocrisies of straight society (Biscuit's homophobia and her contraction of HIV, for example), but rather a sympathetic portrayal of those afflicted who cause others no pain and simply want to love and find everyday fulfillment.

The narrative also introduces the reader to Yo's father, the equally complex Crescencio Ramírez, a Mexican gardener who works for the Palm Desert well-to-do set. More than a stand-in for the working-class Chicano community that keeps the desert alive and beautiful for middle-class characters like Eliana and her husband, Crescencio brings to the story not just a Mexican machismo but an outsider's deep awareness and sensitivity that cuts through the racism that clouds people's vision of the world and their engagement with others. As Crescencio contemplates "his lost world" (22)—Mexico—and the death that surrounds him, he watches his dying employer and secret love-interest, Eliana, and imagines death rushing into her body's "emptied, confused" spaces (174). The reader soon realizes that, at least in Sheila Ortiz Taylor's invented world, he is left with little air to breathe. Crescencio's loss of his wife and lesbian-identified daughter leads to his suicide at the novel's close. And then there is the character Leonard Lowe, who turns out to be more than meets the eye: an architect by day and a cross-dresser named Lowella by night. And, there's the Chicana character named Marina Lomas, a name newly acquired after fleeing her abusive husband. Here, the narration celebrates the love that develops between Marina and Yo. The narrator naturalizes their love, describing on one occasion how Yo's arms open "like a cactus flower" and how their embrace makes Marina feel as if her body is "hot petals and sizzling liquids: agua caliente" (88). However, rather than Marina's new name and relocation leading to grand emancipation that might romanticize a mestiza lesbian nomadism as de facto resistant to patriarchal oppression, the narrator reminds the reader that she has been forced to become once again a woman "of no history at all" (50).

Concluding Remarks

In this analysis of Chicana authors Ana Castillo (self-identifying publicly as straight and/or ambiguously bisexual/bi-curious) and Sheila Ortiz Taylor (publicly out as lesbian), we see that both writers invent an array of characters: straight, gay, lesbian, bisexual. That is to say, they are writers of fiction that use the power of empathy to enter into the imagination of those within and outside their own experiences to invent fictions that then powerfully engage the reader's imagination. Of course, that one has crossed over into the mainstream (Ana Castillo) and the other has not (Sheila Ortiz Taylor) speaks to the specific socio-historical contexts within which their fictions circulate. It is a fact that "out" authors like Ortiz Taylor—and also Terri de La Peña, Alicia Gaspar de Alba, Alma Luz Villanueva, Ibis Gomez-Vega, Emma Pérez, and Cherríe Moraga, to name a few—have not crossed over. Their works are published by small presses and with limited distribution. As mentioned already, in the case of Moraga's long history as a playwright, she continues to face tremendous resistance and a lack of production support; her last two plays, in fact, have not been produced at all. What does this say exactly? It says that while Chicano/a writers are free to invent worlds outside of their experience, when those worlds are filled with queer/lesbian-identifying characters and themes, they encounter the closed doors of mainstream publishing houses.[3] On the one hand, Castillo's texts represent a wide spectrum of sexual experience; she is known and marketed mostly as a writer of feminist "ethnic" fiction. On the other hand, Ortiz Taylor, who began her career with the lesbian-explicit and lesbian-exclusive *Faultline* and *Southbound,* is known first as a lesbian, second as a writer of ethnic fiction. The tangible material result: Castillo is published with the titan Doubleday and Ortiz Taylor with the small presses Naiad and the University of New Mexico Press.

This has always been true of lesbian-authored and lesbian-themed fiction. Take, for example, the many lesbian authors writing books during the early part of the century: only Radcliff Hall's *Well of Loneliness* made it into the mainstream; or, take Djuna Barnes, who was championed by T. S. Eliot but whose only big publication was *Nightwood*—all the rest of her fiction was published by small presses. While many taboo subjects eventually made their way into the mainstream (Henry Miller's and later Nabokov's descriptions of sex with minors, Joyce's descriptions of Bloom masturbating in *Ulysses,* as I mention in the Introduction to *Brown on Brown*), the articulation of gay and lesbian sexual identity and experience in fiction continues to remain a taboo subject. Now, if we add race as an ingredient in the mix, this touches off even deeper fears. I think of the gay Chicano author Arturo Islas, who in the mid-1970s wrote *Dia de los Muertos,* an explicitly gay novel with a Chicano first-person narrator. After receiving over thirty rejection letters and spending nearly a decade revising and writing out its gay content, he finally managed to publish it as *The Rain God*—a novel greatly trimmed of its original Chicano *caló* and its queer characterization. (For more on this, see my *Dancing with Ghosts: A Critical Biography of Arturo Islas.*)

Whether brown, white, straight, and/or queer, authors want to be read; writers need to make a living by writing so they require large publishers with big distributions. The small press is important, but usually the scope of its production isn't sufficient to support a writer. (Hence, the big legal battles that ensue between author and small press, such as Denise Chávez's ten-year fight with Arte Público to re-secure her rights to her first novel, *The Last of the Menu Girls.*) All the gay/lesbian and straight Chicano/a writers that I've talked with want to make a living at writing, and to do this, their writing must cross over. This doesn't mean that they have to compromise their aesthetic values but that writing strategies must be worked out—especially if they are writing about the taboo subject of (inter)racialized queer/lesbian sexuality.

The analysis of Ana Castillo and Sheila Ortiz Taylor also demonstrates that these two Chicana authors must variously employ genre and narrative technique to strategically engage, seduce, then disengage a reading public that might otherwise resist entering into their queer/lesbian border-erotic worlds. And, arguably, Castillo uses a double voice—writing to and against the mainstream—in ways that make her fiction more appealing as crossover material. This does not mean to suggest that she "sells out"; her skill at crafting fictions that complicate and challenge at every turn is undeniable. Those that sell out are writers who reproduce cliché in formulaic writing, as with, for example, a writer like Himlice Novas, who in her novel *Mangos, Bananas, and Coconuts* represents sans irony or self-reflexivity a hyper-exoticized Latina protagonist whose various phases of desirability are likened to bananas, mangos, and coconuts. Novas's novel lacks the double voice of Castillo, which makes her novel one of pure consumption and not one that aims to open readers' eyes to other ways of seeing and experiencing the world. Chicana writers like Ana Castillo can create fictions that can speak both to a mainstream United States and to a multiple cultural and hybrid subject by creating new possibilities for metaphors, imagery, syntax, and rhythms and for identity in a double-voiced borderland textual space. Perhaps Ana Castillo is an example of an author who is constantly discovering new ways to negotiate the articulation of a Xicanista identity within the mainstream. *So Far from God, Peel My Love Like an Onion,* and *Loverboys* prove that to be the case. In *Coachella* more than any of her previous novels, Sheila Ortiz Taylor, also, employs a double voice to create a world populated by a variety of characters—white and brown, queer and straight. It remains to be seen whether her image as a lesbian author first and a writer of ethnic fiction second will change now. It remains to be seen, then, if indeed the Chicana lesbian writer's use of a double voice narrative strategy that at once speaks to the mainstream and challenges its readers will be allowed to play with other writers and imagined worlds in a much larger literary sandbox.

CHAPTER 5

Edward J. Olmos's Postcolonial *Penal*izings of the Film-Image Repertoire

In March of 1992, Chicano actor Edward James Olmos released his directorial debut, *American Me*. In this film, Olmos opened cinemagoers' eyes to the multilayered terrain—psychological, sexual, social—in his creative representation of a Chicano youth turned gangbanger in East L.A. As the film unfolds, Olmos (as director and as the story's protagonist) begins to break new ground in Chicano cinema by revealing the Chicano subject's internalizing of neocolonial models of oppression. Olmos's interweaving of connotative and denotative detail both at the level of the story (plot, characters, events, themes) and at the level of the telling (the cinematic narrator's use of music, mise-en-scène, editing, voice-over narration) makes for a film that is both implicitly critical of neocolonial practices that continue to inform mainstream ideology and critique the heterosexism and homophobia that exists within the Chicano/a community.

Briefly, *American Me* (scripted by Floyd Mutrux[1]) unfolds as follows: We first meet the protagonist Santana (played by Humphrey Bogart–styled tough guy Edward James Olmos) as the bars slam and he enters Folsom State Prison. The story begins to unwind as Olmos recalls the complicated contours of his past (his interior monologue-as-voice-over filling the film's narrative diegetic space). A series of flashbacks first takes the audience back to his inception: his mother, Esperanza (played by Vira Montes), is brutally raped by white Navy sailors on the night of the Zoot Suit riots (June 3, 1943). Then Santana's voice-over leads the audience into his life as an alienated teenager in the late 1950s, when he formed his gang, La Primera, in East Los Angeles. After several sequences that show gang camaraderie between Santana and his "number one crime partners," white boy J.D. and Chicano, big-eyed Mundo, the audience soon finds them all behind bars in Juvenile Hall. Here Santana knifes in the jugular the much-feared, white-sodomizing rapist, which fast-tracks him into Folsom State Prison. The audience catches up with Santana and his *clica* eighteen years later. La Primera has transformed into La Eme, the factually based Chicano Mafia that today controls most of the pushing, pimping, and gambling that goes on inside California state penitentiary walls. In the late 1970s, Santana and J.D. are paroled and struggle to adapt to a very transformed outside world. An act of desperation that seals Santana's fate (he orders the sodomitical rape and murder of an incarcerated Italian, the son of his arch-competitor), along with Santana's inability to reform (he sodomitically rapes love-interest Julie, played by Evilinda Fernández), lands Santana behind bars once again. Diegetically speaking, as the film comes to an end, we are closest in story time to the moment when we first meet Santana, at the film's start. The story's tragic denouement (six members of La Eme stab, then tier-drop Santana because he shows "weakness") brings the film story full circle.[2] However, while the film's story is centrally focalized through Santana's consciousness, it nonetheless gives over a little extra diegetic time to Julie and Santana's younger brother, Paulito (played by Jacob Vargas). After Santana's death (and logically the place where the film story should cease), the camera-narrator continues to tell the story: Julie is described leaving the barrio and on her way to night school, and Paulito sniffs glue with another *chavalito* and, from behind the wheel of a '56 Chevy, fires a bullet at some innocents.

There's more than the break-the-cycle moral to this tale of redemption. As Santana experiences a 180-degree turn to his sense of self and community—his encounter with Julie (who identifies him, not so incidentally, as an oxymoronic, bifurcated man-infant) opens his eyes to his own participation in the genocide of his peoples—we see him struggle symbolically to break away from a deep-seated Euro-Spaniard supermacho legacy. Santana's struggle, finally, is about how he breaks free of age-old binaries—colonizer vs. colonized, bully vs. sissy, male vs. female, *activo* vs. *pasivo*, buggerer vs. maricon, hole maker and holed one—that continue to inform and control from within the Chicano/mestizo subject today.

Not surprisingly, perhaps, the plot makes major shifts after the story's three rape events: The first rape, of Esperanza, marks Santana as a proverbial *hijo de la chingada* (as did the rape of the Maya and Aztec peoples by Cortez et al.); as a result of the rape of his mother, his taciturn father, Pedro (played by Sal Lopez), cuts him off emotionally, so Santana turns to the streets and forms his alternative male-male social matrix. The second and third rapes take place in the same temporal moment (the camera-narrator uses an increasing jump-cut tempo to juxtapose Santana's sodomitical rape of Julie in an apartment with that of the sodomitical rape and murder of the Italian in prison by Santana's henchmen, Puppet (played by Danny De La Paz), Mundo (played by Pepe Serna), and El Japo (played by Cary Hiroyuki Tagawa). The rape and murder of the Italian leads to a small apocalypse in the barrio and alienates Santana from Julie. As a result, Santana questions his raison d'etre; he shows weakness.

However, the rape scenes work as more than kernel events that shift the plot. Director Olmos's use of the rape scenes creates a film that, on the one hand, uncritically reproduces the anal encounter as abnormal and perverse, as an act of physical violence that leads to the mass destruction of the heterosexual matrix. For example, in a post–anal-rape repentive moment just before Santana's death, he writes in a letter to Julie, "Here in this cage . . . behind these bars, I can read, I can learn, I can *make love,* but it's distorted." And, of course, when the double anal rape scene leads to an apocalypse in the barrio, one can't help but read this against our AIDS-panicked mass culture that associates anal intercourse (men "taking it like a woman") with suicide and disease, especially in poor ethnic enclaves. Other examples abound. For example, as soon as the character Little Puppet gets out of the male-male–only pen, homosexual panic sets in; he swiftly marries. And, while same-sex encounters are suggested (some to a greater degree than others, as with Santana's open declaration that he can make love in prison), it is only to assert the heterosexual encounter. For example, when J.D. (played by William Forsythe) gets paroled and struts his stuff down the penitentiary's tier, the character Mundo says, "Get laid out there for me"—as if "getting laid" can happen only in the civilian, heterosexually coded world.

The film's machismo complex rechannels the homosexualization of desire back toward the heterosexual object. Heterosexuality swallows all that threatens an economy built on male-female biological reproduction and that ensures the safe passage of power from father to son. Even though the prison system functions to sexualize Santana's desire as anal-directed, for the civilian system to work this must be considered only as a means to a better, heterosexual end. In a post-anal encounter scene, Julie reproduces this heterosexist tendency when, angrily resisting Santana's apologia, she likens his death drive ("you'd kill me") to anal sex ("No, you'd fuck me in the ass"), thus reproducing the opposition: life is heterosexual (vaginal); sex and death are homosexual (anal) sex.

Certainly, however, *American Me* does interrogate the Chicano macho/bully paradigm—the hyper-exaggerated machismo of the male inmates calls attention to varying shades of the same impulse evinced by many Chicano men (such as Santana's taciturn, fly-off-the-handle father) in their violence against women and children. The camera-narrator identifies Santana's macho behavior as the origin for the series of events that leads to the Italian godfather's circulating of uncut coke that kills off dozens of Chicanitos. And the film is critical of Santana's self-victimization, a self-identification that transforms his initial alienation from the Father and from society (his noncitizen status as a Chicano) into a subject firmly entrenched in the very power that alienates peoples of color. Through the camera-narrator's critical lens, we see how the drive to acquire power as a way to authenticate Chicano subjectivity only leads to Santana's internalizing of a will-to-bully that destroys more than saves his family.

Along with the film's denotation of the sodomy as perverse, the sodomitical rape scenes carry an equally strong connotation of the colonial encounter. Namely, not so unlike the erstwhile conquistadors, Santana penetrates and, according to the heterosexist code, humiliates the Other (i.e., Julie). While their lovemaking begins in the heterosexualized missionary position, he's confused; something deep within is triggered—a legacy of Euro-Spanish sexual domination of the *indio/a*. To control and synthesize the "exotic" female-qua-new-virgin territory, he violently turns Julie over on her face, humiliates her, and penetrates her. Here the act of buggering (undesired by the bottom and thus a rape) connotes much. Importantly, it speaks to a history of transatlantic *colonial* libido that penetrated (anally, orally, and vaginally) the New World Other. As José Piedra claims in his essay "Nationalizing Sissies," the construction of a discourse by the conquistador/colonizer that prohibited racial mixing to maintain purity of the Euro-Spanish bloodline was simply a way for the colonizer to justify the buggering, or "sissyfying," of the New World Amerindian men and women. In other words, like the colonial fear of/desire for the New World male hole (mostly), the drive was always ultimately to maintain the purity of the Euro-Spaniard heterosexual lineage. José Piedra contends that the women remained "the hidden object of desire enacted by the sissy who operates in her stead just enough to save the bully from admitting to a gay connection" (371). And, in the big fear/desire dialectical scheme of things, Piedra informs, the "sissy becomes less of a man or a lesser man and more than a woman. In a parallel fashion, the bully becomes more of a man upon treating a lesser man as a woman" (371–372). This is to say, the machismo complex isn't new. The double-rape is simply a modern-day version of the colonizer's violent penetration, humiliation, and annihilation of the indigenous peoples—this time, however, enacted by the very progeny that came of the anal-to-vagina slippage during the Conquest.

Furthermore, the sodomitical act in *American Me* resonates with narratives seen in the early conquistador and colonizer texts that, by describing the New World Other as "sodomites," "pederasts," hybrid hypergenitalized men/women-animals, justified Euro-Spaniards' realization of their own closeted transgendering desire. José Piedra writes of colonial takeover as the colonizer (the "bully") keeping the New World subject (the "sissy") in a "suspended libidinal state" between, he maintains, "maleness and femaleness, hetero- and homosexuality, or 'worse.' Fantasized as androgyny, hermaphroditism, virginity, or celibacy, the sissy's 'in-betweenness' serves as the ultimate butt of macho rhetorical inscription, physical intervention, or both" (371–372). In other words, while Olmos invents a filmscape that questions macho codes of conduct that oppress women and children, the film also speaks to the process of internalizing the colonial model of controlling the Other and releasing of Self in the sodomitical act.

The rape sequences and Santana's apparent turn toward heterosexual norms in the post-anal encounter (he seems to visually repent with furrowed brow and head bowed low after he violates Julie) lend themselves to yet another reading. The film is being more critical of the sodomy-as-rape code than we see at first glance. If we consider the camera-narrator's heavy gesture toward revealing the more complicated pre-Columbian cultural terrain, the film also works to destabilize hypersexualized representations of the Other. We can reread Santana's rape-cum-repentance less as his sexualization in terms of *lacking* the "correct" hole (vagina), but rather as his move into a sexual in-between zone that threatens the male-male power structure of La Eme. Santana's "weakness," then, identifies his move into a more ambiguous top/bottom, *activo/passivo*, strong/weak identification that, by resisting age-old binaries (macho vs. sissy), threatens La Eme's male-male, teleologically heterosexual goal-directed, capitalist economy.

Santana's tragedy, in a sense, is that he enters a more complicated sexual zone not confined to binary oppositions. As a result, he is penetrated (stabbed) to death by six of the male-male, macho initiates. When mestizo-identified masculine desire is versatile and/or ambiguous, it threatens the system—national, sexual, racial—founded on constructed dichotomies that function to contain, to control, and to uphold (even if cloaked as *raza*-emancipating, like La Eme) the white, heterosexist, middle-class status quo.

It's not so much, then, that Santana must be annihilated because of his show of the dreaded detumescent "weakness" felt in his heterosexualized postlapsarian blues. Rather, it's his coming into an unfixity of sexual identity that leads to his annihilation. Such an ethnosexual, unfixed sexuality threatens the status quo precisely because it is uncontainable and, in its crossover movements, invisible to even the best of panoptic, ethnosexual surveillance structures. Santana's "weakness," then, is also his strength. As he crosses from *activo* to *passivo* he crosses into an ethnosexual borderland identity that threatens the status quo. Indeed, the camera-narrator, along with the character portrayal, betrays not so much a heterosexualized, vagina-redirected Santana, but rather a character who comes into an in-between ethnosexual identity that is both bully/top (the heterosexual macho, anal penetrator) and also sissy/bottom (anally penetrated).

Filling the Wrong Filmic Holes

I've briefly laid out the so-called surface (denotative) and deep (connotative) structures that make up the various messages readable in *American Me*. It isn't so surprising that the film conveys several layers of meaning. Films, we know, are as open to multiple layers of interpretation as, say, the novel. This is partly the result of the filmic text's lack of a time-present, that responding interlocutor (unlike the real-time of uttered quotidian speech) that would, according to his/her response (whether social-, racial-, sexual-, gender-conditioned), shape the outcome of the story/exchange. Of course, this isn't to say that *American Me* is a tabula rasa open to all sorts of interpretive squiggles. Indeed, the camera-narrator's auditory and visual channels and the story itself intertwine (intentionally or not) and cluster around certain nodes of meaning. It is not completely out of left field, then, to read Santana's ultimate show of "weakness" as the move into an unfixed identity zone informed by a legacy of anal-colonization when, for example, the film story begins with the Navy gang rape sequence that spins the audience's mind into allegorical re-memories of the sexual conquest of the New World.

However, this *raza*-informed audience frame doesn't necessarily guarantee a postcolonial reading of the film. For example, as Luis Valdez told a reporter for the *San Jose Mercury News* just after *American Me* hit the big screen, "My response then was that it was a diatribe against Latinos. . . . This is a genre (street-crime movies) that's been offered to me many times. It's not what I relate to. I believe in the cinema of triumph" (Feb. 29, 1992). Valdez wasn't alone. Other Chicanos/as in Los Angeles and throughout California more vehemently attacked the film for its negative portrayal of the Chicano community.

Few reviewers and critics picked up on anything but the film's ghetto/gangbanger code, leading either to extreme pans or celebrations; of course, there were few peeps about the film's complicated meddling with sexual middle grounds. For example, in the March 30 issue of the *New Republic*, Stanley Kaufmann took the opportunity to wax negative, writing that *American Me* is just "one more story of boys being led by ghetto conditions into drugs and crime, of gangs as the only available validation of self, of consequent prison, of crime in prison" (26). That same month, and seemingly with the same breath, Brian D. Johnson commented on how "Hollywood's most visible crusader of Hispanic causes" (Olmos) failed to "rehabilitate the tired formula of the prison movie" (*Maclean* review, 51). Johnson doesn't hold back here, writing, "The violence, which is both visceral and frequent, verges on exploitation. And the movie becomes a vicarious excursion into underworld exotica" (51). Might the use of "visceral," "exploitation," and "vicarious excursion into underworld exotica" betray something more than Johnson's dislike of the sculpted, brown male body?

American Me certainly is a film that focuses on gangs and prison life; at the beginning of the film the camera-narrator announces its self-proclaimed affiliation with the prison-film genre: "prison doors clank, keys jangle and an unidentifiable voice commands, 'Open mouth . . . lift up your nut sack . . . bend over . . . grab your ass and give me two good coughs.'" However, Kaufmann et al. seem to be stuck in their own preconceptions of how a prison-film story unfolds; they've missed the many complicated, often contradictory codes that make *American Me* more than a simple rehabilitation of "the tired formula of the prison movie."

Turning Holes Inside Out

Kaufmann's lack of critical appreciation doesn't surprise. Valdez's distaste does. The release of *American Me* in 1992 marks an important moment in Chicano/a film history. In the past, Chicano/a film had focused on constructing positive images and celebratory stories to undo nearly a century's worth of the silver screen's "greaser" and/or Malinche/virgin stereotypes. Hollywood's essentialized ethnosexual phantasmagoria stretches back to the 1910s with silents like *Tony the Greaser* (1910), *The Greaser's Revenge* (1914), and of course the more (in)famous *Birth of a Nation* (1915). For white filmgoers over time, we've been imagined only as lazy lay-abouts (our super-large sombreros give us nap-ready penumbral shadows) inclined to deviousness; and we've been ill-tempered, hot, heterosexual lovers (often the more Euro-Spanish phenotypical mestizos) as well. Negative and essentializing, yes; but would Hollywood production money allow Latinos to even role-play such blunderous stereotypes? Charlton Heston is cast as the Mexican protagonist Vargas in Orson Welles's *Touch of Evil* (1958), and in *Viva Zapata!* (1952) Marlon Brando (with the help of gobs of brown shoe polish) gets to step inside the brown skin of our national hero. Even Floyd Mutrux originally scripted the character Santana in *American Me* to be played by Al Pacino.

Then there's the Latina/Chicana in Hollywood, who are mostly thrown into the gushy, I'm-hot-salsa roles: in *Fools Rush In* (1997), for example, Salma Hayek paints her lips thick with red and speaks with a Mexicanized, Spanglish lisp to portray a histrionic peasant-girl who is saved by a Euro-Anglo knight in shining armor (played by Matthew Perry). Then there's *The Perez Family* (1994), with Marisa Tomei's representation of a Cubana who emerges on Miami's coastline clad in a wet T-shirt. In the mainstream-lauded *Colors*, Dennis Hopper has actress Maria Conchita Alonso portray the Chicana character as hot-blooded and willing to betray her community; the virtual barrio apocalypse at the film's close is depicted as her fault.

All this is to say that Luis Valdez's work to create a cinema of triumph is important. (Of course, Valdez isn't the only one. There are others, such as Gregory Nava, Alfonso Arau, and documentary filmmaker Lourdes Portillo, who also have been working to put the Chicano/a subject on the representational map.) However, we must not exclude the negative characterization if it can complicate the Chicano/a representational terrain, something I think Olmos's *American Me* attempts to accomplish. As Robert Stam and Louise Spence aptly point out in terms of the production of ethnic film images generally, "The insistence on 'positive images,' finally, obscures the fact that 'nice' images might at times be as pernicious as overtly degrading ones, providing a bourgeois facade for paternalism, a more pervasive racism" ("Colonialism, Racism and Representation," 3). Valdez is a case in point. While his films *Zoot Suit* (1981) and *La Bamba* (1987) make explicit the racism that exists in our every day, and make huge strides in giving substance to Chicano/a character identity as it is informed by history, culture, and race, the films do so at the expense of uncritically reproducing and even celebrating a destructive machismo. For example, in *La Bamba* Valdez's protagonist Ritchie Valens (played by Filipino Lou Diamond Phillips, an odd choice given Valdez's otherwise aggressive moves to cast Chicanos/as) comes into his manhood once he loses his virginity to a dark *mexicana* prostitute when he crosses over for the first time from California to Mexico. Valdez cuts to the postcoital moment with Ritchie waking up, not next to the *mexicana* seen in the last take, but next to his brother, Bob; they are lying in a dust-ridden *curandero*'s shack where they are initiated into pre-Columbian faith. The *mexicana* is barely around enough even to be a body; nonetheless, she works as a vehicle for the homosocial bonding between the brothers. Valdez is well versed in Maya and Aztec epistemology. Here, on a connotative level, Bob and Ritchie's bonding comes to symbolize the cosmic super-bonding between life and death, between the two male-coded, diametrically opposed gods Tezcatlipoca and Quetzalcoatl. While, however, Valdez gives much weight to this homosocially inscribed cosmic moment (the *curandero*'s totem is linked with Ritchie's song "La Bamba," ensuring its climb to the rock chart's number one spot), age-old gender essentialism surfaces. The brown woman's vagina acts only as a device to present a pre-Columbian symbolic underlay; in the legend, Valdez lets slip, the supermasculine Tezcatlipoca was a macho who violently raped Xochiquetzal, both female and god. (The trauma led her to transform herself into a transgendering god worshipped by straights and bents alike.)

Unfortunately, while Chicano cinema in general is marginalized, films by Chicanas are doubly so. Few films by Chicanas/Latinas have crossed over; most continue to receive support only from small-budget independent production companies. And while the mainstreamed *Mi Vida Loca* (1993) focused on the socioeconomics of Chicana *clicas,* its representational politics are arguably suspect; it was directed by an already semi-established *gringa,* Alison Anders. If the de-essentialized presence of Chicanas is doubly marginal, then brown cinema that deals with ethno-queered characters is triply marginalized. It is worth mentioning Darnell Martin's *I Like It Like That* (1994), where a limited amount of screen time is given to the fleshing out of a cross-dressing Puerto Rican character. Of course, Chicano/a scholars such as Chon Noriega, Ana Lopez, and Rosa Linda Fregosa, among others, have done much to open eyes to the heterosexism and homophobia that inform much of Chicano cinema.

This chapter, however, isn't meant to be a retrospective of Chicano/a cinema; yet I want to give a sense of the Chicano/a cinematic backdrop—with all of its genitalizing components—against which *American Me* is set. Indeed, understanding the backdrop allows us to understand how to decipher such a film narrative more fully.

Oddly, the very critics who reveal the gender essentializing that takes place in Chicano cinema fail to see *American Me* as anything but a film that reproduces the machismo complex. Kathleen Newman, for example, concludes her essay "Reterritorialization in Recent Chicano Cinema" by proclaiming *American Me* a failed attempt to "deterritorialize" the U.S. patriarch-serving, nation-state (95); because of its violence toward Chicanas, she informs, it fails to "reterritorialize the State . . . as a neutral site of equality and justice for all citizens" (104). Newman interprets the double-rape scenes "as actants" that simply move "the narrative to a conclusion wherein gender is disconnected from character and redeployed in the service of epic" (99). And Rosa Linda Fregoso attacks *American Me* in her book *The Bronze Screen* because, like other gang exploitation flicks, it reinscribes patriarchal politics of gender instead of promoting a non–gender-essentialized cultural nationalism. There is a way to read *American Me* that takes a different, frissive stroke—indeed, one that acknowledges the macho-complexed gender issues but that also investigates the complicated in-between area where nonnormative sexuality and race/ethnicity crisscross.

Cream Puffs and Tough Daddies

American Me is a Chicano film that shares affiliation with the prison film genre. *American Me* operates within the generic codes that traditionally identify trans-ethnic prison film: the protagonist's incarceration, socialization, will-to-power (book learning and/or godfatherization), epiphany, then liberation (through death or parole). Of course, prison films, given that they usually represent the "deviants" of our society, usually work as a microcosm of the panoptic surveillance systems used to control the genitalized Other (marked by class, race, sexuality) in mainstream society. Some films reveal the machinations of control, while others simply reproduce for the comfortable, middle-class audience the blueprint for social control that allows the movie-goer to breathe a sigh of relief. For example, in such prison films as *Midnight Express* (1978), *Bad Boys* (1983), *Blood In Blood Out: Bound by Honor* (1992), *Pulp Fiction* (1994), *Bad Girls in Prison* (1998), and Hector Babenco's *Carandiru* (2003) the camera-narrator constructs imaginary frames that separate the screened Other from a "real" theater-going audience. With such a distancing frame in place, same-sex desire can be represented because, as it always boldly announces, there is no alternative; same-sex lovemaking (men-men, women-women) is coded as a result of the lack of "natural" heterosexual coupling within the walls. In such films, inmates are portrayed as half-people; and because prison flicks inevitably focus on racially and socially genitalized groups (black and Latino), race and class are implicated. We don't really see films that focus on white-collar criminals; and when we do, as with *The Shawshank Redemption* (1994), the white-collar criminal is usually wrongfully incarcerated.

John McNaughton's low-budget *Bad Girls in Prison* is a good example of how Hollywood heterosexually codes same-sex desire. In *Bad Girls*, it seems that outed Hollywood actress Anne Heche (blacklisted after *Seven Days, Seven Nights*, when audience response groups couldn't suspend sexual-orientation disbelief) is a heterosexual *femme fatale* in the civilian world but swiftly morphs into a hot lesbian once behind bars. The quick shift suggests that she was simply donning the mask of heterosexuality. This could have proved an interesting reversal that naturalized lesbian sexuality, and revealed heterosexuality to be artifice. However, because while a heterosexual she's figured as a self-serving, murderous woman on the outside, her innate queerness only acts as that well-known pathological backdrop to give substance and motive to her deviant (criminal) self. And, as the audience discovers of those "girls in prison," they apologize for their same-sex desire. When the camera-narrator gives the audience a sequence that presents a hot, steamy, interracial, woman-on-woman shower scene, the inmate Melba explains to another: "I used to go out with boys on the outside, but there ain't none in here."

In male-prison flicks, the teleology is always directed toward the deeply de-sired heterosexual encounter equated with freedom—the outside; sexual encounters are also tied into power. The same year that *American Me* caused a certain frisson, director Taylor Hackford released *Blood In Blood Out: Bound by Honor*. The camera-narrator informs the audience: while in the prison yard, turf is divided by race, and when a new inmate arrives, especially a *guero* (mixed Anglo and *mexicano*), and enters the yard, borders collapse. White, black, and brown inmates variously whistle and holler: "Baby cake," "How about being my candy," and "Be my bitch." Miklo, the light-skinned (racial crossover), effeminate Latino is genitalized and the object of the (hard-bodied and soft, big and small) inmates' erotic gaze. Oddly, this is the only moment during the film when the different races are shown to be at one; the same-sex fetishist act functions to racially democratize the prisoners. And, once Miklo realizes that power resides in his gaining control of his same-sex sexuality, he gains power. However, the film ends up presenting the same-sex desire as anything but a democratizing agent. In a back-kitchen scene, Miklo role-plays a bottom, only to kill an inmate in order to escape and make off with a bag of money and a list of clients to peddle drugs to on the outside. The pattern—transracial tops that fetishize bottoms and bottoms who try to become tops—repeats itself and reproduces heterosexualized patterns of hierarchical power.

The locating of power in such films is heterosexually directed; the prison-inmate characters ultimately want a patriarchal power to survive and make it to the outside world to engage in "normal" heterosexual sex acts. The top/bottom mise-en-scène present in *American Me* is part of a larger, tough-guy filmic canvas. When Santana struts with a slight back-to-the-side cant, his bad-boy image (top) resonates with a panoply of Hollywood toughies: Humphrey Bogart, Lon Chaney, James Cagney. In Michael Curtiz's 1938 *Angels with Dirty Faces*, for example, James Cagney talks the talk ("don't be a sucker") and struts the strut; he's popular with the juvenile delinquents because he is the macho apotheosized—as the Italian- and Irish-identified gang kids recognize, he is not a "cream puff." We can certainly read much into *Angels*. For example, it's hard not to read the swift return of Cagney, once paroled, to his childhood crime-partner now turned soft-priest as a drive to return to a prelapsarian homosocial relationship. And, as in *American Me*, it is finally Cagney's turning soft (becoming a bottom) that leads to his death in the electric chair.

Before moving on, however, I want to mention one prison film that gives texture to a more sensual representation of male-male love and desire. Alan Parker invents a camera-narrator in his film *Midnight Express* (1978) that portrays the character Billy Hayes (played by Brad Davis)—in a Turkish prison for attempted drug smuggling—making love to his love-interest. The camera-narrator's auditory channel fills with a smooth, rhythmical romantic melody and the mise-en-scène fills with a soft-hued light. The camera-narrator doesn't distinguish between top and bottom; power relations are suspended and the same-sex encounter is sanctioned. The moment breaks, however, when Billy pulls away his wandering, soaped-up hand and informs his partner, "I have a girlfriend"; his heterosexual panic snaps into place and the moment is lost. Of course, while the camera-narrator begins to depict same-sex love in a more complex light, it does little to complicate the representation of the racial Other. The camera-narrator readily shows scenes of the Turkish guard visually devouring Billy Hayes's pure-white, boyish-looking body. Finally, then, *Midnight Express* conveys uncritically the white character as remaining a "pure" (heterosexual) and the racial Other as "impure" (perversely queer).

It is by no coincidence that the camera-narrator of *Midnight Express* codes a stabilized same-sex drive as perverse and racial. Not only do films like *Midnight Express* resist presenting the possibility that a same-sex identity can exist in and of itself (and not as the negative antithesis to heterosexuality) with its own means and ends, but Parker presents the same-sex identity as that which is foreign and a threat to white civilization; Billy's drug-smuggling entrepreneurial spirit is intimately linked with his individualism, smarts, and sense of duty to his girlfriend. Queer sexuality, on the other hand, is coded either as a slip due to the lack of women in prison or, more importantly, as exotic and freaklike. This perverting of the exotic, racially "alien" isn't new to Parker, nor to film texts in general. We see a similar codification of the non-Western (Judeo-Christian) Other in those early Euro-Spanish–penned conquest chronicles of the New World. In "Loving Columbus," José Piedra discusses the need for the conquistadors to construct a hypersexualized space—hermaphroditic freaks, sodomites, and violent, arrow-shooting Amazonian lesbians—that constructed the New World as a sexual "gray zone" in order to justify both the brutal genocide and colonization of the peoples as well as the conquistadors own anal/vaginal rape of New World men and women (240). For example, the Euro-Spaniards' fear of those inhabitants of *isla mujeres,* whom they label *amazonas* (which breaks down to mean "love zone" in Spanish), betrays a copresent desire to penetrate the unidentifiable (uncontrollable) Other and assert the law of the Phallus. For director Parker, like the Euro-Spaniard conquistadors, the construction of the Other as sexually perverse served to test the limits of the Euro-self, as well as to justify their enactment of S&M-styled sexual fantasies to brutal ends. For this reason, José Piedra reminds, the construction of the New World Other as a hole *requiring* Euro-Spanish filling necessitated the textual (symbolic) formation of the Caribbean archipelago as a "theater of gender and sex freaks" (238).

Hol(e)y Freaks

The textual construction of Other as sexual freak doesn't take place just in a far-off, exotic land in Parker's *Midnight Express,* or only in a modern-day type of *isla mujeres* or *isla hombres* (prison). The hypergenitalizing of the Other also takes place in films located on outside-world, U.S. turf. Of course, the Other-as-sexual-freak is often transposed from, say, sodomitical male inmates and/or Turkish guards to society's outcasts on the outside. For example, in Quentin Tarantino's much lauded *Pulp Fiction*, the kernel event that marks the film's push toward the final denouement comes when a pair of inbred, redneck white boys engage in the sodomitic rape of the black gang-overlord character, Marsello (played by the hugely sized, muscled, and deep-voiced Ving Rhames). To Tarantino's credit, he creates a scene that brazenly foregrounds exactly this fear/desire dialectic that informs white, heterosexist maps of power; it is the two rednecks who not only are marked by codes of hypermasculinity (they drive Harley's, pawn weapons, wear Marlboro Man denim outfits, and are lavishly tattooed) but keep a black-latex–clad male "gimp" chained up in their basement, absolutely submissive to their desire for the anal-only encounter. The black latex has zippers only for the gimp's mouth and anus, emphasizing the rednecks' fetishistic transformation of the male sexual subject into a hole-only–object.

Unfortunately, however, Tarantino slips back into that narrative of the colonizer-as-savior, and the complicated relief-mapping of the perversions of white heterosexuality vis-à-vis race deflate. Bruce Willis—the Hollywood quintessence of safe, white-boy heterosexual masculinity—arrives to save the black Other, and thus the civilized, heterosexual world, from the destructive, sodomitical Other. Actor Bruce Willis enacts a modern-day re-creation of yesteryear's European colonists who set out to "save" the dark, savage Other.

Traditionally, the silver screen uncritically represents the interrelations of race, sexuality, and class that lead to white, middle-class heterosexual violence toward the Other in order to maintain power. Films like *Pulp Fiction* and others that sequence same-sex encounters (mostly anal rapes) more often than not simply reinscribe the heterosexual values. John Boorman's *Deliverance* (1972) is yet another case in point. The story's plot-turning, pivotal event takes place when the four suburban, middle-class, male characters are anally raped by two Appalachian hillbillies. But first, while the film doesn't directly deal with race, its camera-narrator's mise-en-scène does transpose the ideologically racialized codes that traditionally represent the brown/black as Other onto the white trash hillbillies. Briefly, in the film's opening sequence the camera-narrator sets up a contrast between the suburbanites who speak and gesture slowly to engage the "noble savages": the hillbillies are presented as somehow wise and impenetrable (they don't speak a word), and they "naturally" dance when another mimics on his banjo the melody of the suburbanite's guitar strums. Of course, the rafting trip, all about the middle-classers getting to be at one with their masculinity and nature, is a neat transposition of the 17th- and 18th-century European colonial narratives wherein the Euro-Anglo, tired of his mundane existence, penetrates and makes holes in the jungle less for conquest and more for that return to a prelapsarian at-oneness promised by the brown/black primitives.

Race and class transpose easily here. So, when the infamous sodomitical rape scene takes place (the character Bob/Chubby, played by Ned Beatty, is covered in brown mud and squealing like a pig while a redneck sodomitically rapes him), race, class, and sexuality cannot help but crisscross. Not only do the "noble savaged" hillbillies transform into the heterosexual male character's worst nightmare, but the camera-narrator locates them within the same space (primitive and savage) that historically represented brown/black New World bodies. The film, then, is not only a narrative that plays into a white, middle-class fear of the return of the repressed (white-trash-qua-blacks), but by the film's end the heterosexual, middle-class norm is reestablished. In the film's final sequence, the camera-narrator's mise-en-scène presents the character Ed (Jon Voight) in bed cuddled next to his sleeping white wife and newborn. And, Ed, the character who showed weakness at the film's beginning, transforms into a testosterone-driven *überman* once his heterosexual masculinity is threatened. He single-handedly hunts down his "savage" rapist and saves his fellow rafters.

Pulp Fiction, Deliverance, and other films that represent sodomy as *contra natura* (primitive and savage) also form a contextual backdrop that allows for a deeper connotative reading of *American Me.* If read against a homographic and colonialist narrative backdrop, the film reveals a less clear-cut depiction of queer/bisexuality as *contra natura.* Indeed, unlike *Pulp Fiction* and *Deliverance,* which make same-sex encounters perverse and therefore reproduce heteronormativity, in *American Me* we see how Santana enters into an in-between sexual identification that complicates straight and bent binary oppositions.

Tumbling Tops and Bottoms

The camera-narrator first introduces the filmgoer to Santana as he enters Folsom State Prison just before his grand, multiple-knife-penetrations death—and just before his story unfolds as a series of flashbacks. Before story time begins, then, we have an imagistic impression of the protagonist—Edward James Olmos as a solemn, older, macho character; we glean this from the series of "focal character" shots (Santana's perspective) the camera-narrator uses to open the film:

- Camera-narrator pans down from gray wall with "Palm Hall" black-letter stenciled on it to medium shot of back of prisoner's head as prison door opens and the body walks forward and guard follows.
- Camera-narrator cuts to frontal shot; medium long shot with character's head and chest framed by prison-door barred window. The character

walks forward into the shot (with red-lettered "Exit" inscribed above doorway) and into a medium shot. The audience can now identify the character as actor Edward James Olmos.

- Camera-narrator employs noise of a door opening and closing and guard's voice within the auditory channel: "bend over, grab your ass, give me two good coughs."
- The film's thematic-identified music score fills the auditory channel and an accented woman's voice (we later identify as Julie's) can be heard at the level of the discourse: "you are like two people: One is like a kid, doesn't know how to dance, doesn't know how to make love. The one I cared about. The other one I hate, the one who knows, who has this rap down, who kills people."
- Camera-narrator fade shot into a slow pan from medium to close shot of protagonist (Santana) reading Tolstoy in cell: "Until now I would have thought it a sign of weakness to listen to what you said that night. I see that you were right. I am two people. One was born when I met you. The other one began in a downtown L.A. tattoo parlor."
- Camera-narrator fades to flashback sequence.

That the camera-narrator identifies Olmos as the protagonist isn't surprising. When Olmos appears in a film, he carries with him clusters of adjectives accumulated by his previous roles. So even without the mise-en-scène of prison interior, the actor Olmos's presence functions as the descriptive, signifying pure macho. I think here of Olmos's tough-guy image as Lt. Castillo in the TV series "Miami Vice," his portrayal of the pachuco in Valdez's *Zoot Suit*, as well as the Chicano patriarch in *Mi Familia* and *Selena*. His image as a macho Chicano has acquired a stable meaning—a kind of quintessence of the top/buggerer. Not surprisingly, then, audiences are apt to resist the recodification of Olmos not only as a top, but as bottom as well. So, while the rape scene disturbs, there is an equal amount of confusion and discomfort when the actor who signifies machismo suddenly turns over for us. This shift between top and bottom should be of little surprise. It's a myth that in same-sex relationship patterns sexual preference and role-playing behavior are etched in stone as a binary oppositional. The grand denouement arrives when Olmos-as-Santana is stabbed to death and becomes the receptor (unlike Julie, he is willing here) to the gang's penetrating blades.

While the death scene certainly brings into high relief the subtextual politics of prison same-sex identity (penetrations and humiliations that depose tops for bottoms), as the film unfolds the filmgoer witnesses not only Santana's transformation into a top, but how even an identity as a top isn't so hard cut. There's the story of Santana's socialization into a top/*activo*. As the older

Santana-as-narrator rhymes, "I thought I knew it all. . . . ended up in Juve Hall and the shit got even deeper" (literally). Santana flashbacks to the night in Juvenile Hall when a white boy, just after sodomizing Santana, threatens, "Say one word about this and they'll be shit on my knife, not on my dick." The knife conflates phallus with violence and humiliation (we see this throughout). In the postcoital moment, Santana jumps the white boy from behind, wrestles him to the bed and, as he takes the knife and plunges it into the white boy's body (a very sexualized scene where the boy's eyes roll up as his mouth opens and he gasps ecstatically and blood spurts sporadically), Santana becomes the top. However, for Santana there's more than just posturing as a tough guy for the other men. He's a top with a hard-core exterior but one whose small gestures and offhand comments betray a love (romantic even) for his "number one crime partner," J.D., as well as desire (physical mostly) for the hard-bodied, chisel-jawed Asian inmate El Japo.

Like many homosocial exclusive cliques (including the most homophobic of male gangs, sport teams, and Greek fraternities), ass slapping, crotch grabbing, and "fag" identifying labels betray a complicated fear of and *desire for* dialectic that informs the male-male sexual identity. Considering that Santana and J.D. belong to a *clica,* then, their open signs of affection betray a similar dialectic. J.D. often calls Santana "Chavala" (in Spanish this is slang for sweetheart, or fiancée, and is sometimes used to identify a *passivo*/maricon). However, there's more here than meets the eye. While we never see them cross those lines that define Hollywood heterosexual romance (no tongue kissing, no romantic scores, and no candle lighting), you can see them struggle with an intimacy that wants to push across such lines. Of course, J.D. and Santana (and Mundo) set in motion the male-male desire as teenagers, when they needle (tattoo) each other in the closet-like space of a mausoleum. As adults, J.D. and Santana show acceptable signs of affection, such as little pecks on the cheek—even longing glances. For example, the camera-narrator pauses to describe a long scene wherein a newly paroled J.D. looks deep into Santana's eyes just before he leaves Folsom State Prison; and, perhaps more obviously, once on the outside and living that much prison-desired heterosexual lifestyle (Mundo tells J.D., "Get laid *out there* for me"), they exchange longing glances across a courtyard while dancing with their respective love-interests. At one point, too, the camera-narrator describes a prison scene with J.D. fighting back tears for Santana just before his death—tears that betray a push across those lines that traditionally separate the macho from the maricon.

For all of Santana's macho presence, the camera-narrator rarely shows him alone in the penitentiary. Either J.D. or the Asian character *fill* the mise-en-scène when Santana is in the spaces of the prison yard and storage rooms.

However, Santana's interaction (gestures, dialogue, bodily exchanges) differs for each, depending on context. For example, it is unclear even who is top and who is bottom when the camera-narrator describes Santana with J.D.; they both manifest hard and soft qualities when together. Yet it is J.D. who, in the end, remains purely *activo* by effectively signing Santana's death warrant.

While it seems clear that Santana is the *activo* with the Asian character, the Asian himself in a different context (the rape of the Italian) can switch roles. Importantly, one context that determines the type of *activo/passivo* interaction between Santana and his male lovers, subtextually speaking of course, is race. For the *guero* J.D., who is phenotypically marked as "white," his final interaction with Santana is one that de facto aligns whiteness with the *activo* role: he signs Santana's death warrant. On the other hand, Santana's engagement with the Asian character, El Japo, plays into confining stereotypical images of the Asian as bottom/sissy in hierarchies of erotic images (especially seen in U.S. white-ga(y)zed porn). El Japo is hard-bodied and without a voice. He is physically strong, but without an agency unhitched from Santana's über-*activo* will to power. He hovers around Santana as an obedient bottom. Once El Japo comes to exist sans Santana (Santana is paroled), his will and action are tied to Santana but no longer as a mute, passive bottom. Codes of behavior turn upside down. As one of the rapists who forcefully sodomize the Italian (under Santana's direction admittedly), El Japo transforms from the submissive "Rice Queen" (a pejorative label used in gay porn) to a violent top, which not only shows how context shapes sexual behavior, but how sexuality shifts refract the traditional hierarchies of power that would normally confine the Asian on the outside. In the equations of Italian-as-white (a symbolic stand-in for globalized, capitalist, white-based power) vs. Asian-as-subaltern (symbolic of those without power and lacking fundamental claim to turf in the nation-state), El Japo is accepted by like-subalternized subjects, the Chicanos. As he ties down the Italian, gags him with a ripped-open bag of rice (scribbled with red and black Asian ideographs), then sodomitically rapes him, the Asian not only inhabits a different sexual identity (*activo*), but reverses age-old racial hierarchies of power. The Asian isn't so much a "yellow rice queen," after all.

This isn't to say that I condone violence if it subverts racial and sexual oppression. Rather, I delineate the characters' more fluid *activo*-to-*passivo* roles as determined by context—a context that resonates beyond the confines of the story world and spills into master narratives of race and sexuality. Santana, then, role-shifts according to context (racial, inside/outside, spatial) and so too do the male love-interests. Santana role-plays the *activo* with the Asian (the camera-narrator describes the Asian as somewhat adoring) and plays a softer role (una "chavala") with J.D.; we even get a glimmer of jealousy in Santana's eye when he sees J.D. dancing with a woman. Nor do J.D. and the Asian character conform to an either *activo* or *passivo* role type; they, too, shift according to context.

A Repository of Tradition between the Cracks

Of course, all of the characters' movement between the macho and sissy role belies the friction that generates character arcs and epiphanies but does not lead to the traditional cinematic denouement: the white heterosexual coupling and promise of biological reproduction. What Santana's interactions with his love-interests leaves the audience with is his story—a story generated out of the rape of his mother, punctuated by his being raped, then becoming a rapist but ultimately being sustained by his male-male interactions. Certainly there is much in the film that directs our reading of Santana's nonbiological reproduction as a deficiency. After all, in one of the film's penultimate sequences, he concludes his autobiographic letter to Julie, "You Julie . . . were the door to another life, where my seed might have been reaffirmed." Stereotypes of women as repository aside, that his melancholia gravitates around his inability to have his "seed" affirmed strongly lends to a reading that positions male-male sexual interaction as *lack*. This is further emphasized when, addressing his male-male environs as a void, he continues to write, "I've brought back to this *hole* some life which I'm trying to use." However, while it is certainly his encounter with Julie that functions as the impetus to the writing of his autobiography, it is nonetheless an autobiography that speaks to homosocial (and homosexual) socialization. Namely, his story is the surrogate offspring of his male-male interactions. His story, with its mnemonic devices and circular patterns, is the concrete product of male-male intercourse (that which sustains and even generates the story) that will survive Santana. So, while women play an important role in Santana's formation, it is ultimately his story that acts as his lineage (just consider the screen time given to the men and also how the kernel events turn around the male characters).

Of course, while Santana's nonbiologically procreative presence threatens the heterosexual codes and leads to his annihilation, his nonbiologic scion survives him; the penning of the letter to Julie and the film itself (his voice-over narration) function in the form of recorded testament as a surrogate lineage. Like his namesake, Saint Anna, Santana is biologically barren. Unlike Saint Anna, whose narratives worked as convincing supplications to the Heavenly Father and who soon found herself impregnated with the Virgin

Mary, Santana's narrative leads to a biological (heterosexual) reversal of his fortune. While his story isn't of the biological reproductive kind, it does exist as an alternative savior-narrative intended to save future generations of Chicanos/as from self-destruction.

Not only does Santana represent an alternative, nonbiologically produced savior narrative that dialogues with and subverts Judeo-Christian religious paradigms, but his coming into his role as a storyteller who leaves behind the concrete artifact of his written story/testimony for future generations positions Santana within a long line of asexual, bisexual, homosexual spiritual figures traditionally responsible for holding together communities before and during the Conquest. (The Zuni Indian bisexual "berdaches" were similarly revered as the repository of tribal tradition.) For example, in the late-15th century Fray Ramón Pané wrote in his proto-ethnographic study of the Arawak Indians that "hay algunos hombres que *practican entre ellos,* y se les dice behiques (there are some men who practice among themselves and are called *behiques)*" (quoted in Piedra, "Nationalizing Sissies," 392; emphasis mine). While the Euro-Spanish, Catholic ideologue certainly had good reason for constructing the indigenous medicine man as a sexual Other ("hombres que practican entre ellos")—a fool-proof conversion/genocide justification narrative—José Piedra recovers similar evidence from native records that suggest the *behiques* were not only revered as keepers of Arawak tradition, medicine men, and tellers of stories, but also as queer. Piedra's research reveals the close link between the *behiques* and the age-old myth of the Guaganaona, popularly known in the Afro-Hispanic Caribbean as "The-One-Without-Male-Ancestry." According to historical and present Hispano-Caribbean language and lore, the mythic Guaganaona, not so unlike the *behiques,* is "transgendered."

Santana's inhabitation of that sexualized in-between storytelling zone lends itself to a transposing of the Guaganaona myth-template. José Piedra briefly classifies the sexualized symbolic spaces the Guaganaona inhabits: "First, this entity is the Being of the Yucca, a 'female' root fetishized as the penis—and more specifically, a penis engaged in a male self-satisfying, masturbatory action. Second s/he is the Sea, a female power that once held the transatlantic male voyagers in the palm of her hand. Third, s/he is 'The-One-Without-Male-Ancestry,' an originating force with no male models or need for phallic instruction or introduction—a less-than-traditional phallic 'resolution'" ("Nationalizing Sissies," 393). Santana functions symbolically as female and male: he's a quintessential Chicano macho who brings home the money and physically protects *la familia*—and he is the community storyteller (a position in Latino culture traditionally inhabited by women and/or asexualized, old, and impotent *curanderos*). On the one hand, while Santana's story functions to save his community (as his voice-over spills out into the discourse for the audience to hear), on the other, materially it is a story penned as a letter in the confines of his prison cell; his story contains that inherent quality of the epistolary form: the masturbatory, s/he auto-erotic. He's the Being of the Yucca. Second, Santana comes into a more fluid sense of sexual identity, not so coincidentally, just after his first splash in the Pacific Ocean. (The camera-narrator weighs this scene as a kind of New World baptism, but with a precolonial spiritual tinge.) It is after his tryst with heterosexual love-interest Julie at the beach that, while standing knee-deep in the ocean, the "she"-coded storytelling act passes symbolically from Julie to Santana; after this sequence, Santana becomes his own storyteller.

As Santana crisscrosses gendered roles in the act of penning his biography, he disrupts the hierarchical economy of (neo)colonial desire. In a symbolic sense he becomes Piedra's identified "s/he . . . Sea" that can powerfully turn upside down, even destroy, those transatlantic male Euro-Spanish voyagers. This is to say that Santana fulfills the criteria by becoming a modern-day avatar of the Guaganaona/*behique*. He comes to inhabit a sexual and gender (even a trans-Chicano/Latino/Carib) identity that is similar to "The-One-Without-Male-Ancestry" and that ultimately exists as an alternative "originating force" to the traditional vagina/penis binary system.

Santana's coming into a sense of himself as a storyteller stretches his identity not only across different sexual- and gender-coded roles, but also across cultures. His coming into a symbolic transgendering subjectivity resonates with the complex Aztec deity—Xochiquetzal. According to the legend, after being raped by the macho war god, Tezcatlipoca, the hetero-procreating goddess Xochiquetzal re-marked her body as sexually ambiguous to fend off the hands of the heterosexual macho gods. In his essay "Legends, Syncretism, and Continuing Echoes of Homosexuality," Clark L. Taylor concludes: "Xochiquetzal was male and female at the same time, and in her male aspect (called Xochipilli), s/he was worshipped as the deity of male homosexuality and male prostitution" (82). Santana's coming into this storytelling self coincides with his coming into a sexually ambiguous space, paying tribute to Xochiquetzal's male and female "aspects."

There's more to Santana's entering into that storyteller-self place that symbolically links him with the bi- and same-sexual *mexica* mythology. Xochiquetzal is the deity most associated with flowers; the Toltec empire itself was celebrated in its day as the Fourth World, also called the world of the flowers of Xochiquetzal. With Xochiquetzal symbolizing same-sex love, flowers have come to be associated with homosexuality (referred to as *xochihuan*, literally "flower owner" and the verb *te-xochuia* [to use flowers on someone]). Not so coincidentally, perhaps, *American Me* over-determines the flower. The flower carries a double hetero/homo valence, first, as a straightforward representation (ode, even) to heterosexual romance. For example, there is an abundance of flowers at the wedding of the Little Puppet character (played by Daniel Villareal). The flower is also associated, ironically, with Santana's inception, where it signifies the macho, heterosexual violence toward Chicanas by whites as well as Chicanos. The sequence unfolds as follows: Close up of father Pedro applying a gauze strip to his arm where a freshly black-inked "Por Vida" is tattooed across a tattooed blood-red rose. (In Aztec iconography, black and red are colors associated with the macho deity Tezcatlipoca.) The camera-narrator shifts to a medium long-shot of the sailors' breaking into the tattoo parlor and subsequently gang-raping Esperanza. Then the camera-narrator pans left and away from rape scene to pause momentarily at various, colorfully drawn flowers and butterflies (*placa* examples) on the walls and inside glass cases. (Of course, the butterfly-filled glass cases also gesture toward the colonial project to classify (control and contain) not just the New World flora and fauna, but also the marvelously wondrous ethnic-object specimens.) However, as the story unwinds, the flower is associated less with either an idyllic heterosexual love and/or violent macho desire. Certainly the rape of Esperanza is as violent as it comes. However, there's the suggestion, with the iconographic copresence of the butterfly and flower, that in violence something new is born. Indeed, the flower motif begins to resignify a more positively coded male-male intimacy. Often the moments of intense, sensual intimacy between the inmates take place while they needle each other with flowered tattoos. Moreover, in Santana's death scene, after Mundo asks Santana, "are you *coming out* ese?" and Mundo tells him, "you gotta lotta heart, carnal, maybe too much," there is a cut to a slow-motion long shot that follows Santana's fall from the tier down to his death. During this sequence Santana's body forms into a flower of sorts: flailing arms and legs together with a patterned blood stain on his chest suggest the filament/stigma/style and surrounding calyxes and loose-hanging sepals of the flower. In Santana's death there is not only the sense of something reborn but, if we're to read against the legend of Xochiquetzal as the film's codes suggest, then he comes to inhabit the subjectivity of *xochihuan*—or, the "flower owner," a figure that symbolizes and celebrates sexual in-betweenness.

(Neo)Colonial Backdoors

Santana's coming into a complicated in-between sexual identity as he tells his story is the subtext to *American Me*. Interestingly, although the film critic Rita Kempley negatively reviewed the film for the *Washington Post,* she identified it as a "cruddy, *K-Y-jelly-coated* look into the prison house" where inmates are represented as "ethnically *cannibalistic.*" Kempley unwittingly reproduces those conquistador narratives that perversely genitalize the New World subject. Of course, her comment speaks to those denotative codes that allow, for example, the audience to transpose the Zoot Suit riots of 1943 onto the brutal conquest of the Americas. We know now that for the Euro-Spaniards to justify their conquest and genocide of Amerindian peoples, they genitalized and made "perverse" the ethnic subject; this act also allowed the Euro-Spaniards to set up a convenient libidinal system that would legitimate their frictive synthesis, sans biological miscegenation, of the sexualized Other. And, this violent penetration and violent synthesis of the hypergenitalized Other (Amazonas, pederasts, queer men and women) didn't always take place along a heterosexual axis of desire. As José Piedra maintains, "many Spaniards secretly adopted sodomy to provide human contact and sexual release while skirting the dangers of miscegenation. . . . In the end, sodomy and homosexuality become transatlantic forms of birth control as well as metonymic expressions of male-centered elitism and imperialism on both sides of the Atlantic, as well as a unifying macho-saving feature of transatlantic colonialism" ("Nationalizing Sissies," 397–398).

Importantly, as Piedra further identifies, the Conquest included the Euro-Spaniard's not only sodomizing the Other, but also the macho, elite indigenous male's sodomitical desire. The camera-narrator doesn't exactly equate Pedro's macho behavior (the male tattoo artist penetrates and stains Pedro's arm) with that of the belligerent white sailors, but both coexist in the same sequence, and both represent different degrees of macho behavior that hides a same-sex desire. (With whom do the sailors really share their fluids?) Recall, too, that Bernal Diaz's gifting of his much favored boy-page, Orteguilla, to Moctezuma was more than just a token of his friendship. It was a *warped* expression of his desire to exchange fluids with the elite male other. There's much subtextual evidence to suggest that Moctezuma and Cortez shared fluids across Orteguilla's body. According to Diaz's journals, Orteguilla was referred to as a female (often referred to as *la malinche,* the name used to identify Cortez's female mistress, Doña Marina) and a *pasivo.* Orteguilla is the hole that is filled (textually and physically) by both macho elites as they engage in a same-sex desire perverted by their heterosexual/*conquistador* ideological baggage. This is to say, the film not only sets up an easy time/space transposition of the 1943 rape and consequent marking off of Santana as a bastard (the product of the U.S. military's violent penetration of the barrio-as-New-World-hole in need of filling) with the conquistador encounter, but also delineates the heterosexual macho's (white and brown) violently twisting up of a deep desire for the holes.

Utopic Slits and Ends

The film continues to make explicit the conflation of vagina with anus in a heterosexist, neocolonial twisting up of desire, especially when it comes to Santana's buying into an economy of power built on the in-flow and out-flow of drugs and capital from within prison. Not so unlike the white, sailor-boy rapists, Santana internalizes the he-who-controls-the-hole-has-the-power model. Women's holes are used in this economy as a way to ensure citizen-like rights to Chicanos; the women are used by the men to make prison environs homelike. For example, the camera-narrator's auditory channel plays the song "Slipping Into Darkness" by the 1970s band *War* while the visuals describe the following: an above, tilt-angled medium-long shot of an unnamed white female character (previously seen with J.D. in the prison visiting room) lifting up her dress, sitting on a toilet, then removing a balloon-like object from her vagina that she then flushes down the toilet. Cut to a closeup of a black sewer pipe and a rapid pan, left, as flush sound continues. Cut to a medium shot of the pipe as the camera follows it vertically downward. The shot pauses with a shot of a half-naked inmate fishing out shit and the balloon-object with his hand. The scene ends with a medium shot of the inmate (now identifiable as the character Puppet) opening the balloon, tasting white powder, sealing it, then squeezing K-Y jelly onto it and visibly inserting it into his anus.

The flow of cocaine from vagina to anus to mouth/nose promises the inmates inside a momentary, albeit imaginative, escape to the outside. Santana peddles in drugs that promise to make the inmate feel whole in a hole full of men that is marked off as lack. By controlling the flow, Santana participates in the reproduction of a desiring system that marks off the prison as the place inhabited by the fragmented, lacking subject. He mistakenly believes that his acting as valve controller to the opening and closing of the flow of desire in and out of various bodily pipes and holes will allow him to emancipate himself and *compañeros.* On one occasion he informs Julie, "before if somebody wanted something from you like your manhood and they were stronger than you, they just took it. We changed all that."

At the very least, the theoretical postcolonial queering of *American Me* might reveal just why someone would harbor such anger toward the gendered, racialized, sexualized Other. By taking into account the narrative's surface structures (the men's internalized colonialism that leads to violence against Chicanas), as well as the deeper, precolonial and colonial layers (Santana's coming into an ambiguous sexuality that threatens the order of things), we can read *American Me* as a richly imagined narrative that opens audience eyes to the racism, homophobia, and heterosexism that pervades all aspects of society.

Re-visioning Chicano/a Bodies and Texts

In this concluding chapter, I want to return to several issues raised (directly and indirectly) throughout *Brown on Brown*. As I've already discussed at some length in Chapter 1, there are some critical entanglements that inform much of U.S. (borderland and postcolonial queer) cultural and literary studies today. There is the conflation of the fiction of narrative with the facts of our everyday existence. There is the fusion of cultural studies scholarship with political activism. There is the conflation of en masse resistance to real sites of power with individual acts of resistance based on identity politics. However, as I've begun to untangle and clarify, while narrative fiction, verbal and visual, can open one's eyes to social and political injustice, it is not the same thing as the massive organizing and protesting of real people that historically has transformed the social and political arena. Historical, social, and political facts can inflect borderland queer literature and film, but the fiction of such narratives (its organization according to aesthetic convention) should not be made subordinate to such facts. This is not to say that we cannot study cultural phenomena such as borderland literature by and about the gay/lesbian Chicano/a experience to better understand our world. However, to better understand queer Chicano/a literature—or any cultural phenomena—does not alter the real conditions of our everyday life, nor does it work to magically transform real sites of power. To believe any differently is to divert our work as scholars whose research might lead to verifiable—or falsifiable—conclusions and therefore give us a deeper understanding of the cultural products of humanity in all their complexity and variety.

Let me conclude with several general points regarding literary and film interpretation: what it can and cannot achieve. First, in regard to its cultural studies component, it should be less wishful and more realistic. To be that, it would have to stop pretending that a small cadre of academics decoding cultural phenomena have the power to change the world in the same way as the working population can when it organizes itself independently and moves towards the achievement of its self-designed goals. If borderland queer (and straight) literary and film (cultural) studies are to have any value today, we must turn to rationalist and empirical methods of gathering and analyzing data and formulating hypotheses that might help us better understand the reality we live in and the actions that really transform it. For borderland queer (and straight) critical studies to move forward, we need to be sensitive to how literature and film are organized according to verifiable elements that make up their aesthetics: those verifiable elements like style, point of view, tempo, tense, and so on that writers employ to engage readers in specific ways.

The call to question the role of the literary scholar and the function of literary interpretation (queer or straight, Chicano or Anglo) in and outside of the classroom has resurfaced of late. The skepticism over what theory can actually do (especially poststructuralism's "aporia," "slippage," and *"différance"*) to intervene and resist is warranted. At the conference on theory held at the University of Chicago on April 11, 2003, *New York Times* journalist Emily Eakin opened her report by observing that "These are uncertain times for literary scholars. The era of big theory is over. The grand paradigms that swept through humanities departments in the 20th century—psychoanalysis, structuralism, Marxism, deconstruction, post-colonialism—have lost favor or been abandoned. Money is tight. And the leftist politics with which literary theorists have traditionally been associated have taken a beating" (9). That the question of theory's role in and outside humanities departments today didn't get much airtime suggests that theorizing the slippage of signifier and signified has done little to make good on its promise: to resist, intervene, and transform a world increasingly marked by barbaric acts.

Others are skeptical of theory that confuses those facts that make up everyday reality and the words and structures that make up literature. Such scholars as Robert Alter, John Searle, and John Ellis question the poststructuralist doxa: that *verba* magically suffices to radically change human *res*. And, already a decade ago, Frederick Crews expressed skepticism about the ability of the "discourse radicals" (his term) to resist, intervene, and transform real centers of power. Moreover, Crews identifies poststructuralism's allergic reaction to positivism as well as its aversion to clear thinking and writing, declaring it of little service to those oppressed groups with which it claims an affiliation. And there have been other voices of dissent more squarely situated within the scholarly Left. I think here of the sharp bites and barks Terry Eagleton began making in his essays that began appearing regularly in the late 1990s (collected and published by Verso as *Figures of Dissent*). In these essays he holds little back, identifying poststructuralist theory as an "offshoot of science fiction" (*Figures of Dissent*, 1) and calls its so-called "dialectical thinking"

(160) an anything-goes-eclecticism that, in the name of social transformation, only ever served up a "restrained, reformist sort of politics" (165).

Eagleton and others identified the dangers of the apriorism that permeates poststructuralist theory especially when tied to a political agenda. When such scholars expressed criticism, however, they were shrugged off as either too old-school Left, reactionary, and/or apolitical. Today, other scholars have approached poststructuralist theory with the idea of sifting the fine from the coarse in order to salvage what might be useful: Paula Moya's Chicano/a–based redeployment of Satya P. Mohanty's "postpositivist realism," Gayatri Spivak's postcolonial-based "strategic essentialism," and John McGowan's U.S.-cultural-studies–based "pragmatic pluralism." Each in her or his own way explores problems that poststructuralist theory raised but did not answer. Several such questions include: What is the role of intellectual work in and outside the classroom? Can work in the classroom become a model of social democracy? What is the function of literary interpretation? Can it transform minds and therefore direct political action?

To answer these necessary and important questions, scholars like Moya, Spivak, and McGowan attempt to yoke a humanist belief in universals (to know those facts that make our world unjust and that are necessary for us to fight for true democracy) together with a belief that reality is indeterminate and socially constructed. They consider the intellectual a kind of "cultural worker" who has the power to transform the minds of students through literary analysis and, therefore, ultimately to transform the psyche of the body politic. Yet, their cultural workers must also acknowledge the material reality of how each subaltern community is oppressed by an identifiable oppressing power (colonial, capitalist, or otherwise). For example, Paula Moya's Chicano/a redeployment of postpositivist realism, which first appeared in the introduction to her coedited volume *Reclaiming Identity: Realist Theory and the Predicament of Postmodernism*, aims to couple a poststructuralist (reality as discursive construct) and an essentialist (feminist/Nativist) mode of formulating identity and experience. Moya's postpositivist realism says there *can* be an essential (biological and racially constituted) Chicana subject; that is, an individual who experiences the world according to her perception of herself and her interaction with a world where opportunities and resources are distributed according to her being identified as a type: brown and woman. At the same time, while Moya believes that identity determines how we experience the world in specific ways (hence her critical stance toward poststructuralist theory that proposes the indeterminacy of identity), she is also careful to declare that as a postpositivist realist, she is not a "naive empiricist" (2). So while she posits a localized experience of the social and political, she believes that knowledge of reality is not objective; like the poststructuralist theorists, she, too, believes that all observation and knowledge—and therefore reality—is mediated. So, while Moya puts forward arguments in favor of objective knowledge, she ultimately falls back on the relativist and constructivist notion that "knowledge is not disembodied, or somewhere 'out there' to be had, but rather that it comes into being in and through embodied selves. In other words, humans generate knowledge, and our ability to do so is causally dependent on both our cognitive capacities and our historical and social locations" (18), the key words here being "causally dependent."

Moya's tautological coupling of an empiricist and a constructivist position is not unique. Spivak's "strategic essentialism" and more recently McGowan's "pragmatic pluralism" attempt to do the same. They, too, experience discomfort with poststructuralist theorists who consider the subject and world to be only discursive constructs and so claim that decoding texts and symbols will radically alter the world; decoding hegemonic discursivities will not transform a society, but rather it provides a soft cushion for political complacency. In their different approaches, Moya, Spivak, and McGowan believe that to level the socioeconomic playing field by making education and freedom of expression an equal right for all would require the locating of real sites of power to make visible real targets for social transformation. So, whether identified as "postpositivist realists," "strategic essentialists," or "pragmatic pluralists," they are obliged to recognize patterns and structures even when they posit their various theories of cultural resistance. Yet, identifying patterns and structures would be equivalent to believing in a reality that is objectively out there. Hence, the surfacing yet again of the tautological bind.

So, in spite of their skepticism, each believes that if humans work in and through language, then decoding how we work and think within language will lead to new ways of interpreting and understanding the world and will augment the type of social transformation that takes place by real people. Yes, they acknowledge that real subaltern subjects are violently oppressed. However, because social injustices continue to exist, they believe one way or another that strategic cultural work *is* necessary for social transformation to occur. That is, they still consider *verba* as being able to alter *res*.

Democracy or Cultural Relativism?

Moya's "postpositivist realism," Spivak's "strategic essentialism," and McGowan's "pragmatic pluralism" are relativism dressed up anew. Namely, each presents another way of stating that what we know of the world and our selves is contingent on theories that are themselves contingent on other theories. The equation "reality is text" has been present in one guise or another in the different versions of poststructuralist theory. As Steve Woolgar (a constructivist-relativist sociologist of science) has put it, poststructuralism "is consistent with the position of the idealist wing of ethnomethodology that there is no reality independent of the words (texts, signs, documents, and so on) used to apprehend it. In other words, reality is constituted in and through discourse" ("On the Alleged Distinction between Discourse and Praxis," 317). Now, of course, the denial of an extratextual reality is not only counterintuitive (nobody in everyday life confuses words with their referents, nobody believes that the *word* "salt" will make his meat taste better), it is oxymoronic (literally, pointedly foolish). If the world is a text, or if as Jacques Derrida said, *"rien hors le texte"* (there is no outside-the-text), all but a few sciences must be superfluous: grammar or linguistics would suffice for us to know or to investigate how all matter — from atoms and subatomic particles to human brains and societies — functions.

This becomes especially apparent when McGowan identifies "the principle of democratic egalitarianism" (*Democracy's Children*, 264) as culturally and historically constituted and not a transcendent truth. Here, for example, he states that a "humanist society can make decisions in the absence of truth" (264). His formulation is tautological. It suggests that we can transform an empirically verifiable reality with tools and information that aren't verifiable and whose meaning is relational and contingent. In *The Politics of Interpretation,* Patrick Colm Hogan clarifies, "If I see something as an orange, this has nothing to do with essences, but means only that I construe certain experiences in relation to a schematic hierarchy and in the context of present interests and practices" (61). What Hogan exemplifies is that there is no question of the presence or absence of the orange (in the sense of *essential* presence or absence) but only one of interest, in this case, in that the orange is perceived as a result of verifiable biological and cognitive mechanisms. Our perception of things is, as Hogan nicely clarifies, "partially accurate and partially inaccurate understandings of the world. They are based upon our previous understandings, including those codified in our linguistic competence, but they are not confined to these. And their accuracy is a matter of the way relevant intentionally discriminated things happen to be, and not the way supposedly essentially discriminated things are (or are necessarily)" (61). Namely, the orange, like all things that make up reality, provides that object that can generate common grounds of interest and information based on empirically verifiable evidence.

To put it more plainly, for Moya, Spivak, and McGowan to even be able to state that truth/fact is socially constituted relies on the rules of language that are based on shared understanding of grammar, syntax, and semantics. If there was an absence of truth and empirically verifiable reality, real social change could never happen; it would mean that because I was born in Mexico and raised Chicano my brain works differently than the brains of Anglos born and raised in the United States, and therefore my reason—thought, language, algorithmic process—operates differently than that of others in the United States. In other words, if we were all social constructs, then no communication could take place between intellectual and worker and thus no collectivities formed for political activism. In such a relationally contingent world, no action would be possible to realize a shared goal of making a truly democratic nation-state. To return to the point made above about the orange, it is good enough that we perceive and verify things and their effects in the world. Claiming that knowledge is relative and that objects and subjects are socially constituted will only muddy our path toward realizing the true ideals of democracy.

The upshot: As long as we try to hold together contradictory positions (empirical and social constructivist), we will always find ourselves straddling an unbridgeable gap. Rather, we must untangle such tautological knots in order to begin to more satisfyingly answer questions posed about the role of the critic and theory generally. We know from our experiences that reading and interpreting literature and film can open eyes to different ways of existing in the world; we know that we can gain something in the process of reading and interpreting a novel—our experience of an Other—even when we are fully aware of its fictionality. However, we must ask, is it really possible for our work as Chicano/a scholars and teachers of queer Chicano/a literature to influence and single-handedly transform the values and attitudes of the many millions of people required for real social transformation? Can we tell our students that the work done in the classroom in analyzing, say, Ana Castillo's *So Far from God* or Sheila Ortiz Taylor's *Coachella* is a form of political activism? And, can we really liken the place of the classroom to a democratic space where legislation and policy take place?

Method or Madness

I press further by asking, What is our function as teachers of literature? Should we shun method, as some have suggested in the formulation of a "pragmatic pluralism"? Method is in the air we breathe. Every part of our everyday survival as *Homo sapiens sapiens* requires the teaching, learning, and practicing of method. We go to school where methods are employed to teach reading, writing, and algorithmic skills: We need to learn rules in and out of the classroom—words in a certain order and hierarchy within this order—to communicate; carpenters learn which tools to use and in which particular order to build houses for shelter; architects and engineers follow methods to design such structures; pilots learn which instruments to use, and in what order, to fly us safely through skies. Even the most randomly conceived of cultural forms require method. Harry Gamboa and the other avant-garde Chicano artists that made up the collective Asco ("nausea") defied convention a la *rasquache* in *fotonovelas*, mail art, and "No Movie" films to disturb and disrupt both a Chicano nationalist and an Anglo-American mainstream cultural image repertoire. Gamboa and his fellow artists pushed the envelope on representation but were still constrained by the media they chose to use. In painting, for example, this meant choosing from the limited number of colors that the eye can perceive (determined by cognitive and biological constraints) and following an order by which they are applied. And the list could go on ad infinitum. This is to say that creation that involves any kind of conception or innovation has to follow a method. If we take pause to think about this, we realize that it is precisely the learning of method with its respectively defined parameters that advances our knowledge about the things and activities that fill our world. (To learn to build a bridge does not require the learning of the method for flying an airplane, for example.) Indeed, all the minutiae of our everyday existence entail the teaching, learning, and practicing of method.

Certainly, interdisciplinary work is important for the study of queer Chicano/a literature and film. I'm all for learning what we can from other disciplines—recent advances in cognitive science, linguistics, and evolutionary biology certainly shed new light on our understanding of how literature works—and the knowledge in each discipline is produced precisely because of the use of method. Each field of inquiry is productive and even predictive precisely because it limits the number of directions it pursues. For example, the physicist follows a certain method when formulating a hypothesis, knowing that for the hypothesis to lead to any tangible results, it must have limits. Certainly, these limits are not fixed for all eternity. However, whether in the field of science or in the study of literature and film, we need to impose limits to *what* we intend to investigate or argue and we need method to explore this *what*. In literature and film there is no limit to what can be imagined by a writer and/or director, and thus we could discuss and imagine an infinite number of elements that make up fiction.

Queer Chicano/a literature and film—like all phenomena that make up our culture—are the products of complex human beings and therefore are as limitless as we are. This doesn't mean, however, that when writing, interpreting, and/or teaching queer Chicano/a literature and film that we should follow no method with no limits. Just as we do need to employ method, we also need to reduce the number of elements and questions to formulate a hypothesis that might potentially lead to an explanation of the text at hand. If done well, bounded inquiry based on rational method can have great predictive power. More precisely, it is the reduction of the number of concepts explored in, say, narratology that can explain an unlimited number of literary and cinematic phenomena: concept of voice, point of view, and the like. Of course, using the tools of narratology is not the only method for analyzing an *American Me* or a *La Mollie*, but it does offer great explanatory power.

Needless to say, we shouldn't impose limits that stifle scholarly and creative exploration. Rather, we impose limits in order to build on and revise what we know of queer Chicano/a literature—and the world generally. If there is no method and no limit, then anything goes and whatever we say or argue has no particular importance. For example, sociolinguistics (or "pragmatic linguistics") eventually ran into a dead end because its field of inquiry had no boundaries. Though systematized in the 18th century in the work of Fontanelle, the taxonomy itself as a way to understand language had no limits. Language is a very complex phenomenon associated with millions of human activities and behaviors that are difficult to systematize. Because the terrain was too large, the predictive capacity of sociolinguistics turned out to be worthless. (Chomsky realized that for linguistics to have any predictive power, it must follow the scientific principle of reduction and abstraction. Hence, his formulation of a "universal grammar" in his reducing the number of linguistic features that appear in all languages.) If everything goes in the large field of culture (all that is the product of man's activity), then culture is everything, and thus as a field of study too large a domain of inquiry to be productive. Just as we must have method (argue, test, and refute) to survive, we must also set limits to our field of inquiry or else we simply produce *flatus voci*.

As scholars of Chicano/a literature (straight and queer), we can use method to understand better what the critics *make*. What we make are hypotheses based on theories, analysis, and arguments that can be furthered by reaching out to other fields that use the same empirical methods to arrive at their own conclusions. As teachers of Chicano/a literature, we need to provide students with the methods for sorting the seed from pulp. Teaching students that eclecticism is better than rigorous method, as some scholars propose, or that to reduce is to destructively essentialize, or that subjects and the world are discursively constructed, moves us away from the means by which we can build, verify, refute, and revise our understanding of how Chicano/a literature—and film—works.

Indeed, method (with its disciplinary limits and tools to test hypotheses) allows us to formulate within specified boundaries and limits a number of elements that make up a teachable system that can be passed on as a tool for a next generation of scholars to learn, revise, and build upon anew. Without limits to literary exploration, we can conjecture limitlessly because all is contingent and arbitrary. As Chicano/a literary scholars we should be affirming the place of method in opening up the possibility for exploratory advancement.

Democracy in the Classroom?

Without a clear understanding of how knowledge is arrived at, any type of statement can be made in and outside the classroom: there is no *hors texte*, or there is only the color red, or, in the case of McGowan, the classroom is a democratic space where we can enact a "pragmatic pluralism." McGowan elaborates that it is within the space of the classroom that "negotiations, compromises, arguments, and procedural steps [that will lead to] collective decisions" can take place (*Democracy's Children*, 267). Using the pragmatic pluralist method in the classroom will create an egalitarian and collective space where "differences and interdependencies" (6) are valued, and that will ultimately, according to McGowan, help pave the way for the making of a democratic nation-state. In response, I ask, Can teaching Chicano/a literature and film (queer and straight) in the classroom foster democratic ideals of equality, freedom of speech, and tolerance for all taste and opinion? Is the classroom a sacred space that somehow exists outside the totalitarian-like institution of the university? If we diffuse authority in the classroom do we resist a colonial and/or capitalist racist, homophobic, and heterosexist hegemony? I ask these questions because there are many scholars who believe that this is all possible within the classroom. We need to pause, reflect, and clarify what we can and cannot do in the classroom.

If authority is everywhere, then it is nowhere. There must be an identifiable center of authority in the classroom that provides useful limits and rules as required by its respective disciplinary methodological contours in order for students to learn and become independent thinkers. The teacher has trained for a certain amount of time (sometimes years and years) and has acquired a knowledge of things that the students cannot and do not have simply because they have not been able to devote as much time and energy to study as the teacher has done. This means that the teacher has completed a series of tasks and has to be qualified to introduce concepts and categories and tools to deal with the verifiable elements that constitute his or her particular discipline. And, to suggest that power in the classroom is everywhere follows a belief that power is everywhere. This is necessary, of course, if one believes that we can enact resistance and political intervention through language and cultural phenomena. However, not only does it participate in a formulation that dislocates power and permanently erases it from real sites (the state apparatus of the real ruling class and the owners of the means of production that assert "real" power through executive, legislative, and judicial institutions) but it dangerously allows academics to sit comfortably in a small corner of the world and think that their work decoding signs somehow magically destabilizes and transforms master narratives of oppression. Rather it is the teaching of method that will provide the clear-sighted thinking necessary for students to see things as they are in and outside the classroom—an outside where real political activism takes place.

It is our job as teachers not to regard the classroom and/or the interpretation of literature as the ersatz means of "empowerment" and "liberation" in lieu of the actual mobilization of an autonomously organized youth and labor force. Perhaps the best way to further the goal of realizing a true democracy is not to confuse the classroom with the democratic politics shaped through the work of millions of people. Perhaps the best way for us to further democratic goals is to encourage the learning of methods that can verify facts to build our understanding not just of Chicano/a literature and film but of the world we inhabit. Perhaps our role is to encourage students to turn to other fields of inquiry, not to become specialists in those fields but to see how research might help us better understand how we function universally.

What Can Borderland Literature Do?

This still leaves us the question, how do texts shape our values, attitudes, and actions and those of our students? When we pick up, say, John Rechy's *This Day's Death* and have stepped into the shoes of his biracial, queer protagonist's experiences of L.A.'s demimondes, has anything more than our imagination been transformed? When we step back into our reality, has the experience of this fictional world transformed us or even transformed our reality? Common sense already suggests that reality will not have been transformed. But, if such a queer borderland narrative fiction has the power to open our eyes to other ways of being, doesn't it then have the power to change the way we think and therefore act in the world? As such, doesn't it indirectly have the power to transform reality?

Certainly, queer borderland literature can be a resource for us to better understand the world. And like any field of knowledge that sheds light on human activity and the world we inhabit (physics, for example, helps us understand how gravity works), it has the potential to change our attitudes toward this world. However, to transform our reality requires human action—and this in the hundreds of millions. Likewise, when we study or teach literature, this doesn't change the development or nondevelopment of, say, capitalism. As history proves, regardless of whether or not we study and teach literature, capitalism developed; the merchants that transformed society into capitalist marketplace didn't do so by knowing literature any better.

So why do we teach literature if it is not, as McGowan proposes, to further our aims of creating a true democracy in the classroom? We study literature to discover, for example, how an author like Ana Castillo, Sheila Ortiz Taylor, John Rechy, Richard Rodriguez, and/or Arturo Islas uses specific narrative tools to engage the readers' imagination. We study literature to know better how those black marks on the page can create images and sounds in the mind of the reader. We study how literature's formal features and organization become meaningful in a serious, playful, ironic, or tense manner. We study literature to understand better how the reader suspends disbelief. We study literature to understand better why we feel the pleasure and pain of a character while simultaneously aware of its ontological status as fiction. We study literature to explore how a novel like *The Miraculous Day of Amalia Gómez* uses point of view and temporal disjunction to engage in new and novel ways how we remember. We study literature to understand better how the universal human capacity of storytelling might shed light on our capacity to tell the difference between deception and truth, hostility and love, in our everyday social encounters. We study the verifiable elements (point of view, style, temporality, genre, mood) of literature to understand better how writers use such tools to engage their readers. And, while it is important for us to know the research in other fields (cognitive psychology, linguistics, and history, to name a few), it is with the aim of better understanding how literature works. For example, we can posit the not completely unfounded hypothesis that poetry manifested itself before the novel because, as deduced by cognitive research on brain development, rhythm has a mnemonic function. Such research from psychology labs and/or neuroscience gives us useful information in that it allows us to better understand our different engagement with prose and poetry. And, if we can understand better how language functions by turning to recent research in linguistics—proving that there is no direct link between language and thought—then we can understand how art might stimulate those thought processes that take place prelinguistically. This might lead to a further understanding of how nonlinguistic images form in our mind after we read words on a page.

To reiterate several points made at the beginning of *Brown on Brown*, history and politics do inflect queer borderland literature and film. And as such the novels, short stories, and film that I study here all reflect both critically and artistically on hegemonic patriarchal, heterosexist features of capitalist society. Indeed, their use function is as an aesthetic object that spins out of their massive capacity to create engaging possible worlds—and not in their putative function as political doctrine. Again, to reiterate a point made earlier in the book, I don't mean aesthetics in the old-school sense of a given text being inherently more beautiful than another, but rather in the sense of how an author or director makes memorable an everyday experience, event, or story by reframing and organizing it according to aesthetic structures. Such aesthetic reorganizing can create a "protected space" where we might be able to "reconcile those impossible narrative seams in our own lives" (6), as Ben Sifuentes-Jáuregui suggests in his book *Transvestism, Masculinity, and Latin American Literature.* Using the tools of narratology, history, Chomskyean linguistics, cognitive science, and so on, allows us to discover, engage, and share such protected spaces and allows them in turn to acquire the tools necessary for critical and sharp interpretive thinking about themselves as subjects, their identities, and their potential political engagement in the world beyond the classroom.

The only meaningful way in which queer Chicano/a literature and film (by and about) can have value is precisely in our understanding better how they are organized as aesthetic objects and how they communicate with and effect their readers and audiences alike. Finally, then, as I've begun to demonstrate in *Brown on Brown,* Edward James Olmos, Ana Castillo, John Rechy, Sheila Ortiz Taylor, Arturo Islas, and Richard Rodriguez all bracket reality and engage a variety of storytelling techniques to invent literary and film landscapes filled with bisexual/queer/lesbian Chicano/biracial characters who inhabit invented worlds that *disengage* readers/audiences from delimiting preconceptions of race, gender, and sexuality.

Notes

Introduction: Narrative, Sexuality, Race, and the Self

1. I understand the unconscious to consist of those functions not hardwired to the circuitry of consciousness; thus I avoid using terms such as "repression" to move us away from theories of the unconscious as a repository of repressed memories and desires. As recent research in neuroscience and evolutionary psychology shows, emotional and "automatic" cognitive behavior, as well as other nonconscious mental activities, are unconscious not because they are repressed trauma as per Freud's formulation, but because that is the only way for a person to function and the species to survive. Automatisms (reflex reactions, emotions, and so on) are an essential part of humankind's evolved mental equipment.

2. "Reality" in the sense of everything that is *out there* (as established by consensus and not by definition) plus the mind, and that necessarily includes a sense of the relationship between mind and what is *not* the mind.

3. Unlike yesteryear's neuroscientific research based on the nonliving brain, technologies such as the FMRI (functional magnetic resonance imaging scan) and PET (positron emission tomography scan) have allowed scientists to measure more accurately the biochemical and neuronal processes and their affiliated affective and cognitive operations in living human brains (healthy and damaged).

4. The "principle of identity" says that if all properties present in X are also present in Z, then X is identical to Z because you cannot discern a difference between X and Z. Their properties are indistinguishable. Stated otherwise, if all is gray, then there are no colors because all properties of everything overlap with the property of gray and therefore gray does not exist. (See Leibniz, *Discourse on Metaphysics*, 1988.)

5. Image making and its affiliated goal-driven intentionality are central to the evolution of the human self as they form the central elements of our universal capacity for "worldmaking"; that is, our ability to inhabit holographically a past and a future in the present. The activation of this universal worldmaking capacity—much like Noam Chomsky's hypothesis of our universal grammar—requires environmental stimulus to activate genetically hardwired biochemical and neuronal processes that evolve as we grow from infant to adult into an increasingly sophisticated and complex worldmaking capacity.

6. In the Stone Age, humans grouped in more or less small communities that allowed them to transform nature through their work as gatherers and hunters and toolmakers, and, by transforming nature (satisfying their needs), they also transformed themselves. As time passed, work became more and more socialized and so involved more and more organization and coordination of increasingly large numbers of people. So, as communities grew, our ancestors had to find new ways of transforming nature: domestication of animals, cultivation of crops, the invention of more sophisticated tools. When our ancestors began to organize work on a much larger scale to ensure the survival of increasingly expanding communities, society itself began to transform into one divided by manual and intellectual labor. Hence, the rise of clerical workers, priests, architects, musicians, and painters, for example, who did not have to depend on manual labor to survive. The increasingly sedentary life of the community led to the private ownership of land by individuals, families, and/or clans. With private property and the tools to cultivate this private land, two main institutions appeared: the church (any institution that regulates the beliefs of the community) and the state (which has the force to guarantee private ownership or state ownership of the land). Indeed, the state in its origin is directly related to power (force) and to property. The self is thus the human mind/body that belongs to a community-bounded territory controlled by a state and a church. At the same time, the self is from birth till death an individual.

7. This does not mean an absolute deterministic sense of self. There are many examples of, say, the working class and/or trade leaders defending the interests of the bourgeoisie, and of those born of the bourgeoisie adopting and fighting for the interests of the working class. And, perhaps less willfully, we see how certain historical moments (the 1929 stock market crash, for example) have given rise to huge shifts in sense of self that result from dramatic changes in the individual's material conditions.

8. We are fast approaching a stage in our evolution when we might be able to reproduce without these determining biological facts: cloning as asexual reproduction. Even in such cases, however, because of the sociobiological material basis of human reproduction, we are still constrained by the laws of evolution; that variety gives more opportunity for positive adaptive mutation necessary for the survival of the species. Given our biological machinery, if all zygotic reproduction stopped we would work against evolution and therefore lead our species to an ultimate dead end.

Chapter 1. Querying Postcolonial and Borderland Queer Theory

1. Other important feminist and queer Chicana anthologies published during this late-1980s and early-1990s period include the Latina Lesbian History Project's publication of Juanita Ramos's *Compañeras: Latina Lesbians* in 1987 (reprinted by Routledge in 1994), Arte Público's publication of María Herrera-Sobek and Helena María Viramontes's *Chicana Creativity and Criticism* (1987), Aunt Lute's printing of *Haciendo Caras: Making Face, Making Soul* (1990), and the Third Woman Press publication of Carla Trujillo's *Chicana Lesbians: The Girls Our Mothers Warned Us About* (1991).

2. We see such a comparative approach also in queer Latino/a theory. For example, in *Queer Latinidad: Identity Practices, Discursive Spaces*, Juana María Rodríguez analyzes a number of "unsanctioned" objects produced by Chicano, Cuban, and Puerto Rican artists and activists that open up "interpretive possibilities for the representation of queer *latinidad*" (8). In her so-identified "rhizomatic reading of *latinidad*" (22), she

destabilizes heteronormative and racist ideologies that naturalize sexual and racial differences. We also see this "transethnic" move in such queer postcolonial excavations and representational texturings as those in the following edited collections: John Hawley's *Postcolonial and Queer Theories,* Peter Drucker's *Different Rainbows,* Hoshang Merchant's *Yaraana: Gay Writing from India,* and Ruth Vanita's *Queering India: Same-Sex Love and Eroticism in Indian Culture and Society.* Within the field of Native American studies, there is Will Roscoe's volume *Living the Spirit: A Gay American Indian Anthology,* which recovered a genealogy of queer tribal healers.

3. In Leo Bersani's *Homos,* for example, he identifies a *homo*-ness as a "nonthreatening supplement to sameness" (7) and as a "homosexuality without sexuality" (121) by resuscitating Gide, Proust, and Genet, all while uncritically reproducing a primitivist representation of the ethnosexual queer as Other.

4. We see a similar maneuver in Roland Barthes's "The Death of the Author," an essay heavily influenced by Derrida. For example, Barthes writes: "In the multiplicity of writing, everything is to be *disentangled,* nothing *deciphered,* . . . writing ceaselessly posits meaning ceaselessly to evaporate it, carrying out a systematic exemption of meaning. In precisely this way literature (it would be better from now on to say *writing*), by refusing to assign a 'secret,' an ultimate meaning, to the text (and to the world as text), liberates what may be called an anti-theological activity, an activity that is truly revolutionary since to refuse to fix meaning is, in the end, to refuse God and his hypostases—reason, science, law" (146). And, like Derrida, Barthes's infinite semiosis reaches into the theological heavens.

5. On the same page in *Speech and Phenomena* where Derrida characterizes *différance* as "neither a *word* nor a *concept*" he also states: "difference more properly refers to what in classical language would be called the origin or production of differences and the differences between differences, the *play* [*jeu*] of differences. Its locus and operation will therefore be seen wherever speech appeals to difference" (130).

6. In *Of Grammatology* Derrida writes, "Thus as it goes without saying, the trace whereof I speak is not more *natural* (it is not the mark, the natural sign, or the index in the Husserlian sense) than *cultural,* not more physical than psychic, biological than spiritual. It is that starting from which a becoming-unmotivated of the sign, and with it all the ulterior oppositions between *physis* and its other, is possible" (47). He continues, "*The trace is in fact the absolute origin of sense in general. Which amounts to saying once again that there is no absolute origin of sense in general. The trace is the difference* which opens appearance and signification" (65).

7. Ernest Gellner identifies Freud's hydraulic model as a "hydro-hermeneutics" (93) that as the "driving force behind the agitation of our mind is related to powerful instinctual forces, with a deep physiological basis, and related to the biological needs of survival and procreation" (93). Importantly, Gellner asks whether Freud's "sketchily constructed model of sluices and channels and chambers and locks and water-wheels [is] in any way scientifically serious, as opposed to being mere metaphor" (*The Psychoanalytic Movement,* 93).

8. In Freud's words, "we have arrived at our knowledge of this psychical apparatus by studying the individual development of human beings. To the oldest of these psychical provinces or agencies we give the name of *id.* It contains everything that is inherited, that is present at birth, that is laid down in the constitution—above all, therefore, the instincts, which originate from the somatic organization and which find a first psychical expression here [in the id] in forms unknown to us" (*An Outline of Psycho-Analysis,* 14).

9. As formulated in *The Ego and the Id*, the ego accomplishes this restraining function by bringing the psychical apparatus into relation with the world, acting as a repressing mechanism and performing its defensive operations in ways that are most often automatic without ceasing to be ruled by what Freud calls the "reality principle." The repressing mechanism rejects from consciousness those ideas and impulses which threaten the stability of the ego in its function of connecting the psychical apparatus with the external world, channeling them towards the id. The connection with the environment involves all conscious and deliberative processes, including an awareness of all sorts of external entities and their characteristics as well as the perception of the subjective qualities of experience (odor, taste, color, and so on) and the recognition of other humans as intentional beings like oneself. Other ego's skills are the capacity to use and understand human symbolic representations, to establish logical and causal connections, to conceive ideas and communicate them through language and other means, and so on. In his book *An Outline of Psycho-Analysis*, Freud lists the principal characteristics of the ego in a way that merits its lengthy citation:

> In consequence of the preestablished connection between sense perception and muscular action, the ego has voluntary movement at its command. It has the task of self-preservation. As regards *external* events, it performs that task by becoming aware of stimuli, by storing up experiences about them (in the memory), by avoiding excessively strong stimuli (through flight), by dealing with moderate stimuli (through adaptation), and finally by learning to bring about expedient changes in the external world to its own advantage (through activity). As regards *internal* events, in relation to the id, it performs that task by gaining control over the demands of the instincts, by deciding whether they are to be allowed satisfaction, by postponing that satisfaction to times and circumstances favorable in the external world or by suppressing their excitations entirely. It is guided in its activity by consideration of the tensions produced by stimuli, whether these tensions are present in it or introduced into it. The raising of these tensions is in general felt as *unpleasure* and their lowering as *pleasure*. It is probable, however, that what is felt as pleasure or unpleasure is not the *absolute* height of this tension but something in the rhythm of the changes in them. The ego strives after pleasure and seeks to avoid unpleasure. An increase in unpleasure that is expected and foreseen is met by a *signal of anxiety*; the occasion of such an increase, whether it threatens from without or within, is known as *danger*. From time to time the ego gives up its connection with the external world and withdraws into the state of sleep, in which it makes far-reaching changes in its organization. It is to be inferred from the state of sleep that this organization consists in a particular distribution of mental energy. (14–15).

10. Freud's ternary model can be summarized as follows: At a certain moment in the life of the child (more or less after the age of five), part of the energy from the id that had been channeled into the ego starts becoming differentiated once again and, in this process, creates a new agency which will be in charge of forwarding or hindering the pleasure-seeking aim of the id in ways that differ from those used by the ego. The resisting forces of the ego are based on its connection to the external world and its submission to the reality principle, while those of the superego are based on its internalization of parental and (more largely social) ideals and moral values. In the superego one finds a combination, as it were, of the realistic thinking of the ego and

the irrationality of the id. Children's dependency is relatively long and teaches them to obey both the reality principle and the precepts, wishes, and moral dictates of parents and/or other persons in position of authority upon them in order to secure their approval, avoid pain, and obtain pleasure. After a certain time, the judgmental, censorial, and punitive or rewarding parental action is internalized and becomes the child's own moral code. Thus, the parent's authority, as assimilated by the child, becomes an agency of his or her psychic apparatus. The child's insertion in society follows a similar path, since the prohibitions, demands, precepts, critical judgments, and other practices in the child's environment become part of the larger process of socialization.

11. Already in 1856 (the year Freud was born) German physician Otto Deiters identified dendrites and axons in nerve cells; a few years later, it was proved in the work of Ernst Brücke, Emile du Bois-Reymond, and Ewald Herring that nerves could be stimulated not only electrically, but also chemically. In the "Project" Freud alludes to such a knowledge base, stating that "the main substance of these new discoveries is that the nervous system consists of distinct and similarly constructed neurons, which have contact with one another through the medium of a foreign substance" (89). (See also Zvi Lothane's *In Defense of Schreber: Soul Murder and Psychiatry.*) And, two years after Freud wrote the "Project for a Scientific Psychology," British neurophysiologist Charles Sherrington conducted experiments (for the Spanish historiographer Santiago Ramón y Cajal) to determine how signals traveled from one neuron to another; this led to the conclusion that the neurons were independent cells and did not form, as previously believed, a continuous network). In 1900, Sherrington further demonstrated that certain nerve cells could turn signals on and off. Whereas Ramón y Cajal won the Nobel Prize in 1906 and Sherrington in 1932 for their discoveries, Freud never did take home the prize. (Neither was he rewarded based on his creative ability, an option used by the Nobel committee to honor Bertrand Russell in 1950). For more on the history of the exploration of the brain, see Robert-Benjamin Illing's essay, "Humbled by History."

12. According to Saussure, the two components of the sign (the "signifier" and the "signified") are psychological ("mental") entities and they are not separable. In other words, contrary to a widely shared misconception, the Saussurean notion of the sign excludes all possibility of a split, a parting, a hiatus, a void, or a slippage between these two components. The sign can only exist and function as a sign, that is, as the most basic unit of linguistic communication, if it remains whole, if it is the undivided mental unity of an acoustic image (what is known as a "phoneme") and a concept (a "meaning"). Many theorists have confused the "signified" (a "concept," a "meaning") with the referent (of necessity, "something" exterior to the sign), thus judging themselves entitled to separate the "signifier" from the "signified," misconceiving the "signifier" as a "word" and the "signified" as a "referent," all the while believing that they are following Saussure's theory of sign and language.

13. J. L. Austin follows a long line of scholars of structural and philosophical linguistics—Ferdinand de Saussure, then later Leonard Bloomfield and Edward Sapir in the United States, and Roman Jakobson in Russia and several other countries—whose work followed a mainly descriptive and taxonomist approach in their attempts to know how language and our linguistic faculty function. However, their work failed to explain some obvious features of language, such as the fact that "the repertoire of sentences is theoretically infinite," the fact that humans are already able to make use of this faculty in a very complete way since infancy, when their exposure to linguistic phenomena is very limited, and "the fact that any language can be used to convey any

proposition, from theological parables to military directives," a fact that "suggests that all languages are cut from the same cloth," as Steven Pinker has recently repeated in his *The Blank Slate* (37).

14. In an interview Foucault says that S&M will open the possibility for "an acting out of power structures by a strategic game that is able to give sexual pleasure or bodily pleasure" ("Michel Foucault: Sex, Power, and the Politics of Identity," 27). He adds to this a discussion of how role-play, ritual, and even real physical pain can offer us a way to enter into and transform the psyche (collective and individual). And, in his vision of a future where "economy of bodies and pleasures" is not subject to the "austere monarchy of sex" (*History of Sexuality*, 159), Foucault proposes an aestheticization of self/pleasure that ultimately stands in resistance to external laws. It is only in Foucault's theory centered on the self that the realm of absolutely unregulated pleasure can be conceived and that the positing of resistance to discursive power relations in the "normal" real world can take place. In this theory there is no place for actual collective solidarity, only for self-centered play.

15. In *Racial Castration*, David Eng aims to decode Asian American subjectivities where non-normative desire actively ruptures dominant, discursively constructed epistemologies and ontologies. His Asian American queer desiring subject is posited as a counter-discourse that unsettles "existing categories by exposing their complicity with those regulatory systems that kill desire" (6).

Chapter 2. John Rechy's Bending of Brown and White Canons

1. Although not a focus of discussion in this chapter, Rechy engages with, then redeploys, the genre of the picaresque in *The Life and Adventures of Lyle Clemens* (2003) to destabilize racial, ethnic, and sexual essentialist categories. The sexually polymorphous and ambiguously biracial protagonist, Lyle Clemens, sets off from his U.S./Mexican bordertown home to L.A. (via Las Vegas) on a quest to discover himself. As his episodic adventuring reaches a final crescendo, he finds his greatest source of vitality after he strips himself (literally, outside L.A.'s Egyptian Theater) of all identity categories: "His body was calm, his voice firm. More people gathered about him, responding to the triumphant words he sang in a voice that was entirely his own: *I was once lost, but now I'm found, Was blind, but now I see!*" (324).

2. Rechy's ever-expanding list of novels also made it possible for scholars like David William Foster to analyze the trends and departures present in his work in toto. In *Sexual Textualities*, Foster identifies Rechy's shift from "specifically homoerotic depictions" (81) in novels like *Marilyn's Daughter* to a more racially explicit representation of sexuality and gender in a novel like *The Miraculous Day of Amalia Gómez*.

3. For a detailed and insightful analysis of Rechy's story "El Paso del Norte," see Theresa Meléndez's "*El Contrabando de El Paso.*"

4. Unlike *The Sexual Outlaw*, which offers an overt critique of the Foucaultian position that believes ritualized violence and sex in S&M can be a politically resistant act, in Rechy's later *Rushes: A Novel* S&M is uncritically incorporated into his narrative schema as a transgressive site of resistance. (For more on this, see Jonathan Dollimore's *Sexual Dissidence*.)

5. In *The Miraculous Day of Amalia Gómez*, Rechy's narrator describes a similar invasive light, but this time it is racialized: "Suddenly light poured down in a white pit.

Squad cars rushed to block the side exits off the boulevard. Police motorcycles tangled in and out of lanes. Young Mexican men rushed out of cars. Some were pushed to the ground. There were screams. The police pulled out their guns" (44). And, increasingly, Amalia notices "sun-glassed Anglo police prowling the area like leisurely invaders in their black cars. She saw young Mexican men—boys—sprawled against the walls while cops frisked them" (44).

6. The character Manuel provides an intertextual link with Rechy's earlier novel *Bodies and Souls* (1983). In this novel, he appears as a much more fleshed out, effeminate gay character who inhabits L.A.'s complexly layered demimonde. In "John Rechy: Bodies and Souls and the Homoerotization of the Urban Quest," David William Foster provides an analysis of Manny Gómez's obsession with having a Christ figure tattooed on his chest (in the image of a cock and balls) as an act racially and sexually reinhabiting an otherwise oppressive Christ iconography. Moreover, this act symbolizes Manny's own sense of being a victim within a homophobic Chicano community and a racist mainstream society.

7. Amalia is not exactly like Bloom—especially when it comes to his orientalist phantasmagoria. For example, when Bloom walks streets in the red-light district of Dublin, he describes a prostitute as "a pigmy woman" (429); and, during one of his many flights of fancy, Bloom orientalizes Molly in "Turkish costume" with "opulent curves [that] fill out her scarlet trousers and jacket slashed with gold. A wide yellow cummerbund girdles her. A white yashmak violet in the night, covers her face, leaving free only her large dark eyes and raven hair" (439).

8. John Rechy likes the number three. He mentions in his Foreword that it took him three months to write *Numbers*; in *This Day's Death*, Jim Girard makes his third trip in three months to L.A.

Chapter 3. Arturo Islas's and Richard Rodriguez's Ethnosexual Re-architexturing of Metropolitan Space

1. As discussed at length in Chapter 2, there is the gay Chicano author John Rechy, who set all of his novels after *City of Night* (1963) in urban centers. However, as also discussed in Chapter 2, his novels were not identified as Chicano until long after the publication of *City of Night*.

2. See my biography of Islas, *Dancing with Ghosts*, where I discuss at length his writing of *La Mollie and the King of Tears*. He wrote the novel in a flurry between October 1986 and January 1987. However, the text remained unpublished until 1996, when, ironically, one of the many presses to originally reject the manuscript, the University of New Mexico Press, published the novel. There is little difference between the manuscript Islas intended to publish and the posthumously published version. Certain scenes are trimmed down—less characterization of la Mollie, for example—but minimally. The text itself (style, technique, genre, and mode), and especially the moments in the novel that reveal the tropes or ideas of queerness I analyze in this chapter, remain unchanged from the manuscript dated June 1987 to the 1996 published version. To emphasize this point, I will henceforth reference both the original (June 1987) manuscript housed in Stanford's Special Collection Library and the Skenazy-revised published novel.

3. The pairing of Islas and Rodriguez might seem a little odd, considering that they didn't see eye to eye on issues such as affirmative action and bilingual education. Islas

was outraged with the conservative voice in Rodriguez's *Hunger of Memory*, but *Days of Obligation* radically turns away from that voice, allowing the earlier ideological distance between them, at least textually, to lessen.

4. At a certain point in the transition from manuscript to published novel, the line "sneaky like the border patrol, waiting to pull you in just when you think you're free" (69) was added to Louie's sense of remembering his past in El Paso. The line is not in the June 1987 manuscript. Yet the published version similarly projects the sense that Louie's memory is strongly racialized and in constant threat of being policed by characters like la Mollie who threaten to deny him an affirming sense of a Chicano-infused self-knowledge.

5. Louie's reaction to the male-male erotica differs in the June 1987 manuscript. Here Louie remarks, "It was eerie, man, and I recognized the old demon lust winking in the background of all them pictures I couldn't erase from my head. . . . Maybe the whole thing felt strange to me cause there wasn't no women in that room and women always bring something mysterious into any room" (198–199). While the sentence differs from that of the 1996 novel, both reveal Louie's exaggerated ("strange cause there wasn't no women") heterosexual role play. Moreover, like the novel, the manuscript includes Louie's frequent slips—such as his comment about the "cute little waiter" (58)—that suggest a hesitating desire to move into a male-male libidinal economy.

6. Louie also walks through the Castro at dusk in the June 1987 manuscript. However, the manuscript adds to Louie's struggle with his sexuality a sense of his troubled history with alcohol: "In my heavy drinking and drugging day, I couldn't never figure out how come they called that time of day the Happy Hour. It was anything but happy for me and all I wanted to do was drink away my fear of the dark that was coming on like a big, wet and heavy wool blanket all smothering and dark and scarier than a pillow Othello uses to snuff out his darling Desdemona" (93).

Chapter 4. Ana Castillo's and Sheila Ortiz Taylor's Bent Chicana Textualities

1. While Moraga and Anzaldúa's edited collection of essays, poetry, and fiction by women of color collected in *This Bridge Called My Back* was a spearhead in the Xicana feminist movement, others were already writing on the cultural representation of Chicanas. For example, Judy Salinas's essay "The Role of Women in Chicano Literature" (1979) scrupulously explores and critiques the representation of Chicanas in the works of José Montoya, Rudolfo Anaya, Raymond Barrio, and Rolando Hinojosa.

2. Catrióna Rueda Esquibel complicates the traditional division between straight and queer Chicana fiction. In her essay "Memories of Girlhood: Chicana Lesbian Fictions," she includes Chicana writers like Cisneros and Chávez within the Chicana lesbian canon, "not," she states, "because the characters (or their authors) self-consciously claim a lesbian identity, but because the texts, in their literary construction of such intense girlhood friendships, inscribe a desire between girls that I name 'lesbian'" (59–60). Here, she importantly expands the lesbian/Chicana literary frame to include characters who express a same-sex desire but don't necessarily actualize the desire.

3. Gate-keeping of gay/lesbian fiction does not take place just within the realm of publishing conglomerates; it is also pervasive in the academy at large. In a recent survey of University of California campuses, it was determined that 41 percent of faculty decided against including gay/lesbian-themed texts in their courses. This isn't always

because a given professor rejects the texts outright, but because of well-founded fears that students will negatively evaluate the course. Since evaluations are used to determine tenure and pay raises, often the decision not to teach gay/lesbian-themed books is motivated by economics and not homophobia. (For more on this, see Karla Jay and Joanne Glasgow's *Lesbian Texts and Contexts: Radical Revisions.*

Chapter 5. Edward J. Olmos's Postcolonial *Penal*izings of the Film-Image Repertoire

1. Floyd Mutrux takes the screenplay's title, "American Me," from Beatrice Griffith's sociologically informed book on post-WWII U.S. gangs. The title and content have now been retooled by Mutrux, who focuses less on Griffith's original taxonomy of the male pathological type and more on developing a complex characterization of the biographical Chicano gangster Cheyenne, who was a founding member of the Mexican mafia and murdered in prison in 1972.

2. Including Santana, the group makes up seven. This number resonates with symbolic significance. According to Amerindian mythology, Rafael Pérez-Torres writes, "Aztlán names the Mexican homeland—the land of seven caves (Chicomostoc), the palace of the Twisted Hill (Colhuacán), the place of whiteness (Aztlán)—from which the Mexica migrated south toward the central plateau in A.D. 820" (*Movements in Chicano Poetry*, 229).

Works Cited

Abelove, Henry. *Deep Gossip*. Minneapolis: University of Minnesota Press, 2003.

Acosta, Oscar "Zeta." *The Autobiography of a Brown Buffalo*. New York: Vintage, 1972.

Alarcón, Francisco X. "The Poet as Other." In *Chicano/Latino Homoerotic Identities*, edited by David William Foster, 159–174. New York: Garland, 1999.

Alarcón, Norma. "Conjugating Subjects: The Heteroglossia of Essence and Resistance." In *An Other Tongue: Nation and Ethnicity in the Linguistic Borderlands*, edited by Alfred Arteaga, 125–133. Durham: Duke University Press, 1994.

Aldama, Arturo J., and Naomi H. Quiñonez, eds. *De-Colonial Voices: Chicana and Chicano Cultural Studies in the 21st Century*. Bloomington: Indiana University Press, 2001.

———. *Disrupting Savagism: Chicana/o, Mexican Immigrant, and Native American Struggles for Self-Representation (Latin America Otherwise)*. Durham, NC: Duke University Press, 2001.

———, ed. *Violence and the Body: Race, Gender, and the State*. Bloomington, IN: University of Indiana Press, 2003.

Aldama, Frederick Luis. *Contemporary Chicano/a Arts and Letters: Mapped by Interview*. Austin: University of Texas Press. Forthcoming.

———. "Cultural Studies in Today's Chicano/Latino Scholarship: Wishful Thinking, *Flatus Voci*, or Scientific Endeavor?" *Aztlán* 28, no. 1 (2004): 93–128.

———. *Dancing with Ghosts: A Critical Biography of Arturo Islas*. Berkeley: University of California Press, 2004.

———. "*Frontera* Musicscapes: Grinding Up a Bad Edge in Borderland Studies." In *Rebellious Reading: The Dynamics of Chicano/a Literacy*, edited by Carl Gutiérrez-Jones, 95–127. Santa Barbara: Center for Chicano Studies, University of California, Santa Barbara, 2004.

———. *Postethnic Narrative Criticism: Magicorealism in Oscar "Zeta" Acosta, Julie Dash, Hanif Kureishi, Anna Castillo, and Salman Rushdie*. Austin: University of Texas Press, 2003.

Anonymous. Review of *Days of Obligation* by Richard Rodriguez. *Kirkus Review* 60 (September 1, 1992): 1115.

———. Review of *Loverboys* by Ana Castillo. *Publishers Weekly* 243, no. 28 (July 8, 1996): 73.

———. Review of *The Miraculous Day of Amalia Gómez* by John Rechy. *Publishers Weekly* 238, no. 28 (June 28, 1991): 87.

Anzaldúa, Gloria. *Borderlands/La Frontera*. San Francisco: Aunt Lute, 1987.

Arredondo, Gabriela F., Aída Hurtado, Norma Klahn, Olga Nájera-Ramírez, and Patricia Zavella, eds. *Chicana Feminisms: A Critical Reader*. Durham, NC: Duke University Press, 2003.

Austin, J. L. *How to Do Things with Words*. 2nd ed. Edited by J. O. Urmson and Marina Sbisà. Cambridge, MA: Harvard University Press, 1975.

Babuscio, Jack. "Camp and the Gay Sensibility." In *Camp Grounds: Style and Homosexuality*, edited by David Bergman, 19–38. Amherst: University of Massachusetts Press, 1993.

Baker, Samuel. "Ana Castillo: The Protest Poet Goes Mainstream." *Publishers Weekly* 243, no. 33 (August 12, 1996): 59–60.

Bakhtin, Mikhail. *Rabelais and His World*. Translated by Helen Iswolsky. Bloomington: Indiana University Press, 1984.

Barthes, Roland. "The Death of the Author." In *Image, Music, Text*, translated by Stephen Heath, 142–148. New York: Hill and Wang, 1977.

———. *The Pleasure of the Text*. Translated by Richard Miller. New York: Noonday Press, 1975.

Bersani, Leo. *Homos*. Cambridge, MA: Harvard University Press, 1995.

Bhabha, Homi K. "The Third Space." In *Identity, Community, Culture, Difference*, edited by J. Rutherford, 207–221. London: Lawrence and Wishart, 1990.

Bilder, Robert H., Christeine C. Felder, Neil Lewis, David S. Lester, and Frank LeFever, eds. *Neuroscience of the Mind on the Centennial of Freud's Project for a Scientific Psychology*. Vol. 843 of *Annals of the New York Academy of Sciences*. New York: New York Academy of Sciences, 1998.

Birkin, Lawrence. "Desire and Death: The Early Fiction of John Rechy." *Western Humanities Review* 51, no. 2 (1992): 236–245.

Borch-Jacobsen, Mikkel. *Lacan: The Absolute Master*. Stanford, CA: Stanford University Press, 1991.

Brady, Mary Pat. *Extinct Lands, Temporal Geographies: Chicana Literature and the Urgency of Space*. Durham, NC: Duke University Press, 2002.

Brown, Monica. *Gang Nation: Delinquent Citizens in Puerto Rican, Chicano, and Chicana Narratives*. Minneapolis: University of Minnesota Press, 2002.

Bruce-Novoa, Juan. "Homosexuality and the Chicano Novel." *European Perspectives on Hispanic Literature of the United States*. Edited by Genvieve Fabre. Houston: Arte Público Press, 1988: 98–106; reprinted from *Confluencia-revista hispanica de cultura y literatura* 2, no. 1 (1986): 69–77.

———. "In Search of the Honest Outlaw: John Rechy." *Minority Voices* 3, no. 1 (1979): 37–46.

Butler, Judith. *Gender Trouble*. New York: Routledge, 1990.

Cáliz-Montoro, Carmen. *Writing from the Borderlands: A Study of Chicano, Afro-Caribbean, and Native Literatures in North America*. Toronto: Tsar, 2000.

Casillo, Charles. *Outlaw: The Lives and Careers of John Rechy*. New York: Advocate Books, 2002.

Castillo, Ana. *Loverboys*. New York: Doubleday, 1996.

———. *The Mixquiahuala Letters*. Binghampton, NY: Bilingual Press/Editorial Bilingüe, 1986.

————. *Peel My Love Like an Onion.* New York: Doubleday, 1999.

————. *So Far from God.* New York: Doubleday, 1993.

Castillo, Debra. "Outlaw Aesthetics: Interview with John Rechy." *Diacritics* 25, no. 1 (1995): 113–125.

Celan, Paul. *The Straitening (Engführung): 2 Poems of Paul Celan.* Translated by Michael Hamburger. New York: Persea Books, 2002.

Chamberlain, Leslie. *The Secret Artist: A Close Reading of Sigmund Freud.* New York: Seven Stories Press, 2001.

Chávez, Denise. *Face of an Angel.* New York: Farrar Strauss & Giroux, 1994.

————. *Last of the Menu Girls.* Houston: Arte Público Press, 1986.

————. *Loving Pedro Infante: A Novel.* New York: Farrar Strauss & Giroux, 2001.

Chávez, John. "John Francisco Rechy." In *Chicano Literature: A Reference Guide.* Edited by Francisco A. Lomelí and Julio Martínez. Westport, CT: Greenwood, 1985. 323–332.

Christian, Karen. *Show and Tell: Identity and Performance in U.S. Latina/o Fiction.* Albuquerque: University of New Mexico Press, 1997.

Cisneros, Sandra. *Caramelo: or Pure Cuento: A Novel.* New York: Knopf, distributed by Random House, 2002.

————. *House on Mango Street.* Houston: Arte Público Press, 1983. Republished, New York: Vintage Books, a division of Random House, 1991; Knopf, 1994.

————. *Woman Hollering Creek and Other Stories.* New York: Random House, 1991.

Crews, Frederick. Foreword to *After Poststructuralism: Interdisciplinarity and Literary Theory.* Edited by Nancy Easterlin and Barbara Riebling, vii–x. Evanston, IL: Northwestern University Press, 1993.

Cruz-Malavé, Arnaldo, and Martin F. Manalansan IV. "Introduction: Dissident Sexualities/Alternative Globalisms." In *Queer Globalizations: Citizenship and the Afterlife of Colonialism,* edited by Arnaldo Cruz-Malavé and Martin F. Manalansan IV, 1–10. New York: New York University Press, 2002.

Damasio, Antonio. *The Feeling of What Happens.* New York: Harcourt, 1999.

Debord, Guy. *The Society of the Spectacle.* Translated by Donald Nicholson-Smith. New York: Zone Books, 1994.

de la Peña, Terri. Review of *Loverboys* by Ana Castillo. *Lambda Book Report* 5, no. 4 (1996): 14–15.

Derrida, Jacques. *Dissemination.* Translated by Barbara Johnson. Chicago: University of Chicago Press, 1981.

————. "Faith and Knowledge: Two Sources of 'Religion' at the Limits of Reason Alone." In *Religion,* edited by Jacques Derrida and Gianni Vattimo, translated by David Webb, 1–78. Stanford, CA: Stanford University Press, 1998.

————. *Of Grammatology.* Translated by Gayatri Spivak. Baltimore: Johns Hopkins University Press, 1976.

————. *Positions.* Translated and annotated by Alan Bass. Chicago: University of Chicago Press, 1981.

————. *Speech and Phenomena, and Other Essays on Husserl's Theory of Signs.* Translated by David B. Allison. Evanston, IL: Northwestern University Press, 1973.

Diggs, Marylynne. "Surveying the Intersection: Pathology, Secrecy, and the Discourses of Racial and Sexual Identity." In *Critical Essays: Gay and Lesbian Writers of Color,* edited by Emmanuel S. Nelson, 1–19. New York: Haworth Press, 1993.

Dollimore, Jonathan. *Sexual Dissidence: Augustine to Wilde, Freud to Foucault*. Oxford: Clarendon Press, 1991.

———. "Too Hot for Yale?" In *Territories of Desire in Queer Culture: Refiguring Contemporary Boundaries*, edited by David Alderson and Linda Anderson, 214–234. Manchester, UK: Manchester University Press, 2000.

Drucker, Peter. "Reinventing Liberation: Strategic Questions for Lesbian-Gay Movements." In *Different Rainbows: Same Sex Sexuality and Popular Struggles in the Third World*, 207–220. London: Gay Men's Press, 2000.

Eagleton, Terry. *Figures of Dissent: Critical Essays on Fish, Spivak, Zizek, and Others*. New York: Verso, 2003.

Eakin, Emily. "The Latest Theory Is That Theory Doesn't Matter." *New York Times*, April 19, 2003, D-9.

Eng, David L. *Racial Castration: Managing Masculinity in Asian America*. Durham, NC: Duke University Press, 2001.

Esquibel, Catrióna Rueda. "Memories of Girlhood: Chicana Lesbian Fictions." In *Chicano/Latino Homoerotic Identities*, edited by David William Foster, 59–98. New York: Garland, 1999.

Evanson, Brian. Review of *Loverboys* by Ana Castillo. *Review of Contemporary Fiction* 17, no. 1 (1997): 201–202.

Fluck, Winfried. "Aesthetics and Cultural Studies." In *Aesthetics in a Multicultural Age*, edited by Emory Elliot, Louis Freitas Caton, and Jeffery Rhyne, 79–103. Oxford: Oxford University Press, 2002.

Foster, David William, ed. *Chicano/Latino Homoerotic Identities*. New York: Garland, 1999.

———. "Homoerotic Writing and Chicano Authors." *Bilingual Review* 21, no. 1 (1996): 42–51.

———. "John Rechy: Bodies and Souls and the Homoerotization of the Urban Quest." *Studies in Twentieth Century Literature* 25, no. 1 (2001): 196–209.

———. *Sexual Textualities: Essays on Queer/ing Latin American Writing*. Austin: University of Texas Press, 1997.

Foucault, Michel. *History of Sexuality, Vol. 1: An Introduction*. Trans. Robert Hurley. London: Allen Lane, 1979.

———. "Michel Foucault: Sex, Power, and the Politics of Identity." Interview with Bob Gallagher and Alexander Wilson. *Advocate* 400 (August 7, 1984): 26–30; reprinted in *Dits et écrits: IV 1980–1988*, 735–746. Paris: Éditions Gallimard, 1994.

Fregoso, Rosa Linda. *The Bronze Screen: Chicana and Chicano Film Culture*. Minneapolis: University of Minnesota Press, 1993.

———. *meXicana encounters: The Making of Social Identities on the Borderlands*. Berkeley: University of California Press, 2003.

Freud, Sigmund. "Autobiographical Study." In *The Freud Reader*, edited by Peter Gay, 3–41. New York: Norton, 1989.

———. *The Ego and the Id*. New York: Norton, 1989.

———. *An Outline of Psycho-Analysis*. New York: Norton, 1989.

———. "Project for a Scientific Psychology." In *The Standard Edition of the Complete Psychological Works of Sigmund Freud*, 1: 281–397. London: Hogarth Press Institute of Psycho-Analysis, 1953–1973.

Gaspar de Alba, Alicia. "Introduction, or Welcome to the Closet of Barrio Popular Culture." In *Velvet Barrios: Popular Culture and Chicana/o Sexualities*, edited by Alicia Gaspar de Alba, ix–xxviii. New York: Palgrave Macmillan, 2003.

Gellner, Ernest. *The Psychoanalytic Movement: The Cunning of Unreason.* 3rd edition. Oxford: Blackwell Publishing, 2003.

Goethe, Johann Wolfgang von. *Faust: Part One.* Translated by Walter Kaufmann. New York: Anchor Books, 1990.

González, Marcial. "A Marxist Critique of Borderlands Postmodernism: Adorno's Negative Dialectics and Chicano Cultural Criticism." In *Left of the Color Line: Race, Radicalism, and Twentieth-Century Literature of the United States*, edited by Bill V. Mullen and James Smethurst, 279–297. Chapel Hill: University of North Carolina Press, 2003.

Gutierrez, Eric. "Less than a Miracle." *The Advocate* 584 (August 27, 1991): 86.

Gutiérrez-Jones, Carl. "Desiring B/orders." *Diacritics* 25, no. 1 (1995): 95–112.

———. *Race Narratives: A Study of Race, Rhetoric, and Injury.* New York: New York University Press, 2001.

Hames-García, Michael. *Fugitive Thought: Prison Movements, Race, and the Meaning of Justice.* Minneapolis: University of Minnesota Press, 2004.

Hawley, John, ed. *Postcolonial and Queer Theories: Intersections and Essays.* Westport, CT: Greenwood, 2001.

Hernandez, Ellie. "Chronotope of Desire: Emma Pérez's *Gulf Dreams.*" In *Chicana Feminisms: A Critical Reader*, edited by Gabriela F. Arredondo, Aída Hurtado, Normal Klahn, Olga Nájera-Ramírez, and Patricia Zavella, 155–177. Durham, NC: Duke University Press, 2003.

Hernández-Gutiérrez, Manuel de Jesús. "Building a Research Agenda on U.S. Latino Lesbigay Literature and Cultural Production: Texts, Writers, Performance, and Critics." In *Chicano/Latino Homoerotic Identities*, edited by David William Foster. New York: Garland, 1999.

Herrera-Sobek, María, and Helena María Viramontes, eds. *Chicana Creativity and Criticism: New Frontiers in American Literature.* Rev. ed. Albuquerque: University of New Mexico Press, 1996.

Hogan, Patrick Colm. *The Politics of Interpretation: Ideology, Professionalism, and the Study of Literature.* New York: Oxford University Press, 1990.

Houston, Robert. Review of *Face of an Angel* by Denise Chávez. *New York Times Book Review*, September 25, 1994, 20.

Ickstadt, Heinz. "Toward a Pluralist Aesthetics." In *Aesthetics in a Multicultural Age*, edited by Emory Elliot, Louis Freitas Caton, and Jeffery Rhyne, 263–278. Oxford: Oxford University Press, 2002.

Illing, Robert-Benjamin. "Humbled by History." *Scientific American* 14, no. 1 (2004): 86–93.

Islas, Arturo. "La Mollie and the King of Tears." MS. Islas Papers. Stanford University Library Special Collections. M618, box 8, folder 1, 1987.

———. *La Mollie and the King of Tears.* Albuquerque: University of New Mexico Press, 1996.

Jaén, Didier T. "John Rechy." In *The Dictionary of Literary Biography, Chicano Writers: Second Series*, edited by Francisco Lomelí and Carl Shirley, 212–219. Detroit: Thompson Gale, 1992.

Jaimes-Guerrero, M.A. "Native Womanism: Exemplars of Indigenism in Sacred Tradition of Kinship." In *Indigenous Religions: A Companion*, edited by Graham Harvey, 37–54. New York: Cassell, 2000.

Jay, Karla, and Joanne Glasgow. *Lesbian Texts and Contexts: Radical Revisions (Feminist Crosscurrents)*. New York: New York University Press, 1990.

Johnson, Brian D. Review of *American Me*, directed by Edward James Olmos. *Maclean*, March 23, 1992, 51.

Joyce, James. *Ulysses*. New York: Modern Library Edition, 1992.

Katz, Adam. *Postmodernism and the Politics of "Culture."* Boulder, CO: Westview, 2000.

Kaufmann, Stanley. Review of *American Me*, directed by Edward James Olmos. *New Republic* 206, no. 13 (March 30, 1992): 26–28.

Kempley, Rita. Review of *American Me*, directed by Edward James Olmos. *Washington Post*, March 13, 1992, F-6.

Kirsch, Jonathan. Interview with John Rechy. KCRW. November 28, 2001. http://www.johnrechy.com/current.htm.

LeDoux, Joseph, and Jacek Debiec. "Conclusions: From Self-knowledge to a Science of the Self." In *The Self from Soul to Brain*, edited by Joseph LeDoux, Jacek Debiec, and Henry Moss, 305–315. New York: New York Academy of Sciences, 2003.

LeDoux, Joseph, Jacek Debiec, and Henry Moss, eds. *The Self from Soul to Brain*. Vol. 1001 of *Annals of the New York Academy of Sciences*. New York: New York Academy of Sciences, 2003.

Leibniz, Wilhelm Gottfried. *Discourse on Metaphysics and Related Writings*. Edited and translated by R. N. D. Martin and Stuart Brown. Manchester: Manchester University Press, 1988.

León, Luis. "The Poetic Uses of Religion in *The Miraculous Day of Amalia Gómez*." *Religion and American Culture* 9, no. 2 (1999): 205–231.

Lothane, Zvi. *In Defense of Schreber: Soul Murder and Psychiatry*. Hillsdale, NJ: The Analytic Press, 1992.

McCracken, Ellen. *New Latina Narrative: The Feminine Space of Postmodern Ethnicity*. Tucson: University of Arizona Press, 1999.

McGowan, John. *Democracy's Children: Intellectuals and the Rise of Cultural Politics*. Ithaca, NY: Cornell University Press, 2002.

———. *Postmodernism and Its Critics*. Ithaca, NY: Cornell University Press, 1991.

Marez, Curtis. *Drug Wars: The Political Economy of Narcotics*. Minneapolis: University of Minnesota Press, 2004.

Meléndez, Theresa. "*El Contrabando de El Paso*: Islas and Geographies of Knowing." In *Critical Mappings of Arturo Islas's Narrative Fictions*, edited by Frederick Luis Aldama. Tempe, AZ: Bilingual Review Press, 2005.

Merchant, Hoshang. *Yaraana: Gay Writing from India*. New Delhi: Penguin Books, 1999.

Mifflin, Margot. Review of *Peel My Love Like an Onion* by Ana Castillo. *New York Times Book Review*, September 19, 1999, 31.

Molinaro, Mary. Review of *The Miraculous Day of Amalia Gómez* by John Rechy. *Library Journal* 116, no. 13 (August 1991): 147.

Moraga, Cherríe, and Gloria Anzaldúa, eds. *This Bridge Called My Back: Writings by Radical Women of Color*. 2d ed. New York: Kitchen Table, Women of Color Press, 1983.

Morton, Donald. "The Politics of Queer Theory in the (Post) Modern Moment." *Genders* 17, no. 1 (1993): 121–150.

Moya, Paula M. L. *Learning from Experience: Minority Identity, Multicultural Struggles.* Berkeley: University of California Press, 2001.

———, and Michael R. Hames-García, eds. *Reclaiming Identity: Realist Theory and the Predicament of Postmodernism.* Berkeley: University of California Press, 2000.

Muñoz, José Esteban. *Disidentifications: Queers of Color and the Performance of Politics.* Minneapolis: University of Minnesota Press, 1999.

Nelson, Emmanuel S. "John Rechy, James Baldwin and the American Double Minority Literature." *Journal of American Culture* 6, no. 2 (1983): 70–74.

Newman, Kathleen. "Reterritorialization in Recent Chicano Cinema: Edward James Olmos's *American Me.*" In *The Ethnic Eye: Latino Media Arts,* edited by Chon Noriega and Ana Lopez, 95–106. Minneapolis: University of Minnesota Press, 1996.

Novitz, David. *Knowledge, Fiction, and Imagination.* Philadelphia: Temple University Press, 1987.

Nussbaum, Martha. "The Professor of Parody: The Hip Defeatism of Judith Butler." *New Republic,* February 22, 1999, 37.

Olmos, Edward James. *American Me.* Screenplay by Felix Mutrux. Universal Pictures, 1992; MCA Universal Home Video, 2002.

Orteaga, Eliana, and Nancy Sternbach. "At the Threshold of the Unnamed: Latina Literary Discourse in the Eighties." In *Breaking Boundaries: Latina Writings and Critical Readings,* edited by Asunción Horno-Delgaso et al., 2–23. Amherst: University of Massachusetts Press, 1989.

Ortiz, Ricardo. "Sexuality Degree Zero: Pleasure and Power in the Novels of John Rechy, Arturo Islas, and Michael Nava." *Journal of Homosexuality* 26, nos. 2/3 (1993): 111–126.

Ortiz Taylor, Sheila. *Coachella.* Albuquerque: University of New Mexico Press, 1998.

———. *Faultline.* Tallahassee, FL: Naiad Press, 1982.

———. *Spring Forward/Fall Back.* Tallahassee, FL: Naiad Press, 1985.

Pérez-Torres, Rafael. "The Ambiguous Outlaw: John Rechy and Complicitous Homosexuality." In *Fictions of Masculinity: Crossing Cultures, Crossing Sexualities,* edited by Peter F. Murphy, 204–225. New York: New York University Press, 1994.

———. *Movements in Chicano Poetry: Against Margins, against Myths.* New York: Cambridge University Press, 1995.

Piedra, José. "Loving Columbus." *Hispanic Issues,* vol. 19: *Amerindian Images and the Legacy of Columbus,* edited by René Jara and Nicholas Spadaccini, 230–265. Minneapolis: University of Minnesota Press, 1992.

———. "Nationalizing Sissies." In *Entiendes: Queer Readings, Hispanic Writings,* edited by Emile L. Bergman and Paul Julian Smith, 307–409. Durham, NC: Duke University Press, 1995.

Pinker, Steven. *The Blank Slate: The Modern Denial of Human Nature.* New York: Viking, 2002.

Pratt, Mary Louise. "The Short Story: The Long and Short of It." *Poetics* 10, no. 2/3 (1981): 175–195.

Pribram, Karl H. "A Century of Progress?" In *Neuroscience of the Mind on the Centennial of Freud's Project for a Scientific Psychology,* vol. 843 of *Annals of the New York*

Academy of Sciences, edited by Robert H. Bilder, Christeine C. Felder, Neil Lewis, David S. Lester, and Frank LeFever, 11–19. New York: New York Academy of Sciences, 1998.

Ramos, Juanita, ed. *Compañeras: Latina Lesbians, An Anthology*. New York: Routledge, 1994.

Rechy, John. "El Paso del Norte." *Evergreen Review* 6, no. 1 (1958): 127–140.

———. Interviewed by Debra Castillo. "Outlaw Aesthetics: Interview with John Rechy." *Diacritics* 25, no. 1 (1995): 113–125.

———. Interviewed by Jonathan Kirsh. KCRW, November 28, 2001. http://www.johnrechy.com/current.htm.

———. *The Life and Adventures of Lyle Clemens*. New York: Grove Press, 2003.

———. *Marilyn's Daughter*. New York: Carroll & Graf, 1988.

———. *The Miraculous Day of Amalia Gómez*. New York: Arcade Paperback, 1993.

———. *Numbers*. 1st ed. New York: Grove/Atlantic, 1967.

———. *Rushes: A Novel*. New York: Grove Press, 1979.

———. *The Sexual Outlaw*. New York: Dell Publishing, 1977.

———. *This Day's Death: A Novel*. New York: Grove Press, 1969.

Rodríguez, Juana María. *Queer Latinidad: Identity Practices, Discursive Spaces*. New York: New York University Press, 2003.

Rodriguez, Richard. *Brown: The Last Discovery of America*. New York: Viking, 2002.

———. *Days of Obligation: An Argument with My Mexican Father*. New York: Penguin, 1992.

———. *Hunger of Memory: The Education of Richard Rodriguez*. New York: Bantam, 1982.

Román, David. "Fierce Love and Fierce Response: Intervening in the Cultural Politics of Race, Sexuality, and AIDS." In *Critical Essays: Gay and Lesbian Writers of Color*, edited by Emmanuel S. Nelson, 209–221. New York: Haworth, 1993.

Rosales, Cecilia. "Chueco Sexualities." In *Chicano/Latino Homoerotic Identities*, edited by David William Foster, 25–46. New York: Garland, 1999.

Roscoe, Will, ed. *Living the Spirit: A Gay American Indian Anthology*. New York: St. Martin's, 1988.

Saldívar, José David. *Border Matters: Remapping American Cultural Studies*. Berkeley: University of California Press, 1997.

Saldívar-Hull, Sonia. *Feminism on the Border: Chicana Gender Politics and Literature*. Berkeley: University of California Press, 2000.

Salinas, Judy. "The Role of Women in Chicano Literature." In *The Identification and Analysis of Chicano Literature*, edited by Francisco Jimenez, 191–240. Tempe, AZ: Bilingual Review Press, 1979.

Sánchez, Rosaura. "Deconstructions and Renarrativizations: Trends in Chicana Literature." *Bilingual Review* 21, no. 1 (1996): 52–58.

Santiago, Silviano. "The Wily Homosexual." In *Queer Globalizations: Citizenship and the Afterlife of Colonialism*, edited by Arnaldo Cruz-Malavé and Martin F. Manalansan IV, 13–19. New York: New York University Press, 2002.

Satterfield, Ben. "John Rechy's Tormented World." *Southwest Review* 67, no. 1 (1982): 78–85.

Shea, Renee. Review of *Peel My Love Like an Onion* by Ana Castillo. *Poets and Writers* 28, no. 2 (2000): 38.

Sifuentes-Jáuregui, Ben. *Transvestism, Masculinity, and Latin American Literature: Genders Share Flesh.* New York: Palgrave, 2002.

Simonelli, Thierry. "La magie de Lacan: Une récréation mathématique." In *Ethique et épistémologie autour du livre Impostures Intellectuelles de Sokal et Bricmont,* edited by Angèle Kremer Marietti, 227–241. Paris: L'Harmattan, 2001.

Singh, Amritjit, and Peter Schmidt, eds. *Postcolonial Theory and the United States: Race, Ethnicity, and Literature.* Jackson: University Press of Mississippi. 2000.

Sokal, Alan, and Jean Bricmont. *Fashionable Nonsense: Postmodern Intellectuals' Abuse of Science.* New York: Picador USA, 1998.

Spivak, Gayatri. "Can the Subaltern Speak?" In *Marxism and the Interpretation of Culture,* edited by Cary Nelson and Lawrence Grossberg, 271–313. Urbana: University of Illinois Press, 1988.

Stam, Robert, and Louise Spence. "Colonialism, Racism and Representation—An Introduction." *Screen* 24, no. 2 (1983): 2–20.

Sternbach, Nancy, and Eliana Orteaga. "At the Threshold of the Unnamed: Latin Literary Discourse in the Eighties." In *Breaking Boundaries: Latina Writing and Critical Readings,* edited by Asuncion Horno-Delgado et al., 2–23. Amherst: University of Massachusetts Press, 1989.

Tatum, Charles. "The Sexual Underworld of John Rechy." *Minority Voices* 3, no. 1 (1979): 47–52.

Taylor, Clark L. "Legends, Syncretism, and Continuing Echoes." In *Latin American Homosexualities,* edited by Stephen O. Murray, 80–99. Albuquerque: University of New Mexico Press, 1994.

Trujillo, Carla, ed. *Chicana Lesbians: The Girls Our Mothers Warned Us About.* Berkeley: Third Woman Press, 1991.

Tuan, Yi-Fu. *Space and Place: The Perspectives of Experience.* Minneapolis: University of Minnesota Press, 1977.

Vanita, Ruth. *Queering India: Same-Sex Love and Eroticism in Indian Culture and Society.* New York: Routledge, 2002.

Valdez, Luis. Interviewed by Glenn Lovell. In "This Is the Most Real I Could Make It: Edward James Olmos Hispanic Film's Brutality Stirs Praise, Outrage," *San Jose Mercury News,* Feb. 29, 1992. Morning edition, 1A.

Viego, Antonio. "The Place of Gay Male Chicano Literature in Queer Chicana/o Cultural Work." *Discourse* 21, no. 3 (1999): 111–131.

Villa, Raúl. *Barrio-Logos: Space and Place in Urban Chicano Literature and Culture.* Austin: University of Texas Press, 2000.

Wood, Ellen Meiksins. *Democracy Against Capitalism: Renewing Historical Capitalism.* Cambridge: Cambridge University Press, 1995.

———. *Empire of Capital.* London: Verso, 2003.

Woolgar, Steve. "On the Alleged Distinction between Discourse and Praxis." *Social Studies of Science* 16: 309–317.

Wright, Les. "San Francisco." In *Queer Sites: Gay Urban Histories since 1960,* edited by David Higgis, 164–189. London: Routledge, 1999.

Yarbro-Bejarano, Yvonne. *The Wounded Heart: Writing on Cherríe Moraga.* Austin: University of Texas Press, 2001.

Ybarra-Frausto, Tomás. "Rasquachismo: A Chicano Sensibility." In *Chicano Art: Resistance and Affirmation, 1965–1985,* edited by Richard Griswold del Castillo, Teresa

McKenna, and Yvonne Yarbro-Bejarano, 155–163. Los Angeles: Wright Art Gallery Publication, 1991.

Zamora, Carlos. "Odysseus in John Rechy's *City of Night*: The Epistemological Journey." *Minority Voices* 3, no. 1 (1979): 53–59.

Zamora, Lois Parkinson. *Writing the Apocalypse: Historical Vision in Contemporary U.S. and Latin American Fiction*. Cambridge: Cambridge University Press, 1989.

Index

Lightning Source UK Ltd.
Milton Keynes UK
UKHW012337031219
354522UK00013B/182/P